STRATEGIES FOR SURVIVAL

Cultural Behavior in an Ecological Context

STRATEGIES FOR SURVIVAL

Cultural Behavior in an Ecological Context

MICHAEL A. JOCHIM

Department of Anthropology
University of California, Santa Barbara

ACADEMIC PRESS
A Subsidiary of Harcourt Brace Jovanovich, Publishers
New York   London   Toronto   Sydney   San Francisco

ACADEMIC PRESS, INC.
111 Fifth Avenue, New York, New York 10003

United Kingdom Edition published by
ACADEMIC PRESS, INC. (LONDON) LTD.
24/28 Oval Road, London NW1 7DX

Library of Congress Cataloging in Publication Data

Jochim, Michael A.
   Strategies for survival.

   Bibliography: p.
   Incluαes index.
   1. Man---Influence of environment. 2. Human ecology.
3. Anthropo-geography. 4. Ethnology. I. Title.
GF51.J62   304.2   81-7887
ISBN 0-12-385460-1   AACR2

PRINTED IN THE UNITED STATES OF AMERICA

81 82 83 84   9 8 7 6 5 4 3 2 1

Contents

Illustrations

Preface

This book focuses on the ecological relationships between cultural behavior and its environmental context. It is addressed to all individuals interested in human–environmental interactions, including professional anthropologists and general students of human behavior. The proliferation of ecological studies within anthropology suggests the increasing emphasis given to the systemic context of behavior. The aim of this book is to develop a framework for examining these relationships and for comparing diverse ecological studies within a coherent conceptual structure.

Three general problems characterize much of the literature of ecological anthropology. First, much of the work is strongly materialistic, emphasizing food procurement and exchange. As a result, much behavior often has been unnecessarily excluded from consideration, prompting a backlash of opinion stressing the ideological aspects of behavior as distinct and primary. Second, most studies are particularistic and lack a framework for cross-cultural comparison and generalization. What framework does exist takes the form of an emphasis on a few factors (such as energy, protein, and population pressure), and a limited set of assumptions (for example, minimization of effort or maximization of production). Third, much of the work in ecological anthropology addresses the effects of decisions rather than the processes of decision-making, and can anticipate only optimal behavior. There is little room for suboptimal or maladaptive behavior in most current explanations.

This book is designed in part to address these problems. Specifically, it seeks to construct a general theoretical framework with which to examine the relationship between behavior and its environmental context. It seeks to include any aspect of behavior, to investigate the links between ideological and material factors, to broaden the view of relevant factors and possible assumptions, and to relate the processes of decision-making to their specific context in a manner allowing cross-cultural comparisons. In the process, certain popular forms of ecological explanation will be examined. In addition, specific behavioral examples will be investigated in an attempt to explain patterns of similarities and differences.

I wish to acknowledge my appreciation to countless colleagues who have provided such a stimulating context for the development of these ideas, and most importantly, to Marcy, who is necessary to my survival.

Introduction

Behavior and Ecology

Problems and problem solving seem to emerge together with life.... Life is faced with the problems of survival from the very beginning. Indeed, we can describe life, if we like, as problem solving, and living organisms as the only problem-solving complexes in the universe [Popper 1974:272].

Much of human behavior can be viewed as problem solving. Whether "getting ahead" or "making do," people are constantly trying to solve the mundane problems of survival in their own terms. Many of these problems are rooted in the relationships between people and their natural and social environments. Current dangers of resource depletion, overpopulation, pollution, internal disorder, and international conflict are but special and magnified variants of similar problems that have faced pygmies, peasants, pastoralists, and princes. The perception and context of each individual's problems may be unique or widely shared. Choices of solutions may abound or may be strictly limited by the recognized available means. Solutions may be considered planned or the product of habit and tradition. The choices may be made by each individual or by designated authorities. The goals guiding these choices may be culturally or individually specific. Human cultural diversity can be attributed largely to the varying mixes of these alternative options.

Similar problems are faced by other animal species, and countless viable solutions in the form of morphology and behavior have been attained in the course of evolution through natural selection. The nature of these solutions and their relationship to the species' environmental interactions form the subject matter of evolutionary ecology. Consequently, any general ecological techniques and principles that describe common features of such solutions may be potentially applicable to humans. This is the thesis of ecological anthropology. Such an application may provide a broader understanding of human behavior and a new basis for comparing different human societies. The emphasis here will be on the nature of certain problems and on the context, complexity, and processes of their solutions. Much of the discussion will concentrate on relatively small-scale societies of hunter–gatherers and horticulturalists. Larger and more complex societies face many similar problems, but may differ greatly in the nature and organization of solutions. These solutions, in turn, pose many additional problems of their own that are unique to complex societies, and that will be discussed only briefly.

Chapter 1

The Context of Ecology

1. ANTHROPOLOGY

Ecology is the study of organisms in their natural and social settings and of their relationships to these settings. Humans are unique in that they are found in virtually all settings, and in addition, they can create their own cultural setting. In traditional anthropology, the focus has been on culture as learned norms of behavior, and the emphasis has been on culture as setting humans apart from other animals and the natural world. As a social science, anthropology has tried to explain aspects of culture, and since culture was considered to be a separate and distinct entity, the explanatory terms were also cultural. The immediate causes of cultural traits were seen as being cultural as well.

But humans are animals. They do interact with the natural environment, and their behavior does seem to show some patterning in relation to patterns in the natural environment. The ecological approach in anthropology tries to widen the viewpoint of the discipline to include (and by contrast, often to emphasize) this human interaction with the environment. Cultural behavior is studied not so much for what it is (learned patterns of behavior) as for what it does (provides one means of adaptation).

The ultimate goal of any science is to predict a phenomenon under study (to give the necessary and sufficient conditions for its occurrence) or to predict the consequences of a given set of conditions. To do this, first one has to explain a particular example of the phenomenon, that is, cite its cause. One might look for patterning or for correlations between events and then try to decide the nature and direction of causation. Ecological anthropology is generally at the stage of looking for such patterning or correlations. Only rarely are there simply patterns, and even more rarely can the specific nature of causation be determined. Two major themes stand out from numerous studies:

(1) The complexity of relationships and patterns
(2) The existence of functional alternatives to specific behavior or institutions

3

Recognizing these problems, ecological anthropology is clearly separate from older theories of environmental determinism. The importance of aspects of the natural environment is recognized, but by no means are these aspects seen as prime movers in determining human behavior.

Ecological anthropology is an approach, not a set field or discipline. Its subject matter is as wide as that of anthropology—all people in all times. No fixed problem areas are defined. Any aspect of human behavior may be studied, since it may be directly or indirectly related to features of the natural or social environment. The emphasis may be on structure or function, but since ecology focuses on relationships, explanations should be dynamic and should stress processes. The value of this approach is that it adds to anthropology; it defines new problems and adds new classes of data as relevant to the study of human cultural behavior.

2. SYSTEMS

Ecology is the study of relationships. All relationships can be regarded as transactions or exchanges of energy, matter, or information (Flannery 1972: 400). The goal of an ecological study is to describe, understand, and predict the nature of such transactions—their structure, function, maintenance, and alteration. For living organisms, such exchanges take place on various levels: within the cell, organ, whole organism, local population, community of different species, entire biotic province, and whole world. Ecology deals with only some of these levels, those above that of a single organism.

The basic unit of study in ecology is the *ecosystem,* a set of interrelated species of organisms and their physical environment. An ecosystem is a real entity—a forest grove is a particular kind of environment with certain natural conditions of climate, topography, soil, a variety of plants, and a group of animals from the worms underground to the birds in the canopy, from the tiniest insects to the largest mammals. Here, all the organisms and factors are interacting. The ecosystem is extremely complex, and we can study only those aspects that we can observe and measure. Perhaps the greatest difficulty in studying any real ecosytem, however, is that we have to impose boundaries—often artificial—to define a unit of study that is manageable.

In a real forest ecosystem, there are numerous interactions with materials and organisms from outside. Insects from adjacent fields may pass through and be eaten; forest birds may range far away in search of food; wind may carry sediments and pollen from miles away; and rain and erosion are constantly removing materials. In other words, no real ecosystem is closed, and yet we often have to act as though it were—otherwise we would be tracing relationships forever. The simple fact that the sun is the ultimate source of energy for any ecosystem means that the system is open and that we have to allow at least this input into our study unit.

To some extent, the boundaries we set are determined by our problem of interest. If we want to investigate the entire forest ecosystem, then we would have to include the external factors mentioned. On the other hand, if the focus is on one species of bird, then we could probably narrow our system to those plants and animals with which it directly interacts; other factors could be viewed as constant or at least regular in their effects.

This problem of boundary definition is directly related to our use of the concept of *system*. A system can be defined generally as a group of components or variables interrelated such that a change in one produces a change in all others. Using this concept, once we define those variables that we want to investigate, then we have to include others that can be determined to be related to them in a systematic way. For a study of forest mice, for example, we definitely would include their food resources and predators, but we might exclude, at least initially, animals that feed on rodents other than mice. Note, however, that these other rodents may compete with mice for food, and their removal would affect the mouse population in important ways. This problem of boundary definition deserves emphasis because when we turn to human ecosystems, it becomes more complex, partly because we can observe more diverse interactions and may have greater difficulty in setting boundaries, and partly because humans establish cultural boundaries that may or may not coincide with any natural ones. This problem will be treated in more detail later.

Simple recognition of human interactions with the environment is not, of course, the product of any new, revolutionary thinking by a few farsighted anthropologists. On the contrary, the relationship of humans to the environment has always been a major focus of human thought in the sciences and humanities. Within anthropology, too, these interactions have been central points of study (Hardesty 1977:1–17; Netting 1977:1–7). What is new, however, is the ecological conceptualization of these relationships, which is quite different from previous extreme views.

One extreme position was that of *environmental determinism*. In its strictest form, this held that the natural environment directly affects the psychology and work habits of people, and thus determines the nature and complexity of their culture. In this view, Southern Californians in their warm, benign climate would be lazy and pleasure-oriented, whereas New Englanders, living in a region with great climatic changes and cold winters, would be more industrious and rational. This view, needless to say, would find greater favor in New England.

When such thinking went beyond regional caricatures and purported to explain human cultural development, it became more serious. Africa and South America, in this view, were dismissed from any mainstream of cultural elaboration by virtue of their tropical and subtropical climates and dense jungles. The exceptional civilizations of the classical world—Egypt, West and South Africa, and the Andes—could be discounted because they were obviously experiments doomed to failure.

It is obvious that this viewpoint was intimately connected with racism, paternalistic colonialism, and Western ethnocentrism. Not only are there numerous counterexamples, but also the denial of any active role for people, that is, their reduction to the status of *reactors* to the environment, just does not fit our view of humans. Environmental determinism is still important, however, in that it pervades a good deal of current thinking in rather subtle ways, some of which might be called economic determinism and settlement determinism. In each of these, single lines of causation dominate cultural–environmental interactions, which may provide appealingly simple explanations, but which are belied by our increasing awareness of the complexity involved.

At the opposite extreme was the position that humans differ from other animals by possessing culture and that culture sets them off from their environment. A strict dichotomy between environment and culture was proposed, and the natural environment was reduced simply to a setting or background for the culture. Cultural phenomena such as social organization, residence patterns, rituals, and religions were considered uniquely human, uniquely cultural, and performing functions only in the cultural sphere. An explanation of a cultural phenomenon required only an examination of its relationship to other things cultural; the natural environment could be virtually ignored.

This view was certainly egocentric on the part of humans, but at least it defined the data of anthropology nicely and set the subject apart from the biological sciences. The fact, however, that there is some patterning of cultural and natural features, plus the realization that purely cultural explanations were becoming circular and explaining little, have necessitated a reevaluation of this view. To repeat, humans are animals; they do interact with the natural environment, and their rituals, settlements, and economic institutions do affect this natural environment. The neatly closed, purely cultural system is a theoretical abstraction that bears little resemblance to human societies.

Thus, the middle position, that both cultural and natural phenomena interact and mutually affect one another, has gained acceptance. But there are a variety of viewpoints, a variety of formulations of how such interactions are structured. One of these viewpoints is that of *environmental possibilism,* in which the natural environment as a whole unit sets broad limits on the kinds of behavior and cultural institutions possible. We see nomadic herders in the deserts of the Near East because the environment precludes agriculture; it limits the kind of human adaptation possible. Very evidently it does, but the limits are not absolute. The essence of human technology is to transform the environment. Oil revenues are presently being used in Saudi Arabia to create new agricultural land. Massive irrigation could conceivably make the Sahara suitable for farming. Furthermore, there are areas—around seasonal water courses or oases—where agriculture has been practiced. The simplistic monolithic concept of the environment has to be broken down into its components.

The approach of Julian Steward (1955), who was one of the first to develop cultural ecology as a concept, improved on this environmental possibilism in at least two ways. First, he broke down the environment and culture into specific features to examine their interrelationships. For example, he stressed the kind, abundance, and distribution of resources in different parts of the Great Basin in the western United States and related these to hunting behavior, size and distribution of settlements, and kinship patterns of the Shoshoni Indians. Second, he viewed the environment not simply as setting vague limits but rather as intimately related to aspects of culture. His study of the Shoshoni did not stress that the environment limited these people to hunting and gathering wild foods. Rather, he investigated just how specific resources were obtained, and what the effects of these activities were.

In addition, Steward formulated a model of the relationships between environment and culture that was and is held intuitively by many people. Generally, he stated that some aspects of culture are more directly related to the natural environment that others. In a way, he constructed a hierarchy of descending influence of the natural environment. According to this view, the technology and economy of a society are most directly related to the environment: hunters and farmers both interact most with the environment when getting food. These activities, in turn, set broad limits on the size and distribution of population and on how people regulate this distribution. Thus, social and political organizations are less directly related to the environment. Finally, religion, rituals, arts, and myths are elaborations related to social complexity and leisure time and thus are relatively free of direct environmental influence.

More recently, work in ecological anthropology has stressed the holistic viewpoint inherent in an ecosystems approach, and it specifically has stressed the fact that in a system, any variable can affect any other (Vayda and Rappaport 1968). Broadly speaking, although a hierarchy of relationships might often appear to approximate reality, when investigating any particular aspect of any specific group of people, the complexity of relationships has to be considered. Any aspect of culture—a particular ritual, the selection of marriage partners, or the method of farming—may be related directly to some features of the environment. We should be prepared to observe interactions between any pair of components in our systems, and we should expect that these interactions will be complicated with feedback and multiple implications arising from a single transaction. We must define and subdivide these components into variables that we can observe and measure.

The resulting picture of ecological anthropology is rather formidable. One has visions of human societies being reduced to flow diagrams of boxes and arrows and then, as a final insult, of these diagrams becoming illegible in the inky tangle of their ever increasing and crisscrossing arrows. We may rest assured that mathematics and flowcharts have not yet taken over. Humans are still the central focus of study. Reductionism in the name of quantification has not displaced a recognition of the complex fuzziness of human behavior. Any flowcharts must still be designed with a specific focus in mind, a topic of interest to the investigator. As long as questions and ideas must precede measurement, the central humanity of our science will persist.

3. ENVIRONMENT

Two misconceptions about ecological studies of human behavior seem widespread. The first of these is that the relevant "environment" is restricted to physical and biological factors such as climate and weather, the landscape, plant and animal resources, and other raw materials. These are certainly crucial factors that have been dominant in ecological studies, but they by no means comprise the total environment. An individual's decisions must take into account not only his natural setting but also his family, co-workers and rivals, and the social, economic, and political institutions that define his opportunities and constraints. These latter factors have been the traditional focus of anthropology, which is all the more reason to include them in ecological investigations. Little of human behavior would be meaningful without their consideration. Our study of forest mice, after all, should include the interactions of the local mouse population, the competitors for food and space, and the various animals that prey on them.

The second misconception is that an "ecological study" is equivalent to a description of the environment together with food-getting behavior—topics that have long been portions of traditional ethnographic reports. If this were so, then the ecological approach would narrow the scope of anthropology, not broaden it. But ecology is the study of dynamics. We need to examine not simply human subsistence behavior in a static environment but rather any human behavior in an active, changing environment. We need to examine the interconnections of these various dynamic components of our system. We should include a consideration of the selectivity of human interaction, that is, which aspects of the environment are most important, which are ignored, and what are the criteria and implications of this selectivity?

A realization of such selective interaction brings us to a final point. The "environment" that we as outsiders might observe and attempt to measure for any individual is sure to be different from that perceived by the individual himself. Our description of north coastal Alaska today would certainly include the offshore oil reserves along with the troublesome snow and ice; an Eskimo's perception, on the other hand, would overlook the oil and subdivide the snow and ice conditions into numerous detailed aspects. This distinction between "objective" and "perceived" or "cognized" environments (Rappaport 1968) parallels a broader dichotomy in anthropology between the "etic" and "emic" approaches (Harris 1968)—that is, a distinction between the outsider's and insider's point of view. Though the latter may be difficult to determine, the distinction is valid, and both approaches have a role in ecological work.

If we focus on behavior as problem solving, then an examination of the insider's view, the perceived environment, is crucial to understanding the decisions and solutions. It allows us to investigate the recognition of problems, the awareness of potential solutions, and the evaluation of realized benefits. A more objective appraisal of the environment, by contrast, allows us to evaluate the effectiveness, long-term impact, and secondary ramifications of solutions. It permits an examination of the unrecognized, "latent functions" of behavior (Vayda and Rappaport 1968:491). Furthermore, such an objective view can be defined in terms applicable to many areas, which can be measured cross-culturally. Ecological comparisons of behavior and institutions, consequently, can be based on a common language and set of measurements.

4. ENERGY

The task of measuring and comparing human behavior in relation to the environment require the use of some common dimensions or scales. An exchange of six apples for five oranges can be evaluated, for example, if these are reduced to a common monetary currency. Likewise, the ecological view of interactions as exchanges has suggested a common currency—energy—to which most transactions can be reduced. We know that matter can be transformed into energy; foods, for instance, can be measured for their caloric content. The products exchanged and the work of their transmission can be reduced to caloric equivalents. Even information has been expressed as the degree of organization of matter or energy caused by doing work (Margalef 1968).

Consequently, energy as an ecological currency has gained wide acceptance. Studies of energy contents, energy flow, and energetic costs and benefits have dominated much of ecology and ecological anthropology. Its appeal is based not only on its broad applicability but also on its freedom from cultural context and values. In discussing the sacred cattle of India, Odend'hal (1972) clearly appreciates this freedom:

> A logical and objective method of evaluating the productivity of cattle would be to determine the gross energetic efficiency or the input–output ratio of consumption and production .... The common denominator to which the input and output can be related with most accuracy is not economics, but energetics. The economic value of the parameters involved tends to fluctuate with supply and demand. The caloric values remain relatively constant [p. 4].

However, the focus on energetics is not sufficient; not all exchanges can be meaningfully reduced to calories. Some materials contain much energy that cannot be utilized by humans. Orange peels, eggshells, and coffee grounds in our garbage are trivial examples. More important, we use and exchange many materials for content other than their quantity of calories. Some of these are nutrients including water, protein, vitamins, and essential minerals, and their significance to general ecology is underscored by abundant ecological studies of nutrient cycles. Other substances are important as raw materials. The technological usefulness of obsidian, clay, and copper ore is not defined by the caloric equivalents of these materials. Finally, the information contained in objects is not limited to the *degree* of organization of their molecules but, more important, includes the *nature* of this organization and the *meaning* assigned to it. A birdbath may be as highly organized as a baptismal fount, but the informational contents of the two are vastly different.

Nevertheless, energy is basic to survival, and it continues to form one of several important emphases in ecological anthropology (Vayda and McCay 1975). We can examine the energetic relationships of a group of people along a number of lines:

(1) We can measure their biological needs as these vary with age, sex, health, and activity.

(2) We can examine both potential and actual energy sources, their content and distribution in time and space.

(3) We can evaluate the technologies and techniques of exploiting these resources in terms of costs, material, and personnel, which would allow a calculation of energetic efficiencies.

(4) We can study the other energy expenditures: procuring nutrients, raw materials, and other objects, as well as the many nonprocurement activities. For these we should consider not only costs but also the noncaloric benefits and the consequent reduction in time available for obtaining erergy.

The ultimate aim of these investigations would be to measure the total energy flow—the input and the output, including waste—to formulate the energy budget of the group. The resulting budget can be used as one basis for evaluating options of individual behavior. A particular activity may be considered in light of any energetic constraints, or in terms of its effect on increasing or decreasing the total budget.

5. ECONOMICS

An energy budget is only one of many possible budgets that can be formulated. Others could involve various nutrients and raw materials, land, time, or specialized knowledge with each budget based on an investigation of how these substances are produced, distributed, and consumed. The study of budgets is economics. More formally, economics deals with the "allocation of scarce resources among alternative ends" (Schneider 1974:183). An examination of an energy budget allows the evaluation of the scarcity of energy as a resource; other budgets similarly are useful in ascertaining the role of each of the other factors. Materials, land, or knowledge may be in short supply owing to their distribution, competition, or social and political barriers to their flow.

The allocation of such resources involves decisions about all activities, not simply those involved in food getting. As Odend'hal (1972:20) states, "Perhaps this utilization of energy by humans for nonconsumptive processes is another distinguishing characteristic separating man from other animals. Man uses great quantities of energy for his convenience and comfort." The same applies to human use of materials, time, land, and knowledge. Economics, then, must study the decisions guiding these uses and the processes of choice among the alternative ends.

Economic analysis of these processes requires an examination of (1) all resources, their budgets and possible scarcity; (2) the technological and social factors affecting the possibilities of allocation; and (3) the goals of preferences of the actors (Schneider 1974:191). Thus, we must investigate the constraints on the choices, such as technological capabilities, institutionalized demands, sanctioned options, and activities of other individuals. Equally important, and only recently stressed in ecological anthropology (Rutz 1977; Young 1974:29–30), are the goals guiding the choices among alternative activities. Value systems notoriously have been excluded from discussion by ecological anthropologists because values are nonmaterial and nonreducible to caloric measurement. By viewing behavior as problem solving involving choices, we have a framework for incorporating value systems into an ecological system. No decision is made in a vacuum but is made to attain preferred ends; these preferences may vary among individuals and cultures.

For instance, consider the simplistic, hypothetical example of a farmer facing the decision of what to do with a portion of his land:

(1) He might strive to maximize his monetary profit and grow coffee to sell to a buyer.
(2) He might try to maximize the food calories produced per acre and grow manioc.
(3) He could choose to maximize his production of protein per acre and grow soybeans.
(4) He might attempt to maximize the security of his harvest and select frost- or drought-resistant plants or diversify his crops.
(5) He could decide to strive for maximum production of calories per man-hour of labor and plant rapidly growing crops that require little tending.

(6) He might decide to maximize calorie production per total calorie input and select crops requiring no fertilizers or machine technology.

(7) He could seek to maximize his prestige by planting bananas to make beer or by grazing cattle.

(8) He might try to insure his family's continuity by giving the land to his son-in-law.

Obviously, our farmer has a number of options. Theoretically, many more could be listed. To understand the option chosen, we have to examine the available and perceived options, the desirable ends, and the numerous constraints of crops, climate, soils, technology, market situations, family size, use of other land, other demands on time, and neighbors' activities. The interrelationships of these factors are the subject of ecological anthropology; their effect on the allocation decision can be analyzed in the framework of economics. Monetary efficiency need not be assumed in economics, nor are energetic efficiency or risk minimization necessary components of ecology. Any goal may guide behavior; some goals may be more likely than others in particular situations.

It should be realized, too, that decisions or goals themselves may be in conflict. Each individual must make multiple choices involving numerous aspects of behavior, with each demanding his or her time and energy, and each perhaps guided by a different set of preferences. The result may be that the actual behavior of an individual represents a compromise to these competing demands. No single factor may be maximized. Our farmer may be reasonably efficient according to different criteria, may have relatively little risk of failure, and may be obtaining adequate amounts of calories, protein, and prestige. In other words, he may be *satisficing,* not maximizing; he may be attaining satisfactory amounts of his preferred ends. This possible lack of maximization, of course, does not negate the value of studies that assume such behavior. In some cases, people may indeed strive for maximum efficiency, and investigation may demonstrate this. In other cases, submaximal behavior may be evident only by the discrepancies between expected and real activities revealed by such studies. Certainly, however, such maximizing cannot be assumed to be characteristic of any behavior without empirical testing.

6. EVOLUTION

An underlying theoretical basis for ecological studies is evolution, with its concepts of adaptation and fitness. When we examine the behavior of any organism, we try to understand it, to see the sense in it. Such an attempt implies that some fundamental end is being served by the behavior. Evolutionary theory provides not only such an end but also the means of assessing performance. The end is *adaptation* to the environment, measured by relative *fitness,* or the genetic contribution to the next generation. Consequently, explanations of patterns of animal behavior are usually phrased in terms of their adaptive significance, their contribution to fitness.

A similar desire to make sense of human behavior has led many an- ~rationality approach vs. maximizing approach~ thropologists to view a particular activity not as the solution to a problem, which is the view taken here, but rather as one step toward the realization of an ultimate goal. The distinction is important because in the context of problem solving numerous, often conflicting, and sometimes capricious goals may guide an individual's decisions, whereas in the context of a single unifying goal, the decisions seem to be more harmonious and comprehensible. In recognition of the fact that humans are part of the biological world in which "only one process, natural selection for individual adaptation ordinarily produces goal-seeking behavior" (Richerson 1977:2), many assume that "adaptation" is this basic underlying goal:

> [Human and nonhuman behavior] both function to effect adaptation to the environment and . . . are subject to a kind of selection resulting, *inter alia,* from the fact that individuals or populations behaving in certain different ways have different degrees of success in survival and reproduction and, consequently, in the transmission of their ways of behaving from generation to generation [Vayda and Rappaport 1968:493].

Here we have a direct analogy drawn between the behavior of humans and that of other animals: both are seen as means to the same ends. In view of the many clear differences separating humans from the rest of the animal world, this analogy is startling. It is also very appealing, in that

(1) The diversity of human activities can be brought together within a common framework of understanding.
(2) These activities can be analyzed using concepts and methods developed in evolutionary ecology.
(3) Human evolution can be studied as a continuation of known processes without recourse to concepts of a qualitative leap or a threshold of human consciousness. Humans are different, but perhaps we are only doing many of the same things in different ways.

To assess this possibility, we have to examine the following questions as they pertain to both biological and cultural adaptation:

(1) What is adaptation?
(2) What is the mechanism of adaptation?
(3) Who is adapting? Whose characteristics can we measure?
(4) Are there trends in these measurements through time? Are these goals?
(5) Are organisms maximally adapted? Are they solely adapting?
(6) Can we predict the course of adaptation?

One clear discussion of biological adaptation that is quite suitable for the problem-oriented framework used here is the following:

> It is self-evident that any living species, at least any species not about to become extinct, has a valid set of solutions for certain basic ecological, or biological problems. It must secure food to replenish its energy store, must have a place to live, and a method to reproduce and thus to perpetuate its genes in succeeding generations. Posession of a valid set of such solutions is called adaptedness [Dobzhansky 1974:323].

Clearly, the same definition may be applied to humans, with perpetuation of genes as the ultimate criterion of success. Is such a definition, however, sufficient? Can human adaptation be reduced ultimately to genetic survival? Many people think so, or at least believe that this may be a valuable working assumption (Durham 1976). On the other hand, many others believe that human adaptation must be defined in a broader manner, to allow for the perpetuation not only of genes but also of culture, of "ways of behaving" (Vayda and Rappaport 1968:493). Humans live in groups and share common commitments to a way of life that many of their activities seek to perpetuate. "Better Dead Than Red" is a slogan not easily reconciled with genetic fitness.

Once we admit this broader definition of adaptation, however, we face serious problems. If culture is to be defined as the extrasomatic means of adaptation (White 1949), and adaptation as the perpetuation of culture, then culture becomes a means of perpetuating itself! Perhaps some rewording can help to reduce this apparent circularity. Living humans have a valid set of solutions allowing survival and genetic perpetuation. Culture consists of the extrasomatic (behavioral and ideological) components of these solutions, the chosen motives and the resulting strategies for survival. Human adaptation, then, might involve the perpetuation not simply of genes, but also of a particular set of solutions based on certain goals. Culture does indeed tend to perpetuate itself, and an assumption of cultural conservatism becomes analogous to the observed conservation of biological evolution:

> The class of possible evolutionary futures is highly restricted by the properties of the evolutionary present and the conservatism of evolution. Not only is there a tendency to do nothing, but if anything does occur, it does so in the smallest possible steps [Slobodkin 1977:333].

Additional problems with this definition of human adaptation derive from the difficulties of measuring the persistence of cultural behavior and of reconciling such persistence with the continuous changes in behavior that we can observe. What is to persist? Not the people themselves: births and deaths constantly alter their identity. Not the size of the cultural group, for population growth should be genetically adaptive. The type of economy, the political structure, or the religion? If so, then we cannot say that humans ever have been adapted except for a frozen instant of time. Perhaps we could more easily approach this problem through a systems framework and examine the persistence of the systemic relationships. We could talk of certain variables in our cultural systems being maintained within ranges that permit the continued existence of the system (Rappaport 1968). Yet one of the major criticisms of the systems ecological approach has been that it overemphasizes the stability or equilibrium of cultural systems to the neglect of disequilibrium or change (Vayda and McCay 1975).

Here, again, a rephrasing of the problem may help to suggest a useful approach to the dilemma. People solve problems of survival on their own terms. They choose solutions to the perceived problems that satisfy their goals using available means. Problems, means, and goals that are widely shared may lead to widely shared solutions as well. Problems may change directly through environmental changes; their perception may be altered through communication and experience; the available means may change through accident, invention, or contact; and the goals may change through education or coercion. It is no wonder that behavior is so frequently changing. What may persist in adaptation, then, is simply the possession of any valid set of solutions, together with the acceptance of their validity. The observed conservatism of behavior or the impression of equilibrium of cultural systems may reflect either a temporary stability of problems, means, and goals or the fact that changes must build on the "evolutionary present," that is, must come about in the context of ongoing solutions.

If human adaptation involves more than biological fitness, it may be assumed that the mechanisms of human adaptation also differ from those of biological evolution. Biological adaptation is largely the product of natural selection operating on phenotypes. Through differential survival and reproduction, certain genes attain increasing proportional representation in succeeding generations: "adaptive" genetic traits are transmitted by virtue of their relationship to reproductive success. The ultimate source of genetic variation is random mutations, although more proximate sources may include population interbreeding or genetic recombination.

In an excellent analysis of the evolution of cultural behavior, Durham (1976) discusses some of the problems inherent in a theory of cultural evolution. For any such theory to be complementary to biological evolution, it must incorporate "(1) sources of variation, (2) selection criteria, and (3) mechanisms for the retention of positively selected variants" (Durham 1976:94). Durham goes on to suggest "invention, diffusion, and accident" as sources of variation, and inclusive biological fitness as the major selection criterion. The mechanisms for retention are given less attention but are suggested to include experiences, socialization, and teaching (Durham 1976:94–96). Yet if theories of cultural evolution are to be more than grand analogies, it is essential that we understand these mechanisms. Darwin's evolutionary theory assumed its greatest potential only with the discovery of the genetic basis—the mechanism of the process. The same is true of any theory of cultural evolution; until we understand the mechanisms involved, we are limited to description and analogy.

As Durham states, "Biological theories of adaptation do not yet make adequate allowance for learning and nongenetic inheritance" (1976:90). Learning is the basis of cultural behavior. To understand the mechanism of cultural selection, we must investigate the process by which new behaviors are taught, learned, and retained. We must understand the relationship between adaptation and learning. A behavioral approach to learning, which promises greatest utility in comprehending this relationship, has been suggested by Harner among others: ". . . it seems unlikely that cultural institutions and traits can be successfully passed on through centuries and millennia without having some regular reinforcement for their maintenance" (Harner 1973:152). Our focus should perhaps be on the specific reinforcers for each behavior if we would seek to understand the continuation of that behavior. This focus will be considered later in more detail. By examining learning and reinforcement, we may be better able to deal with some of the unique characteristics of cultural evolution: the selective retention or diffusion of single ideas, the potential rapidity of change, and the opportunity for deliberate change by rational strategizing (Richerson 1977:15).

Much discussion in ecology and ecological anthropology has involved the question of the units of adaptation. Whose fitness and behavior are we concerned with? A major and often useful focus in biological ecology has been on the characteristics and behavior of groups of organisms—populations, species, communities, and entire ecosystems. Recognition of certain patterns in these characteristics has led to investigations into the origins and functions of such patterned behavior, resulting in concepts of group adaptation and group selection (Wynne–Edwards 1965; Gilpin 1975). Populations are seen as units of adaptation, with mechanisms of self-regulation and strategies of evolution. These properties have been extended to ecosystems as well. "The properties of an ecosystem depend on the organisms of which it is formed, but the evolution of such organisms is under the control of a process of self-organization operating in the whole ecosystem" (Margalef 1968:82). Because the components of ecosystems are so tightly interrelated, their cohesion and feedback connections have been thought to cause a higher level of behavior and adaptation. "We theorized that new systems properties emerge in the course of ecological development, and that it is these properties that largely account for the species and growth form changes that occur" (Odum 1977:1290).

There is no doubt that groups possess characteristics separate from those of their component individuals which derive from the organization and interaction of these individuals. Such characteristics—for example diversity, stability, productivity, efficiency, homeostasis, and hierarchical structure—can be measured and compared among groups and through time. Nevertheless, an attempt to account for the origin and function of such properties through concepts of group adaptation faces real problems of "misplaced teleology" (Richerson 1977:3). Natural selection operates through reproductive success, which is the "purpose" of biological adaptation. Explanations based on group adaptation often postulate individual reproductive sacrifice for the sake of the group's persistence, yet this runs counter to our understanding of natural selection. Reexamination of many examples of "group adaptation" has resulted in their interpretation within the framework of individual adaptation; the group consequences arise either by composite interactions or as side effects of these individual activities (Colinvaux 1973:463). Similarly, "ecosystems evolution" has been vigorously denied: "Natural selection does not act upon entire ecosystems but operates through differential reproductive success of individual organisms within communities" (Pianka 1975:847; also see Colinvaux 1973:569; Ricklefs 1973:746).

Natural selection working on individuals or closely related individuals ("kin selection"—Wilson 1975) is the primary mechanism of adaptation. The properties and behavior of higher levels of organization must be explained by this mechanism. Negative interaction within a system is not an example of purposeful or selected regulation on that level (Richerson 1977:19). When we turn to cultural behavior, we find growing agreement that group characteristics must be sought primarily in the behavior of individuals (Durham 1976:93: Vayda and McCay 1975:300). Not just the reproductive interests of individuals, but all of the interests and activities of individual adaptation must be examined. The mechanism of individual adaptation should be considered in terms of decision making. "How to relate the unintended consequences of conscious decisions based on the specific ends of competing management units to the patterned outcome and some goals posited for a whole system remains an ill-defined but crucial problem in ecological and economic anthropology" (Rutz 1977:157). This approach requires, too, that we make no assumptions of group homogeneity. Individual differences in ability, perception, means and goals are as important in human populations as is genetic variability in biological evolution (Vayda and McCay 1975:302). An equally important consideration is the locus of decision making and the possibility that the decisions of some individuals may be imposed on others. Societies may, in fact, have group goals through consensus or coercion, but it is the advantages accruing to the individual for adhering to these goals that must be investigated.

This focus upon individual adaptation and behavior does not deny the existence of group characteristics or the value of their study. Populations may be compared for their diversity, stability, and structure in terms of their age and sex structure of spatial distribution, communities, or systems. Such emergent, "macroecological" properties may be viewed in several ways: as the aggregate of individual decisions and activities, as the result of cooperation by individuals to attain solutions, and as part of the context of such individual behavior. An individual of a widely dispersed population in a highly fluctuating system faces different problems and is likely to make different decisions from one in a crowded, stable situation. A comparison of populations in terms of their aggregate or cooperative behavior or structure of decision making may help to explain differential individual adaptive success. Changes in group characteristics through time may suggest changing strategies of individual adaptation.

Such temporal patterns in group or system properties have been a principal concern of many ecologists. Relatively short-term studies of species replacement in a community have described patterned trends leading to a climax. Long-term studies have depicted temporal patterns in the evolution of ecosystems.

> Succession is in progress everywhere and evolution follows, encased in succession's frame. As a consequence, we expect to find a parallel trend in several phylogenetic lines which can also be recognized as a trend realized in succession [Margalef 1968:81].

Among the trends postulated have been increased in biomass, stability, stratification, complexity, diversity, efficiency of production, and information (Margalef 1968:28–29). Some of these suggested changes have since been found not to occur in every case (Colinvaux 1973:549–550; Margalef 1968:30–32; Slobodkin 1977:334). Others do seem to take place, but the fact has been suggested as trivial; for example, an increase in complexity and diversity of life through time is inevitable in the evolution of life from nonliving matter or in the colonization by plants and animals of an empty landscape (Colinvaux 1973:550–563). There seem to be no consistant trends in evolution or succession other than a general direction, from simple to complex (Dobzhansky 1974; Sauer 1977; Slobodkin 1977; Stebbins 1974). And even this general direction is observable only in retrospect; "It does not follow that the evolution is being directed by some outside agency, or that it has been programmed beforehand" (Dobzhansky 1974:311). In a concurring view, Colinvaux (1973) states

> In the proper Darwinian view of ecology there is no organizing principle behind succession. Successions are not directed by some holistic process of the superorganism. Nor, and this is much more important to modern ecology, are they directed by negative feedbacks of ever-refining ecosystems [p. 571].

Changes in macroscopic cultural characteristics through time have similarly been described as showing general directions or trends. Among those suggested have been increased complexity and diversification, efficiency of energy use, size of social group, carrying capacity, and stability (Durham 1976:95). In the definition and analysis of these trends, many have relied on analogies between societies and organisms, communities, or ecosystems. If such general biological, successional, or evolutionary trends are now considered lacking or trivial, then the value of any analogies is dubious. Certainly we can identify temporal trends in cultural behavior and its complexity—in retrospect. Much of this directionality derives from the simple fact that the present builds upon the past, that present solutions have been constructed in the context of previous decisions. Is there any reason to suspect that the directions have been "programmed beforehand?"

There is, indeed, one very good reason for this suspicion. Humans, unlike other organisms, have an elaborate capacity to plan for the future. "Five-year plans" are uniquely human. People are not restricted to solving immediate problems; they are able to try to foresee possible future problems and develop contingency plans. It is questionable, however, whether this ability is commonly put into practice, whether decisions usually consider future choices and later consequences. The answers to these questions will suggest the degree to which people direct their cultural evolution.

Human adaptation is viewed here as the possession of a valid set of solutions to a variety of problems. Guiding these solutions are diverse goals, only one of which may be reproductive success. Ecological studies of behavior attempt to understand its adaptive significance. It must now be asked whether all behavior is adaptive, and whether humans and other organisms are maximally adapted. In the Darwinian view of biological adaptation, there is every reason to expect less than maximum adaptation, for a number of reasons:

(1) Some traits may be adaptively neutral, that is, they neither increase nor decrease fitness.

(2) Evolution is a process: natural selection is constantly at work, and organisms or their environments may be constantly changing. Thus, at any one time, some traits may exist that were previously adaptive but that are not so in the new situation.

(3) A trait may have multiple effects on fitness, some positive and some negative; selection may have favored its persistence because of an overall positive, but less than maximum, benefit (Dobzhansky 1974:319).

(4) Competing problems or demands may divert energy from reproductive effort (Cody 1974:1156).

The same factors may be operating for humans to reduce reproductive potential from a maximum to a satisfactory level (Terrell 1977:241). In addition, humans can expand their budgets of time and energy for use in activities that have little effect on reproductive success (Durham 1976:104). The broader view of adaptation as valid problem solving, however, can encompass such factors as reproductive neutrality or expanded budgets; these are both components of the problems and their means of solution. The major factors that reduce human fitness in this view must be seen in (1) the difficulties of perceiving problems adequately; (2) the inability of foreseeing all the implications of solutions; (3) the competing demands of simultaneously solving several problems; and (4) the possible inflexibility of learning and behavior in response to changing problems. The result of these factors is that we should not expect the best possible solution to any particular problem; adequacy is sufficient.

A final consideration in this section is the predictability of behavior. Can we predict the course of evolution, the direction of sequential adaptations? Biologists who stress the existence of general trends in evolution argue that we can, at least on the macroscopic level (Margalef 1968:30), whereas those who deny such trends or their significance suggest otherwise (Colinvaux 1973:497). Some of the factors affecting the predictability of evolution are summarized by the following:

> The complexity of the situation is, however, so overwhelming that we cannot predict whether or not an environmental challenge will evoke an adaptive evolutionary response in concrete cases. A response will not occur if genetic raw materials for it are unavailable.... The response to changing environments may be too slow to save a species from extinction.... Finally, a coherent adaptive response to a given environment may be achieved by quite different means [Dobzhansky 1974:318].

One aspect of evolutionary change does, at least, seem to be predicatable. "Evolution will proceed according to the principle of adaptive modifications along the lines of least resistance" (Stebbins 1974:303). This is the evolutionary conservatism stressed by Slobodkin cited earlier.

How predictable, then, is human behavior? By analogy with biological evolution as currently viewed, the answer would have to be very poorly, except for a vague tendency for "cultural inertia" (Durham 1976:99). But there are some promising factors. Terrell quotes Kluckhohn to the effect that "all cultures constitute so many somewhat distinct answers to essentially the same questions posed by human biology and by the generalities of the human situation," and emphasizes the relative constancy of human biology and the variability of the situation (Terrell 1977:245). It is to this situation, to the environment in the broadest sense, that we must look for the questions or problems. It may be possible to analyze and characterize different environments according to their "common problems for life" (Colinvaux 1973:51), and to relate these to biogeographical distributions. Furthermore, it then may be possible to "elucidate general features of hazards and responses and to develop generalizations in terms of such variables as the magnitude, duration, and novelty of hazards, the magnitude and reversibility of responses to them, the temporal order in which responses of different magnitudes occur, and the persistence or nonpersistence of response processes" (Vayda and McCay 1975:297). Obviously, we must realize that more than one solution is possible for a given problem, but such apparent functional alternatives should be examined for their specific differences—their relative costs, speed, and flexibility (Rappaport 1971b) as well as their secondary implications. In addition, different problems might be solved by the same solutions; the adequacy of the solution in each case might be investigated. Finally, solutions may affect or constrain each other and may pose problems of their own. To what extent the general sequences of cultural evolution represent a chain reaction of solutions and secondary problems is an intriguing question. Human behavior may be viewed as dynamic strategies composed of interrelated solutions to problems; its predictability depends on the predictability of the problems and their means available for their solution.

To what extent does "rationality" or "irrationality" effect or interfere with adaptation? To what extent does it alter the definition of adaptability, and the predictability of the problems?

Chapter 2

The Study of Behavior

What are the causes of human behavior? Although biologists might reply in terms of internal chemical processes, psychologists might stress internal motives and desires. Anthropologists have tended to emphasize shared group norms and values, and economists usually have stressed material ends or goals. All of these seem to be correct and to be partially satisfactory answers within each discipline. But what of the relationship of behavior to the environment? Those who stress internal motives, norms, or goals have tended to ignore environmental factors except as they form a background or a set of limiting goods that people can use, should they so desire. At the opposite extreme is the view that the environment is a set of stimuli that trigger human responses—that the environment is the ulti-mate cause of ideological and behavioral effects. Ecological anthropologists recently have treated environmental factors as relatively independent variables in cultural systems, with much of behavior serving to maintain the structure and function of these systems. Cultural evolutionists have taken a longer-term view and have stressed the adaptive nature of the functioning of cultural systems in the context of natural selection.

In Chapter 1, it was pointed out that although anthropologists and ecologists both focus largely on group behavior and group characteristics, they are increas-ingly realizing that an understanding of this behavior must come from the study of the individual members. In dealing with humans, furthermore, we must focus largely on learning as the primary basis of behavior. To comprehend cultural behavior, then, whether in the context of the short-term functioning of societies or their evolutionary change through time, it is essential to examine the mechanisms of individual learning. As suggested earlier, the premise taken here is that a consideration of the reinforcements of specific behavior is crucial for understanding the relationship between learning and adaptation.

In attempts to comprehend behavior, it is common to seek an antecedent cause—an event that *precedes* the behavior in question. Cold air causes shiver-ing and constriction of the blood vessels; touching a hot stove causes a child to withdraw his hand. The psychological model for this type of process is the *reflex*, a stimulus followed by a response. The nature of reflexes is such that (1) there is a threshold of the stimulus below which the response does not occur and (2) as the stimulus increases in intensity, the magnitude and speed of the response increases as well (Millenson 1967:23). Much of our reflex behavior is innate and shared with other animals, but we know from experiments that such behavior can be learned as well through a substitution of stimuli, much as Pavlov's dogs learned to salivate at the sound of a bell.

This reflex, or respondent, model of behavior is attractive. We see cause–effect relationships all around us in the physical world: the moon's pull causes tidal movements of the oceans; droughts cause plants to wither and die. It seems only natural to seek similar causal processes of human behavior. Yet such a view seems to lead inevitably to a position of environmental determinism: humans are reduced to a bundle of reflexes passively responding to outside stimuli. Anthropologists, whether they stress motives, norms, or adaptation, would certainly deny the relevance of such a deterministic model to most human activities. Nevertheless, it seems that many current anthropological generalizations imply this type of behavior. Population pressure is said to *cause* migration, warfare, or agricultural intensification; dispersed resources *cause* high mobility or flexible social organization. In many cases, too, the magnitude and speed of such responses are implied to vary with the intensity of the stimuli. Certainly, these factors show correlations and temporal patterns, but to phrase these in terms of cause and effect obscures the underlying mechanisms and makes it difficult to understand different responses to the same stimulus.

Another, more important model of learning stresses not the antecedents, but the *consequences* of behavior:

> Many of the activities of higher organisms do not appear to fit nicely into a reflex model of behavior. These include the actions of man, which were described long before Descartes as voluntary, spontaneous, willful, and purposeful.... Purposive behavior is behavior that is almost *defined* by its consequences [Millenson 1967:61–62].

Such behavior has been called *operant behavior;* it is strengthened or weakened by the events that follow the response. Consequences that strengthen behavior are called positive reinforcers, whereas those that weaken behavior are called negative reinforcers or aversive stimuli. Any behavior may be strengthened or weakened depending on its effects or consequences (Reese 1966:3). If the act of kicking a stubborn vending machine is followed by the return of our money, we would be more likely to resort to kicking in similar stiuations in the future. Reinforcers are defined operationally—by their effect on behavior. Some seem to be virtually universal or "primary," such as food or electric shocks, whereas others, such as praise or criticism, are learned or conditioned. Even the so-called primary reinforcers do not constantly perform in this manner; to a starving man, food may be a positive reinforcer, but if he has just finished dinner, food may have lost this property.

The study of operant behavior, then, focuses on consequences and seeks causes of behavior in past histories of reinforcement. This focus of behavioral psychology is paralleled in many other disciplines relevant to our discussion. Economists traditionally have emphasized profits, benefits, and other outcomes, and recently have developed "theories of reinforcement of successful (profitable) behavior and elimination of unsuccessful behavior" (Rapport and Turner 1977:372). Economic anthropologists frequently stress "anticipated outcomes," "likely consequences," "satisfactions," or "returns" as major determinants of behavior (Acheson 1976; Dalton 1977; Derman and Levin 1977; Erasmus 1961; Herskovits 1952; Kunkel 1976). General theories of decision making assign a great importance to the possible consequences of various choices (Rappaport 1960). The theory of evolution relies on the effects of behavior on reproductive success, and both evolutionary biology and ecology are incorporating models and techniques from economics such as cost–benefit analysis and game theory with its focus on payoffs (Colinvaux 1973; Rapport and Turner 1977; Smith 1976). In short, these various sciences of behavior utilize methods of analysis that complement the major process of human learning. By adopting such methods in ecological anthropology, we may be able to investigate not only the relationship of behavior to environmental factors but also the mechanisms of cultural selection and adaptation.

But how does this focus on operant behavior relate to internal states, to norms, values, motives, and goals?

> Needs and wants and other motives seem to be closely related to the concept of reinforcers. . . . A person is said to "want" a drink if he asks for it, or otherwise engages in behavior that has previously produced water. The needs and wants refer to the fact that, by a period of their absence, food and water have been made reinforcers [Millenson 1967:364–365].

Values and motives are learned, just as are specific tasks, by personal experience, by imitation, and by verbal accounts. Verbalization of thoughts is subject to reinforcement like any other behavior. Internal states when translated into behavior may be strengthened or weakened according to their consequences. "To say that organisms make responses in order to produce reinforcers conveys no more information than to say that they *do* make responses when these responses have been frequently followed by reinforcers" (Millenson 1967:420).

By emphasizing operant learning, we avoid the deterministic bias of a reflex, cause–effect model of human behavior. Furthermore, this operant emphasis has a number of important implications for anthropological explanations, which will be discussed in the remainder of this chapter.

(1) Any particular response may or may not be reinforced. If it is, however, the reinforcers may occur constantly or only intermittently. Experiments and

observations have demonstrated that although behavior is learned most rapidly with constant reinforcement, it tends to persist and be most resistant to extinction when reinforcement is *intermittent* (Reese 1966:18). Much of cultural behavior has been explained in terms of its effects: warfare reduces population size, potlatches compensate for local food shortages. Criticisms of such explanations frequently cite counterexamples: wars with few casualties or potlatches with little effective food redistribution. A realization of the importance of intermittent reinforcement to maintaining behavior, however, should lead us to expect such counterexamples without discarding the explanations. Warfare may persist if it has only occasionally reduced population. Potlatches may continue to be given if they have occasionally prevented starvation. The identification of such intermittent reinforcement is an important task of analysis.

(2) For behavior to be strengthened, it must be *followed* by a reinforcer, but it need not *lead* to it. There does not have to be any direct functional link between behavior and reinforcer; the sequence may be accidental. Rain dances, hunting charms, and shoulder-blade divination may all be followed occasionally by successful endeavors. From our vantage point we may claim that this success is only coincidentally linked to the behavior, but since these activities are reinforced by intermittent success, they will be learned and maintained. An emic analysis of such "superstitious" behavior might reveal the reinforcers, which an etic study alone could not do. Another task for the investigator, then, is to determine the nature of the linkage between behavior and its reinforcers.

(3) Reinforcement of behavior tends to occur or be possible only in particular environmental situations, and an important part of learning is *discrimination* of the relevant environmental stimuli. Such discriminative stimuli are cues; they carry information that certain responses will be reinforced. Traveling to the hills to gather nuts may be successful only when the color of leaves has begun to change in the fall. Going to a theater may be rewarded only when the price of admission is available. The discriminative stimulus sets the occasion for the response to produce reinforcement. It is because of the existence of such stimuli that we see correlations between environment and behavior, and the development of a kind of control of behavior by the environment. But this control is not deterministic. In a given situation, *any* activities that are reinforced will be learned and maintained. At a banquet table a person might obtain food by waiting demurely, asking for it, demanding it, reaching for it, or climbing up on the table and eating it there. The past history of other reinforcers such as praise, discipline, and social ostracism determines which technique is most likely to occur. Ecological studies must examine patterns of correlation between behavior and environment not as demonstrations of inevitable causal relationships, but as paired cues and responses, bearing in mind that the consequent reinforcement is responsible for this pairing. Behavior that occurs in many cultures in similar environments

may be functionally linked to the possible reinforcement contingencies. Behavior that is transmitted from one environment to another must be reinforced in both. Cultural transmission allows for an increase in an individual's or group's knowledge of discriminatory stimuli and of the probabilities of reinforcement; history augments direct individual experience.

(4) A by-product of the learning process is that discriminative stimuli acquire the properties of reinforcers. Because the possession of money can set the occasion for behavior leading to reinforcers, money can become a reinforcer in itself. Such acquired reinforcers—money, prestige, criticism—obtain these properties through a history of association with primary reinforcers such as food, water, sex, and pain. Many acquired reinforcers, such as money, are generalized, in that by having money, an individual can make many responses, each leading to its own distinct reinforcer (Millenson 1967:238–246). Most human behavior seems to be related to such acquired and learned reinforcers, which seem quite variable among individuals and cultures. In contrast to behavior, which must be currently reinforced (at least intermittently) in order to persist, acquired reinforcers need not be currently paired with primary reinforcers as long as they were paired at some time in the past. Acquired reinforcers may be quite inexplicable in the current environment in which such pairing is not obvious. A miser may hoard money without spending it: it has become an end in itself. Investigation of human behavior must take into account the possible idiosyncrasies of reinforcers and must recognize the importance of the histories of their acquisition. Food energy and offspring may in some sense be ultimate ends, but much of human behavior is directed toward reinforcers with no remaining or obvious relationship to these ends.

(5) Most human activities seem to take the form of an operant *chain,* that is, a sequence of responses and stimuli such that each response produces the discriminative stimulus for a further response. Much of the complexity of behavior derives not so much from complex responses as from the complexity of this chaining process. Behavior may be altered gradually with changing combinations of stimuli and reinforcement schedules. Additional complexity is introduced by two other features of operant learning: (*a*) There are usually a number of possible responses in a given situation, each of which may be differentially reinforced; and (*b*) the reinforcement consequences of a single response may be uncertain, each occurring with a particular probability. A situation requiring the choosing of a group leader might be the occasion for arm wrestling, voting, or coin tossing, and each of these might lead to various consequences. Because of these two features, behavioral chains are characterized by complex branching. In this situation of complexity, we may now speak of "problems" in terms of the discrimination of relevant stimuli, the adjustment to changing stimuli and reinforcement schedules, and the uncertainty of branch points in behavioral chains. "Once the organism has produced a situation for a well-established sequence of behavior,

the problem has ended'' (Millenson 1967:335). An ecological study of the processes of problem solving should examine the changing environmental structuring of stimuli and the degree of uncertainty of reinforcement.

(6) Behaviors are differentially strengthened and weakened not only according to the schedule of reinforcement, but also according to the *value* of the reinforcers. It is clear that food is more rewarding at some times than at others and that ranked preference orders exist among different reinforcers. One key factor that affects this value is deprivation. To a starving man, food is a much stronger reinforcer than it is to one who has just eaten. The value of acquired reinforcers may depend to a great extent on the nature of their original pairing with primary reinforcers. Generalized reinforcers, because they can lead to more options, may tend to have consistently higher values than more specific ones. When ecologists discuss limiting factors or resource shortages, they may be identifying situations of deprivation, and consequently, of potentially high reinforcement value. It should be stressed, however, that deprivation alone will not automatically lead to behavior that corrects the situation. Unless behavior exists for getting to the reinforcer, deprivation alone will not lead to it (Millenson 1967:389). Food shortages during a drought need not automatically lead to compensating activities; they may lead to death.

(7) Another factor affecting the strength of behavior is its cost or effort. The "Law of Least Effort," which is recognized in economics, geography, and anthropology, is equally important in behavioral psychology: "Given two or more alternate chains to the same reinforcer, the organism chooses the one requiring the least work" (Millenson 1967:428). If reinforcement is stopped, responses that require great effort tend to disappear more quickly than those requiring less effort. Furthermore, the amount of work performed and the speed of learning new responses tend to increase as the value of the reinforcer increases (Millenson 1967:383). Thus, ecological examinations of energy costs and efficiency are necessary components to understanding the importance of different activities.

(8) The preceding discussion has been phrased primarily in terms of responses directly strengthened by positive reinforcers and weakened by negative ones. Yet, there are large classes of operant behavior that do not fit this model. Some responses, called *facilitators*, are not themselves reinforced, but make it possible for a second response to lead to reinforcement. Others, called *observing responses*, allow the individual to gather information about the discriminative stimuli present in the environment, giving him the opportunity to refrain from unreinforced responding and to enhance the probability of reinforced behavior. In examining specific kinds of activities, then, we must seek not simply immediate reinforcement but rather the broader consequences that include subsequent responses.

(9) Another class of behavior consists of responses that are apparently

strengthened when they are *not* reinforced. This is *avoidance* behavior: responses that postpone the occurrence of negative reinforcers. It would seem that much of our behavior is avoidance behavior (Reese, 1966:23). We come inside when it looks like rain to avoid getting wet; we pay bills to avoid legal punishment. It should be noted that rather than requiring a special explanation in terms of internal motives, such avoidance can be phrased in terms of direct reinforcement.

The termination of aversive stimuli is (positively) reinforcing, and behavior that performs this task will be strengthened. Dark rain clouds and distant thunder may have become acquired aversive stimuli through a history of association with drenching rain, and the act of seeking shelter, which terminates these stimuli, is strengthened. The avoidance of the rain itself becomes a side effect. In examining any particular activity, we may not be able to discern this history of association and learning, and so we should be prepared to seek explanations in the avoidance of certain consequences as well as in their attainment. In an interesting similarity, evolutionary theory has recognized that the struggle for existence often involves not so much overt competition as its avoidance (Colinvaux 1973:329).

(10) Behavior is most quickly and effectively learned when reinforcement immediately follows a response. Yet many activities may have delayed consequences or side effects. A response leading to positive reinforcement may have aversive consequences much later. Heavy drinking may be very pleasant at the time it occurs, but the next morning's hangover certainly is not. Smoking may lead to an early death, but in the meantime it may provide many positive reinforcements. The immediate rewards for such behavior are responsible for its persistence. There has been a tendency among economic and ecological anthropologists to measure all the monetary or energetic results of an activity and to assume its persistence if the *net* result is positive. Yet, the process of operant learning requires only that the *first* result be positive; later side effects might be much more aversive. The maintenance of certain puzzling "dysfunctional" or "maladaptive" behaviors may be the result of such immediate positive reinforcement (Margolis 1977). Investigators must examine the sequence of effects of behavior as well as their net result.

(11) Humans are not perfect processors of information—a fact increasingly being incorporated into models of decision making and economics (Leibenstein 1976; Ross 1977; Winkler and Murphy 1973). We show biases in perception, limitations of information extraction, tendencies to be tied to initial impressions and past experiences, and emphasis of immediate versus long-term effects. Such imperfections are predictable in the context of operant learning. Our perceptions of "relevant" stimuli and information are learned in the course of past reinforcement properties. One result of these imperfections is that certain behaviors may seem quite inexplicable in their current context. Our "objective" picture of

the environmental stimuli and the consequences of behavior may be quite different from that of the actors. Perceptions learned in the past may not have adjusted to environmental changes. The United States economy is based on a perception of abundant resources that is no longer correct, and we may be (falsely) optimistic about the development of new energy sources because past experience has taught us to be (Watt 1974). Many of our current problems are difficult because they "resemble past situations in which certain responses were appropriate and reinforced" (Millenson 1967:336). Our abilities to plan are limited in part by past experiences and our relative inability to perceive changes in contingencies or long-term side effects.

(12) The individual, not the group, is emphasized in behavioral studies, as is increasingly true of economics and ecological anthropology. We need not assume, however, that a group is simply a collective individual. Just as anthropology has come to stress individual differences in behavior and access to information or materials (Acheson 1976; Kunkel 1976; Salisbury 1975; Vayda and McCay 1975), so too, can a focus on operant learning accommodate individual differences in discrimination, responding, and reinforcement opportunities. Political behavior can be examined in terms of the manipulation of stimuli and reinforcers, and their relationship to consensus, cooperation, coaxing, and coercion.

(13) A common form of explanation of behavior is to cite the behavior's *functions*. As it is commonly understood, a function may be interpreted as either a purpose or as an effect; the first interpretation necessarily implies a goal, whereas the second does not. Anthropological uses of functionalism have examined group behavior and its implications for the group: the function of warfare, for example, may be claimed to be population regulation. One criticism of such explanations is that they seem to attribute purposeful and adaptive behavior to entire groups: "The functional approach often assumes that societies are integrated in terms of the goal of self-preservation and that all, or at least most, institutions and values contribute to this goal" (Richerson 1977:18). If we focus on individual learning and behavior, however, such group attributes are problematic. A society does not behave as a purposeful individual. Moreover, many of the claimed functions are "latent"—unintended and unrecognized (Vayda and Rappaport 1968). How can unconscious goals be pursued?

As a result of these problems, many anthropologists have abandoned interpretations of functional purposes and have stressed the functional effects of behavior (Richerson 1977:20). In this context, functional explanations identify one of several consequences of behavior and give it causal prominence (Brown 1963:110). Warfare kills people, devastates the land, stimulates the economy, and strengthens the central government; the persistence of warfare might be functionally explained primarily by its destruction of excess people. The basis of the choice of the relevant effect is its contribution to the society's maintenance or regulation:

> Clearly underlying all functional doctrines is the fundamental metaphor of the living organism, its several parts and organs, grouped and organized into a system, the function of the various parts and organs being to sustain the organism. . . [Jarvie 1973:33].

A true functional explanation of a trait would require the demonstration that the trait is necessary and sufficient to the maintenance of a system, operating through the process of negative feedback. Unfortunately, most such explanations are weak because the system, its variables, and the requirements of maintenance are not clearly specified (Brown 1963:119). Furthermore, the conditions of necessity and sufficiency are rarely demonstrated, largely because of the existence of alternative means of performing any function (Vayda and Rappaport 1968:496; Yellen 1977:271). Abstinence and abortion can also reduce population, thus being alternatives to war.

Part of the difficulty with such explanations lies with the analogy between social systems and organisms. Society is not nearly so coherent as an organism; it does not survive and reproduce as a unit. There are, nevertheless, patterns of regular behavior and interaction that give society structure, and much of this structure exhibits systematic organization. Feedback relationships in terms of reciprocal responses and effects do exist, but these do not necessarily imply the existence of a cohesive and regulated social system. Indeed, if ecological anthropologists are not trying to explain traits but "are trying simply to show how they work" (Vayda and McCay 1975:295), then such relationships can be investigated without any theoretical metaphors. In fact, anthropologists might accept functionalism as both a valid method and a false theory (Jarvie 1973:35).

Reduced to their essentials, most recent ecological functionalist arguments seek to answer the question, "Why do those people do *that?*" "That" refers to some behavior which appears strange, harmful, or wasteful according to the anthropologists' values. The answers provided usually involve the fitness-enhancing or problem-solving implications of the particular behavior studied. An emphasis on operant learning, on the other hand, leads to two separate kinds of answers: (1) They do it because it is reinforced, and (2) they can survive to behave this way because various problems have been solved.

These answers may or may not be related. There may be no apparent connection between the behavior and any particular problem. If, however, there is some correlation or connection between the two, then at least three possible reasons for this pattern are possible.

(1) The behavior may be solving the problem directly and consciously. Some infanticide, for example, may solve the problem of overpopulation through the

intermediate reinforcement of a lessening of the demands on a mother's time and effort.

(2) The behavior may be solving the problem unconsciously but still directly; the reinforcers are functionally linked to the problem. Among the Tsembaga of New Guinea, for example, it has been suggested that one function of the ritual pig feasts is to distribute protein and increase its consumption at a critical period (Rappaport 1968). The reinforcers, however, would seem to constitute the reduction of disputes and work effort.

(3) The behavior may have little to do with problem solving, but there is a structural not functional link between the reinforcers and the problem domain. For example, a functionalist explanation of the prevalence of potentially dangerous hitchhiking in the United States might stress the beneficial implications of this behavior for reducing air pollution by lowering the number of cars on the road. Support for this interpretation might be sought in the demonstration of a worldwide correlation between level of air pollution and frequency of hitchhiking. Yet the correlation may be spurious and the behavior only structurally linked to the problem through an intermediate factor of the number of cars: the greater the number of cars, the more frequent the reinforcement of hitchhiking is likely to be. In fact, if increased hitchhiking does effect a reduction of the number of cars (thereby reducing air pollution), it also reduces the chances for this behavior to be subsequently reinforced.

Given a focus on reinforced individual behavior, consequently, functionalist explanations should be examined for the *linkage* between reinforcement and problem, a linkage that may amount to nothing more than an accidental correlation between a discriminative stimulus and problem domain. The emic reinforcers must be identified for behavior that etically seems to function to alleviate protein scarcity or to accomplish nutrient balance. Explanations of agricultural intensification that stress the function of dealing with overpopulation or land shortage by increasing productivity per unit area must demonstrate the relationship between this function and the various individual situations, perceptions, and reinforcers. Does the individual in each case suffer a land shortage? If not, what are the rewards for his intensified efforts?

It seems useful, then, to search for functions in terms of the effects of problem-solving behavior. If an activity performs latent functions, it is solving unrecognized problems, perhaps simply as a side effect of its reinforcement contingencies. If the problems seem to us to be too critical to be left to such haphazard solutions, then perhaps we are seeking a too perfectly designed universe. Increasingly, the importance of accidents, chance, and mere side effects in evolution is being recognized (Colinvaux 1973). Certainly, much of the pairing of cues, responses, and reinforcers has initially random characteristics, which are then fixed in the learning process. Adaptive behavior consists of a valid set of solutions to problems—whether the problems are recognized or not, whether the solutions are intended or accidental. Primary reinforcers are intimately related to basic requirements for survival and reproduction As long as these needs are met, then other reinforcers and other problems will guide behavior. Ecological anthropologists must examine and compare specific problems and the relationship of learned behavior to their solution.

Chapter 3

The Context of Survival

1. ECOSYSTEM STRUCTURE AND FUNCTION

1.1. Energy Flow and Trophic Levels

A primary focus of ecological studies has been the flow of energy in the ecosystem. All organisms need energy to survive and reproduce, but they obtain and utilize energy in different ways. The ultimate source of energy input in an ecosystem is the sun. This input can be utilized by green plants through the process of photosynthesis; it is transformed and stored as plant material. Animals that are herbivorous can obtain this stored energy by eating the plants, and they in turn store energy in their body tissues. Carnivores obtain this energy by eating the herbivores, and they in turn may be eaten by other carnivores.

The central process here is the flow of energy along a food chain composed of different groups of organisms. At each stage, energy is converted and stored for later possible use. According to their position in such a food chain, organisms can be classified as belonging to one of the following groups or trophic levels:

PRODUCERS: organisms that can convert solar energy into chemical energy; basically the green plants;

CONSUMERS: organisms that derive their energy from plant or animal tissues; these include *herbivores,* and *carnivores;*

DECOMPOSERS: organisms that break down dead plant and animal material; primarily bacteria and fungi.

An important aspect of this flow of energy is that it is not totally efficient; that is, much energy cannot be passed from one level to the next. A huge proportion—often roughly 90% (Odum 1971:63)—of the available energy is lost through respiration and heat loss. This has given rise to the rule-of-thumb sometimes called the "10% Law," namely, only about 10% of the energy from one level can be captured by organisms on the next higher trophic level.

This law has important consequences for the structure of food chains: the higher the trophic level, the less energy available, and thus generally the fewer the number of individuals and the smaller the total weight or biomass. As a result, most food chains can be represented by *pyramidal* structures, which get smaller with increasing height in food chains. Ecologists have formulated pyramids of energy, numbers of individuals, and biomass to represent this structural principle. As a simple example, white-tailed deer, which are herbivorous, have a typical population density of about 0.04 individuals per acre, or a biomass of 1700 gm per acre. Wolves, which are carnivores, have a much smaller density in the same habitat, around 0.0005 individuals per acre, or a biomass of 19 gm per acre (Jackson 1961; Pearson 1964).

The concepts of trophic levels, food chains, and pyramids are simplications of the real world. An omnivore like the bear feeds on both plants and animals, and so occupies several trophic levels at the same time. Most animals eat many different foods, and are eaten by many different animals, so that simple food chains must be replaced by more complex *food webs*. The more closely our models approximate the real world, the more complex the relationships become. In a food web, it becomes difficult to designate levels, and thus the concept of pyramids is more difficult to apply.

Once we examine ecosystems containing humans, the situation becomes even more complex, for two reasons. First of all, humans are uniquely able to define their own position in the food web and tend to show great flexibility of behavior. Second, humans can change the structure of ecosystems drastically to define their position in relation to energy flow. Several studies of human societies that have focused on energy flow admirably demonstrate this variability and complexity. Among the groups so studied are Eskimos (Kemp 1971), !Kung San (Lee 1969), the Karimojong (Dyson-Hudson and Dyson-Hudson 1969), the Tsembaga (Rappaport 1971a), and West Bengalese (Parrack 1969).

These groups differ greatly in the nature of their energy sources and in the degree of interference with or control over their ecosystem. The Eskimos of the Baffin Island coast derive 63% of their calories from animal products, mainly sea mammals, and before the availability of store-bought foods, the figure was probably closer to 100%.

By contrast, the !Kung of southern Africa, another group of hunters and gatherers, obtain only 32% of their calories from animals, the rest being from plants (and the Hadza of East Africa derive only about 20% from animals) (Woodburn 1968). The Karimojong are African cattle herders who practice some agriculture, and although no precise figures are given, it seems that over 50% of their diet is derived from their domesticated animals. The Tsembaga of New Guinea and the Bengalese of India are both farming groups, and obtain 99% and

94%, respectively, of their calories from plants. These few examples show that humans can vary greatly in their trophic level, from being a pure carnivore to being almost solely a herbivore, with all positions in between.

In agreement with the general pyramidal structure of feeding relationships, human population density shows a partial correlation with relative trophic level: the greater the dependence on plants, the greater the numbers of individuals per unit area (Table 3.1). This correlation is complicated by two additional factors: the amount of interference with the ecosystem by means of domestication, agriculture, and industrialization, and the presence of energy inputs from outside the local system. The hunters and gatherers show the lowest densitities, whereas the others all manipulate their environments to a great degree through herding and farming. The Bengalese, in addition, have intensified agriculture with some irrigation, as well as access to urban energy sources and a wage economy. The question of human population density and its determinants will be considered in greater detail in Chapter 7.

Another point to consider is that humans can differ vastly in terms of the efficiency of their energy budget. The ratio of energy yield to energy cost can be estimated for two of the groups discussed: for the Tsembaga, Rappaport states that this ratio is about 16 to 1, while for the Eskimos this ratio seems to be less than 2 to 1. These figures illustrate part of the range of possible variation but should not be used to generalize about overall relative efficiencies of farming versus hunting and gathering. In fact, as Sahlins (1972) stresses in his studies of primitive economics, agriculture is not necessarily more efficient than hunting and gathering and does not automatically provide more leisure time. For comparison, it is interesting to note that in the American food economy of the 1960s, the ratio of energy yield to input was about 1 to 7.5; we only received about one-seventh of the energy used in agriculture, food processing, transporation, sales, and home preparation (Hirst 1973). Clearly, total energetic efficiency does not characterize our food economy.

Just as humans can define their trophic level, so too can they do much to improve the efficiency of energy capture. In virtually all ethographic studies, it is clear that, among other goals, people seek to minimize labor and to obtain high yields for it. Certain strategies to improve efficiency can be cited for the groups mentioned. The Eskimos, for example, formerly shifted their camps to minimize the distance they needed to travel to hunt and fish. They readily adopted boat motors and snowmobiles because these machines made travel easier and increased the labor efficiency of hunting trips. The !Kung regularly use the closest of their preferred foods and will move camp when the nearby sources are exhausted. The Tsembaga readily adopted the machete because it made clearing work easier, and they prefer to clear secondary over primary forest because it is easier. They normally place their houses quite close to the gardens to minimize walking distance and try to cluster the gardens themselves to reduce the total

TABLE 3.1

Human Population Density and Trophic Level

Group	Population density (No./km²)	Diet (% Animal foods)
Eskimos	0.04	63
!Kung	0.10	32
Karimojong	5.86	>50
Tesembaga	25.00	1
Bengalese	820.31	6

length of fences necessary. The Karimojong move their cattle herds to grazing lands as conditions change; they place no territorial restrictions or obstacles on grazing lands and will often split up herds to match them to local food conditions.

It seems evident, therefore, that efficiency is one overriding concern of most peoples—they seek to increase the ratio of energy yield to input. Another very important concern seems to be the *security* or stability of the energy sources. In the same studies, this concern can be seen to take several forms as follows: (1) strategies to even out energy yields through time and among people; (2) strategies to exploit alternative, emergency energy sources when necessary; and (3) strategies that provide for the long-term conservation of energy sources.

Among the Copper Eskimo, for example, there occurs food-sharing after hunts, and villagewide meals, both of which distribute food among successful and unsuccessful hunters and their dependents. Such practices are supported by norms of behavior and help to provide a stable diet for the whole group. Furthermore, food storage is common, especially after the fall hunt, which secures the winter diet when hunting is more difficult. Since food is stored in bulk and is available to all, this may be seen as a delayed strategy of sharing as well. Other aspects of Eskimos' behavior include the maintenance of flexibility in economic activities. The intensity of winter hunting of sea mammals varies according to the success of the fall hunt and the alternative possibilities for winter. The importance of caribou hunting varies greatly, depending on the availability of caribou and the success of other activities. Summer activities can include open-water seal hunting, basking seal hunting, or fish spearing, depending on the weather. Furthermore, both dog teams and snowmobiles are maintained in the village, so that the dogs can be used in case of mechanical breakdown or lack of fuel. Finally, this group apparently kills just enough animals to eat and not more, despite the new advantages of snowmobiles and rifles, so that the resources are maintained over the long run (other groups of Eskimos have been known to decimate their animal food resources with the acquisition of rifles, however).

The Tsembaga practice no food storage, but they manage to spread out their food yields over time by a process of continuous harvesting year-round. Furthermore, they maintain a great variety of food plants, so that some are sure to survive pests and weather. In weeding and harvesting, they made a great effort to protect tree seedlings, thus promoting forest regeneration rather than invasion by grasses. The tropical forest is thus maintained over time.

The Karimojong regularly share meat and also have large religious sacrifices and feasts, especially in hard times, that serve to distribute food when it is needed most. They use cattle as a medium of exchange to establish social relationships, thus building a network of ties that provide a kind of insurance; if hard times hit, they can rely on help in return. Storage of foods is minimal, but the herds themselves can be viewed as storage on the hoof, since the cattle can be slaughtered if and when necessary. More important, however, the Karimojong regularly use only the live animal products of blood and milk, thereby ensuring continuity of this food source through time. The economic alternatives of agriculture, hunting, and gathering are maintained and vary in importance according to weather, grazing, and condition of the herds.

These various practices that we understand as increasing stability may or may not be recognized as such by the people themselves. Certainly food storage would be, whereas food sharing, cattle exchanges, and feasts might be explained in social terms, not economic. The practices do, however, follow one principle of ecological structure, that is, that stability of an ecosystem is correlated with the number of alternative pathways for energy flow. All these people maintain the following variety of energy sources: (1) alternative food species; (2) stored food; and (3) shared food. Thus, they avoid total specialization, which might mean economic disaster. The focus on energy flow helps to elucidate these effects and, thus perhaps, to explain partly the significance of certain aspects of economics, demography, settlement, and social interaction.

1.2. Productivity

Clearly, there are differences among environments, resources, and economic strategies in their energy content, structure, demands, and yields. Consideration of these differences is critical to understanding human population size and structure, the distribution of different economic types, the processes of food selection, and the relationship among economy, environment, settlement pattern, and levels of social and political organization.

The major environmental zones of the world show differential efficiency of energy capture and incorporation into plant material. Since plants form the ultimate energy source for all animals, including humans, such differences would have great significance for the structure of each food web. Table 3.2 presents some estimates for differences in primary productivity among various habitats. Grasslands are more productive than deserts, and forests more so than grasslands. Managed agricultural systems tend to show equal or greater produc-

TABLE 3.2

Productivity of Various Habitats[a]

Biome	Net primary productivity (kcal/m²/yr)
Desert	400
Grassland	700–4400
Deciduous forest	4800
Coniferous forest	11,200
Tropical forest	20,000
Temperate agriculture	8800–12,000
Tropical agriculture	12,000–30,000

[a] After Westlake 1963:414.

tivity than wild ecosystems. In both types, there tends to be greater productivity in the tropics as compared to higher latitudes, in part due to the greater input of solar energy in the tropics.

Ecosystems can differ too in the nature of their productivity, that is, in the amount and distribution of biomass as plant tissue. Tundras and deserts are marked by having most of their plant biomass in the form of roots and litter (84 and 91%, respectively), whereas forests have between 75 and 78% in the form of stems, leaves, and branches (Kormondy 1969:128). Not only are there different energy contents, but there are also differences in the availability and usefulness of this energy.

Such generalizations are useful, but particular populations of animals, including humans, live in specific local ecosystems, not large-scale biomes. The human environment is not a monolithic whole structure having a single set of effects on humans over wide areas. Rather, there are different microenvironments made up of specific local conditions; humans are aware of these small differences and selectively interact with only certain components of the local natural environment. For example, people commonly take advantage of "unearned resources" or outside energy inputs into a local system by harvesting fish in streams or the ocean or by harvesting migratory birds or mammals that pass through but ultimately derive much of their energy from elsewhere. The use of fossil fuels like oil can be viewed in this way since their energy content came from past ecosystems. Another common feature of human adaptations is the utilization of the so-called "edge effect." This is based on the ecological generalization that borders or transitional areas between habitats (called ecotones) are usually more productive and have a greater variety of species than either habitat alone. Settlement at forest–grassland margins or on riverbanks might be viewed in this way.

TABLE 3.3

Caloric and Protein Content of Selected Plant Foods[a]

Food	Calories/100 gm	Protein (gm)/100 gm
White potato	79	2.1
Taro	92	1.9
Yam	100	2.1
Sweet potato	116	1.7
Manioc	140	1.7
Wheat	330	14.0
Barley	348	8.2
Brown rice	357	7.5
Maize	361	8.9
Bean	340	22.3
Lentil	340	24.7
Cashew	561	17.2
Almond	598	18.6
Mongongo nut	600	28.3
Pinon nut	635	13.0
Brazil nut	654	14.3

[a] After Lee 1979; Watt and Merill 1975.

Another important consideration in evaluating differential productivity is that specific resources can vary greatly in their energy and nutrient contents (Table 3.3). Mongongo nuts, an important staple of the !Kung diet, are extremely rich in both calories and protein per unit weight, whereas most of the other plants in the !Kung diet are relatively poor. Agricultural crops can vary tremendously. Root crops such as yams and manioc are relatively poor, whereas cereal crops such as wheat and maize are much richer in both protein and calories. Legumes like peas and beans are even higher in protein, whereas nut crops like almonds have a very high caloric content, similar to the wild mongongo nut.

In addition, the protein content of various foods can vary in quality as well as quantity. Proteins are made up of amino acids, and of the 22 different amino acids required by humans, eight of these must be supplied in the diet, since they cannot be manufactured by the body. Furthermore, these eight so-called "essential" amino acids must be eaten at the same time but in different amounts in order to be utilized. Individual plant foods tend to be deficient in some of these amino acids, so that different plant foods need to be mixed in the diet for their protein potential to be realized. Observed cross-cultural regularities of such mixtures, such as rice and beans or maize, beans, and squash, increase the effective protein content of the largely vegetarian diet. In evaluating diets, it is necessary to examine the protein in the total daily diet, rather than in individual foods.

Animal foods also vary greatly in their energy and nutrient content and usefulness. Animals such as deer, caribou, bison, and rabbit provide about 50% of their body weight in usable meat, whereas bears, beaver, seals, and birds are about 70% edible (White 1953). The protein and caloric content of animals can also differ greatly (Table 3.4). Even the same animal species can show dramatic changes in weight and protein and fat content from one season to the next. Hibernating animals such as bears show fat accumulation just before winter, whereas many mammals such as caribou, roe deer, and chamois show weight increases just before the late summer or fall rut (Fig. 3.1). Most fish reach their peak weights just before spawning, and for anadromous fish like salmon, this weight is lost progressively as they travel upstream to spawn.

Not only do animals themselves show great variation in energy content, their exploitation techniques also differ in terms of net energy yields. Some factors that seem to be important in determining net yields, in addition to the energy content per unit weight and its edibility, include size of the animal, its population density, its group size, and its predictability of movement (Jochim 1976:22–24). A larger animal provides more meat per kill; a more abundant animal provides greater opportunities for locating and killing; an animal living in large herds provides the possibility of more kills per act of locating the game; and the more predictable the animal, the easier it is to find and capture it. Thus, it is not surprising that large herd animals like bison, wildebeest, or caribou have been the economic focus for many hunters and gatherers, that bears and beaver are often sought out when they are in their dens or lodges and are relatively im-

TABLE 3.4

Caloric and Protein Content of Selected Animal Food[a]

Food	Calories/100 gm	Protein (gm)/100 gm
Caribou	217	20.5
Beaver	248	29.2
Green turtle	89	19.8
Duck	233	21.1
Clam	82	14.0
Cod	78	17.6
Sturgeon	94	18.1
Halibut	100	20.9
Lake trout	168	18.3
Chinook salmon	222	19.1
Eel	233	15.9

[a] After Watt and Merrill 1975.

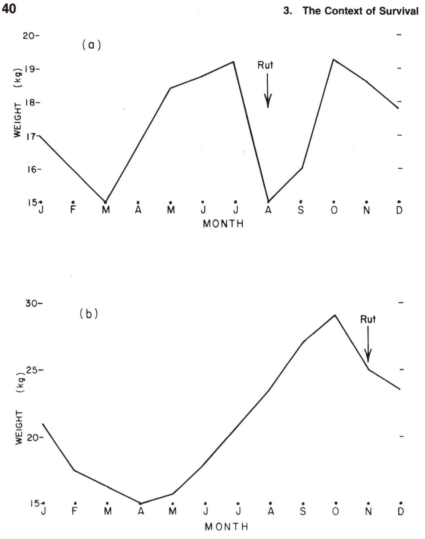

Fig. 3.1. Seasonal weight changes of (a) male roe deer and (b) male chamois (after Wandeler and Huber, 1969).

not always however

mobile, that very small animals are frequently ignored unless they occur in large groups, such as some insect larvae, or that fish and birds are most sought after when they form large groups for spawning or migration. A consideration of energetic efficiency and stability helps clarify some of the basis for food selection and the timing of economic activities.

Certain aspects of technology can be examined from this viewpoint of energetics as well. Snowmobiles and machetes are items readily adopted because they conserve labor for the users. Devices such as spears, arrows, and harpoons extend the reach of the hunter in space, whereas traps, fish weirs, and deadfalls extend his reach in both time and space. These technological devices enable people to harness greater energy, to effect a greater food yield per person. Other features of technology, such as canoes and snowshoes, reduce the effort in traveling and increase the net yield per hunting trip. For example, walking in soft snow at a speed of 4 km per hour requires the expenditure of about 20.7 calories per minute; with snowshoes, the cost becomes only 13.8 calories per minute—a savings of one-third (Spector 1956). From this savings, of course, must be deducted the cost of making and repairing the snowshoes. Snowmobiles represent an even larger immediate savings of energy but are energetically much more expensive to manufacture and maintain.

Turning to agricultural activities, the differences in content of various crops per unit *weight* has been mentioned. Discussion of productivity must also consider the important differences in the yields per unit *land* or per unit *work,* as well as the effects on the soil. Cereal crops, for example, although richer in protein and calories than root crops per unit weight, are poorer in calories per unit area—that is, more calories can be produced per field by growing root crops than by growing cereals. In addition, cereals make greater demands on soil fertility and thus require longer fallow times between plantings or artificial restoration of soil fertility. Legumes like beans, on the other hand, are nitrogen-fixing plants that tend to restore fertility to the soil.

Agriculturalists also have a range of strategies available that will alter their position relative to energy flow. In addition to the differing yields and effects of various crops in different latitudes, there are a number of techniques of farming, each with its own requirements and consequences. Agricultural systems can be classified according to a variety of criteria, one of which is the soil fertility to which they are adapted. Slash-and-burn (or swidden or long-term fallow) farming, for example, is a system that is widely used in tropical and temperate forests and is suited to regions of low natural fertility. In this sytem, fields are cleared by cutting down trees and burning off the brush; the burning breaks down nutrients and returns them to the soil. The field might be in cultivation for 2 or 3 years, after which it loses fertility and must lie fallow or abandoned for perhaps 25 years (there is, of course, a wide variation in these figures, depending on local conditions of soil, crops, and weather). Since new fields must be planted while the abandoned land lies fallow, one family might have only 1.5 hectares of land in cultivation at one time but might require an average total of 12 hectares for a total cycle over the 25-year period.

Depending on local soil fertility and population pressure, this system can be modified by shortening the fallow time through a number of stages. The longest fallow times allow the forest to grow back on the land, and planting can be done directly after clearing. With somewhat shorter fallow times, the forest does not regenerate, and a system called "bush fallow" might be practiced. This is similar to the slash-and-burn technique, but the ground may have to be worked with a hoe before planting since the burning does not effectively clear it.

Finally, in very short fallow times, only grass has a chance to grow in the abandoned gardens, and in such cases, the tough roots need to be broken up by a plow since they are not destroyed by burning. Not only is the plow needed, its use is easier in this system since there are no large tree roots providing obstacles to the plow. In addition, draft animals for pulling the plow can be fed on the grass itself. This "grass fallow" is also called the sectorial or two-field system: a field is planted for 1 to 3 years and then lies fallow for about the same length of time. A family might have 2.5 hectares in cultivation at one time, but require only an estimated average of 6.5 hectares for a total cycle of about 3 years. Note that this savings in terms of total land requirements relative to the longer fallow system is accomplished only by increasing the input of agricultural work. Specific additional techniques and conditions can increase soil fertility and further restrict the land required to support a family, usually with additional requirements of labor. These include the use of manure and chemical fertilizers, the placing of fish in plant hillocks, and the catching and draining of natural silt-bearing floodwaters.

Another way of examining agricultural systems is according to their water supply. Rainfall farming allows one crop per year in areas receiving at least 200 mm of rain per year, although in very hot regions with high rates of evaporation and transpiration, this minimum requirement may rise to 375 mm per year. This can be a relatively easy system, but has some inherent problems. The distribution of rain may be erratic and unreliable, especially in areas receiving close to the lower limit required. If torrential, the rain may cause great erosion and rapid runoff of water and topsoil. Calculation of the total productivity of such a system would have to take such hazards into account, along with the costs of any countermeasures practiced by the farmers.

Many other agricultural systems do not depend directly on rainfall for their water supply, and each system has its own hazards and distinctive set of labor requirements. Floodwater cultivation is practiced in the plains of large rivers such as the Nile, especially in the lower reaches with a low gradient. The water is provided by the annual flooding of the river, and the crops are planted as the floods recede. Fluctuation of flood timing and level may derive from climatic variability closer to the river's headwaters and pose problems of drainage and water control requiring ditches and embankments. Ridged fields and chinampas consist of artificial elevations of dry land built in wet areas, for example, in the Valley of Mexico. Usually, seedlings, not seeds, are planted, and this, together with manuring and mucking, allow three crops per year.

The labor requirements of construction and maintenance in this sytem are extremely high. The reverse of this sytem is the construction of sunken fields, in which the land surface is excavated down close to the water table so that the plants have direct access to the water. This technique, also demanding high labor inputs, is known from the prehistoric occupation of the coast of Peru (Parsons and Psuty 1975). Pot-irrigation is the practice of digging small wells in fields and distributing the water by hand. Although this technique can permit the growing of three crops per year, it is possible only in areas of relatively high water table, usually river plains, and similarly requires much labor. Canal-irrigation consists of the diversion of water by channels dug through natural levees of rivers and into the fields. Although there is a wide range of sizes and form of such canals, they all require rivers or springs with large surface flows, and upstream locations with their steeper grades are most favorable. The construction and maintenance of canals, together with the prevention of salt buildup in fields are among the many demands of this system on labor.

There are numerous other types of agricultural systems, as well as combinations of the above types. Each system differs in terms of its costs in land and labor and in terms of its yields. Discussions of economic productivity must examine each local system according to the various criteria. "Hunting and gathering" and "slash-and-burn farming" are not adequate descriptions of an economy for ecological analysis and comparison. Moreover, expectations about economic systems cannot be based on single environmental measures. It has been suggested, for example, that the general productivity of biomass tends to be highest in the tropics and to decrease with distance from the equator. In light of this generalization, it might appear contradictory that the most productive modern economies (in terms of GNP, food surplus and export, military hardware, etc.) occur in the temperate latitudes. The contradiction can be resolved by an examination of factors other than net primary productivity of the biome. There are numerous contrasts in other features of the environment and economies of the two regions affecting the utilization of this primary productivity.

Tropical environments have a complex and diverse biomass that exists in many different compartments or forms, not all of which are readily useful to humans. Tropical soils frequently are fragile to human interference so that erosion and loss of fertility are huge problems to farmers. The rapid growth rates possible in the tropics may quickly undo human alterations in the environment such as forest clearing, causing a rapid diversification of the simplified human environment. Tropical diversity may include more numerous competitors, parasites, or predators of humans. In light of these problems, many tropical economies emphasize stability at the expense of efficiency. By contrast, the temperate economies tend to emphasize efficiency over stability, and specifically, an efficiency of land and labor use, not total energy use. Consequently, many temperate economies are based on unearned resources from outside their local ecosystems (coal, oil, gas) and are characterized by a large amount of waste by a lack of recycling of energy

[handwritten margin note: also upon shallow line depth]

and materials. Clearly, any expectations about economic productivity based sole-ly upon consideration of latitude and its influence on primary vegetational productivity are so simplified as to be useless. Similarly uninformative are in-terpretations and generalizations based on other single factors, whether these are soil type, crops, or technological efficiency.

1.3. Habitat and Niche

Economic productivity is clearly not directly predictable from the productivity of the natural environment. Similarly, the structure of an economy is not depen-dent solely on the environmental structure. Since economic activities represent the human participation in the energy flow of an ecosystem, it might be supposed that these activities would show a correlation with features of the natural envi-ronment. In certain situations, such a correlation appears to exist. Kroeber (1939), for example, examined the distribution of aboriginal American economies in relation to natural areas—predominantly vegetational zones—and stressed that there was a remarkable correspondence among, not only these two features, but also ethnic groups and complexity of social and political organiza-tion. On the basis of these common distributions, he discussed the concept of *culture area*—a rather homogeneous geographical zone in terms of climate, resources, economies, and social and political institutions, exemplified by the Eastern Woodlands, Great Basin, Northwest Coast, and the Southwest. Despite more detailed distributional analyses that revealed a lack of covariation between specific cultural and natural traits (Hatch 1973:231), the broad patterns of similar distributions remained. These culture areas could be described as the result of similar adaptations to similar environmental conditions or the result of similar selective pressures. They might be more easily understood, however, as similar solutions to similar environmental problems. In this view, the similarity of so-lutions would derive not only from the similarity of problems but also from the similarity of means and knowledge available and from a similarity of goals guiding the solutions.

This neat geographical patterning in North America, nevertheless, is deceptive and poses the danger of encouraging a view of environments and cultures as fixed and simple whole units. Specifically, as Barth (1956) points out, the culture-area approach does not seem to work well in Asia. The distributions of environments, economies, ethnic groups, and cultural institutions do not seem to coincide, and in order to examine and understand these distributions, Barth had to separate and distinguish clearly the concepts of *habitat* and *niche*.

For any organisms, the habitat consists of the biological and physical features of its environment, whereas niche refers to the specific requirements of the organism *[handwritten: in order]* to survive and reproduce. As Odum (1971:234) described them, the habitat is the address of the organism, whereas its niche is its profession. The habitat is the structural setting, whereas the niche is the functional role. More specifically, "a niche consists of the resources a species uses, where it finds them, and the strategy by which it harvests them" (Diamond 1978:323).

Any species of animal may live in a variety of habitats and may fill a slightly different niche in each. One species tends to occupy much the same niche in similar but separated habitats. Frogs have much the same requirements in ponds in Minnesota or Louisiana, sea gulls on the coast of California or Maine, and elk in the high Sierra or Rockies. The elk formerly in Wisconsin and elsewhere in the Midwest, however, occupied a different habitat—flat grasslands, forests, and bogs—and differed from their mountain-dwelling relatives in their behavior or niche accordingly. For many such animals there does seem to be good correspondence between habitat and niche.

A niche may be narrow, meaning that the organism has very specific, limited requirements, or it may be broad, meaning that the organism can survive in a whole range of conditions, that its requirements are many and varied. Accordingly, an organism can be classified as a specialist or a generalist, respectively. Many parasites, for example, are quite specialized for a certain host, whereas a bear is a classic generalist. In any one habitat, however, two different species cannot occupy the same niche for very long. For them to do so would mean that they had identical requirements and thus would compete for everything. In such a situation, one would eventually out-compete the other and prevail; the other would become extinct in that habitat or alter its niche. This principle is known as the "Law of Competitive Exclusion," that is, two species cannot coexist in the same habitat in the same niche (or niches that overlap for crucial resources).

One of the striking characteristics of humans is the huge variety of habitats they occupy. As a species, our biological requirements can be met in most environments. The manner in which these are met, however, is quite variable. The human niche—or profession in Odum's terms—is defined in part by the economy in its broadest sense. All the activities of getting food, shelter, and raw materials contribute to a definition of the niche. It is necessary to differentiate between the concepts of habitat and niche because of the dangers of neat spatial models of segregated populations. An understanding of how different populations can use the same space requires an examination of the nature of this utilization.

Barth (1956) studied the area of Swat, North Pakistan, which is occupied by three ethnic groups who have different economies. The Pathans are sedentary farmers; the Kohistanis practice farming and transhumant herding; and the Gujars are mainly nomadic herders. The Swat area consists of parts of two river valleys separated by high plateaus and mountains. In the south, the valleys are quite wide and the climate hot and dry; in the north, the valleys are much narrower, the climate colder. The Kohistanis were the original inhabitants who occupied the total region. The Pathans were invaders who gradually pushed the Kohistanis partly to the north. The result is that the Pathans now occupy the lower broad river valleys, whereas the Kohistanis are confined to the northern valleys and slopes.

The Swat area was originally regarded as one general habitat by the Kohistanis. They could practice single-crop farming everywhere in the valleys and take their herds back and forth between mountains and valleys. The Pathans, on the other hand, have a different economy and define different relationships with their environment. They plant two crops per year, which can be supported climatically only in the southern half of the area. The Pathans thus occupy a different niche, and consequently subdivide Swat into two separate habitats: one suitable and the other not.

The Gujars are found throughout Pathan territory, but only in the western half of Kohistani territory. Again, they subdivide the same total area into different habitats according to their specific niche. In the southern half of the region, Pathans own or control the higher slopes and grasslands, but use them only for gathering firewood. These areas are used as pasturage by the Gujars, who pay rent in the form of animal products to the Pathans. Thus, a mutual interdependence exists between the two groups. Formerly, the Kohistanis who have a generalized economy used both slopes and valleys in the south, but they were replaced by these two more specialized groups.

Gujars should be more in direct competition where they occur with the Kohistanis because both groups use the higher land for pastures. Consequently, it is remarkable that they should coexist in the northwest. The explanation lies in the economic differences between the two groups and the environmental differences between northwest and northeast Swat. Kohistanis rely a good deal on farming, especially to provide winter fodder for their herds. Owing to climatic conditions, agricultural productivity is lower in the valleys of the northwest than in those of the northeast. Thus the size of the herds supported by fodder crops is much smaller in the northwest. The smaller herds mean that much less of the highlands is used for summer pastures by the Kohistanis, and therefore many pastures are open to use by the Gujars.

Barth was able to elucidate these interrelationships by defining the differences between habitat and niche through an ecological approach. Another advantage to this approach is that it allows the utilization of laws developed in general ecological theory, such as the "Law of Competitive Exclusion." In Swat, the three groups can coexist in the same general region precisely because they occupy different niches. The Kohistanis are generalists and define a very broad niche, whereas the Pathans and Gujars are specialists and define narrower niches, redefining their suitable habitats in the process. Competition should develop only in areas of niche overlap, between each specialist and generalist.

Not only does a focus on ecological niches further our understanding of population coexistence, it also helps to explain instances of spatial displacement and some aspects of behavioral shifts. In a study of Almond Valley, California, Love

(1977) documents the influx of part-time, "retirement" farmers at the expense of local, full-time farmers in terms of their respective niches. The part-time farmers, in general, have access to outside resources not available to the local farmers, such as pensions, savings, or on-going outside jobs. As a result, they can out-bid the local farmers for small parcels of land, with the consequences that over the last 20 years, most small plots of land have passed into the hands of these outsiders. Many local farmers have been out-competed and excluded from these small parcels. Those who remained have changed their techniques of farming to suit their now generally larger farms. Almond Valley appears to have undergone a change from being occupied by one population of rather generalized farmers to a situation in which two specialist populations coexist.

Different species can coexist in the same area in part because they occupy different niches. The manner in which the environment is partitioned by various species has been the subject of numerous ecological studies. A review of 81 studies, largely of terrestrial vertebrates, examined the environmental dimensions along which niches of similar species differed in the same region. The most common dimension was the type of habitat (or microhabitat), followed by type of food and time of utilization (Schoener 1974b). The studies by Barth and Love exemplify cases of human differentiation principally along habitat dimensions. This finding suggests that certain geographic patterns in the distribution of vertebrate niches might be observed. Complex, patchy habitats should be expected to contain a greater variety of vertebrate species than do simpler, more uniform ones. The relative homogeneity of human economies in such regions as the Great Plains or Subarctic Tundras appears to stand in contrast to the greater economic differentiation in regions of increased natural complexity due to topography or other factors.

Such geographic patterns do, indeed, exist and form the focus of biogeographical research. The number of different species, or *species diversity* or density, varies widely among regions. Among the important patterns that have been observed is that species diversity is higher in the tropics than in temperate zones, higher on big islands than on small ones, higher on islands close to continents than on more distant ones, and higher in continental interiors than on coastal peninsulas (Diamond 1973; Schall and Pianka 1978). The correlation of species diversity with latitude is perhaps the most intriguing, since this parallels other latitudinal gradients such as that of incident solar radiation, seasonality, and primary productivity. This latitudinal pattern of vertebrate species diversity, however, has been measured largely in the Western Hemisphere, and does not appear to hold true for Australia. In fact, "species densities of vertebrates in North America increase toward lower latitudes; those of Australian vertebrates do not. Correlations between species densities and abiotic environmental factors for birds and mammals differ on the two continents: correlations are often opposite in sign" (Schall and Pianka 1978:685).

Clearly, geographic patterns of species diversity are not related to single environmental dimensions in a simple manner. An understanding of such patterns requires an examination of a complex set of factors that have been suggested to contribute to their determination, including physical complexity of the habitat, degree of species specialization, degree of competition, intensity of density-dependent mortality, colonization possibilities and history, directional environmental change, and environmental perturbations (Connell 1978). A variety of studies have indicated differential importance of these factors in different areas. The patterns related to island size and remoteness, for example, appear to depend largely upon colonization possibilities together with the high risk of mortality of small populations (MacArthur and Wilson 1967). Discussions of the latitudinal gradient of species diversity, on the other hand, stress competition, specialization, and environmental complexity and variability. High species diversity of tropical regions, for example, has been linked to high rates of competition and specialization in these areas (Diamond 1973, 1978; McNaughton and Wolf 1970). In higher latitudes, the intensity of competition is thought to be less and the niches generally broader because the harsher physical conditions depress populations below the level at which competition for resources becomes limiting.

Competition has assumed a dominant role in ecological explanations of niche structure, in part due to improvements in the definition and measurement of niches (Diamond 1978), and in part due to increasingly sophisticated methods of mathematically modeling competition (Schoener 1974a; Wiegert 1974). Some of the strongest evidence for competition is taken to be the apparently resultant compression of niches in the tropics (Diamond 1973, 1978; McNaughton and Wolf 1970; Pielou 1975). Yet the possibility has been raised that tropical niches show greater overlap rather than greater discreteness (Connell 1978; MacArthur 1972; Pielou 1975). Furthermore, it has been suggested that niche overlap need not lead to intensified competion—overlap might be greatest when competition is least, at times when resources are so superabundant that niche overlap can be tolerated with no selective penalties (Wiens 1977). In addition, an assumption underlying most of the models of competition and niche differentiation is that populations are close to their respective carrying capacities and at competitive equilibrium, yet such equilibria have been placed in doubt for higher latitude environments (Wiens 1977) and even tropical forests (Connell 1978).

The subject of competitive equilibria is of crucial importance to a consideration of niche structure and diversity, but the interrelationships among these factors have been considerably debated. On the one hand, community equilibrium is thought to be caused by environmental stability, which in turn leads to species diversity (May 1973; Pielou 1975). In this view, environmental seasonality and unpredictability decrease diversity by favoring generalist species with niches broad enough to allow flexibility in the variable situation. This view depends on the assumptions that diversity indicates numerous narrow niches rather than extensive niche overlap and that such niche compression results from and avoids the constantly threatening competition. On the other hand, an apparently opposing view, at least for tropical forests and coral reefs, relates species diversity to a lack of environmental stability, to disturbances of moderate frequency and intensity (Connell 1978). Such perturbations are thought to be constantly disrupting competitive interactions that would otherwise lead to equilibria in which the more efficient species would exclude its competitors, thereby reducing diversity. This view assumes that diversity is possible with significant niche overlap because competitive equilibria are not reached.

These two views are based primarily on studies of different types of organisms. The first, linking lack of disturbances with species diversity and discrete niches, derives from research on terrestrial vertebrates, the mobility of which permits them actively to partition their habitats along numerous abiotic and biotic dimensions. The second view results from studies of sessile organisms like trees and corals that define niches more passively through general requirements of largely abiotic factors. When these species differences are taken into account, these two views are no longer necessarily opposing, a fact that emphasizes the need to consider habitats in relation to species' requirements and adaptive potential, a niche is defined by the species' selective interaction with the environment. The breadth of a niche, the number of total niches in a habitat, and the manner of resource partitioning all depend on a variety of interacting factors. Since the structure of human activities, their differentiation, and their interrelationships are likely to have equally complex determinants, any discussions relating economic diversity largely to single dimensions such as environmental heterogeneity, productivity, or population pressure are probably isolating only some of the critical factors.

Significantly, both views on the determinants of diversity demonstrate the growing ecological emphasis of environmental perturbations and variability in relation not only to species diversity but also to behavioral change and adaptive convergence. Anthropology is similarly showing an increased research emphasis on environmental variation and its predictability. Such variation is part of the hazards to survival, and the lack of predictability is a major aspect of many human problems.

2. HAZARDS AND PROBLEMS

Environments are not homogeneous. The uneven distribution of various factors poses tremendous problems for human survival. Some regions have too little rain for farming; others receive torrential monsoons that wash away crops. In some areas, the warm growing season is too short to support agriculture; in others the crops wither and the soils bake in the long summer. The static mixture of such environmental features defines one set of problems requiring adjustments and solutions. Another set of problems derives from the changing features of the environment, such as the alternation of seasonal temperatures, cycles of drought, or directional environmental change. Each of these changes may be characterized by measures of average intensity, spatial extent, and frequency or rate, but each of these measures, in turn, will show a certain variance around this average that indicates the predictability of the change. A region with high average summer rains but with a high variance from year to year will be a much less predictable environment for farmers than another area with a similar average and smaller variance.

A few problems of a general nature will be discussed within the framework of the natural environment, population size and distribution, and competition. It must be emphasized that problems are defined by goals and perspective— Amazonian farmers and hunters must cope with different problems in the same environment. Furthermore, problems as discussed here will differ in their visibility. Some are immediately perceived by all, such as drought, whereas others, for example, soil exhaustion, require a long development or a special knowledge in order to be detected. The differing' visibility and detection of problems should be a major focus of future research. As suggested earlier, many problems may not be recognized as such by the people involved, yet solutions may be provided by their behavior. Research should be directed toward an understanding of how the reinforcements for this behavior are related to the context of the problem.

2.1. Problems in the Natural Environment

2.1.1. Temperature

Ecological studies of limiting factors and their temporal and spatial variation have suggested a number of general environmental problems facing organisms in different biomes. One of these factors of most obvious importance is temperature. Extremes of cold or heat impose limitations and require adjustments in terms of shelter, clothing, and level of activity. Areas characterized by such extremes will show plant and animal communities whose form and behavior are largely temperature controlled. Since humans exploit and alter these communities, such characteristics are of crucial importance.

Regions of relatively low average annual temperatures are characterized by brief growing seasons and scant, rapid-growing vegetation. This floral simplicity and scarcity limits the amount and variety of plant foods (whether wild or cultivated) in the diet, requiring either methods of procuring nonlocal plant foods or else an emphasis on animal foods, and consequently, a high position on the food chain, with resultant implications for human population densities. Wild animal populations must similarly adjust to the limited vegetation, frequently by maintaining high mobility and relatively low densities, and occasionally by periods of inactivity or hibernation. Domesticated animals may need to be kept highly mobile as well, with important ramifications for human settlement and labor organization. An alternative to maintaining high herd mobility would be the supplimentation of wild graze with feed supplies, requiring additional human energy in its procurement and distribution. Human metabolic rates are frequently high under conditions of low ambient temperatures, placing large demands on the system of food procurement and encouraging development of shelter and insulation techniques. In a sense, then, low-temperature environments promote high rates of energy flow to insure the constant production and partial retention of heat and the maintenance of high levels of movement and procurement.

High-temperature environments, on the other hand, promote vegetational growth unless restricted by other factors such as insufficient moisture. With adequate precipitation or ground water, growing seasons are long and vegetation tends to be complex and abundant, encouraging plant collection or cultivation and facilitating the maintenance of high population densities. Obstacles to intensive plant collecting may be posed by the great variety and lack of concentration of single species, prohibiting specialization and easy local collecting. Cultivation must face the problems of field clearance and weeding in such areas of high wild plant growth. In addition, the vegetational variety may encourage faunal diversity, which would discourage specialization on a few animal resources. This same vegetational diversity may result in a limit to the suitable food for domesticated animals, necessitating additional efforts to collect or cultivate fodder. Moreover, vegetational density may pose obstacles to travel, with concomitant increases in costs of economic and social interaction among areas. It should be mentioned too that the high growth rates characteristic of regions of high temperatures would apply to bacteria as well, posing hazards to health, food storage, and house maintenance.

It is, of course, an oversimplification to consider the effects of relatively extreme temperatures in isolation from other factors, but such a simplification is, perhaps, necessary in order to isolate the accompanying hazards. Low-temperature environments necessitate attempts to accelerate and insure the flow of energy. High-temperature environments, by contrast, require attempts to impede, divert, and control the high rate of energy flow in the environment.

Beyond these general characteristics of environmental temperature extremes, the distributional patterns of more moderate temperatures can have significant specific effects according to individual resource tolerances. Corn farming in native North America, for example, seems to have been limited to areas with warm growing seasons of at least 120 days (Kroeber 1939), whereas the greater cold tolerance of barley over wheat accounts, in part, for the differential distributions of these crops (Renfrew 1973). Caribou distribution is related to their upper limit of tolerance of summer temperatures (Banfield 1954). Water temperatures are critical in the distribution, abundance, and behavior of anadromous fish such as Pacific and Atlantic salmon (Netboy 1968; Schalk 1977).

Such resource distributions are important not only in determining their dietary potential but also in the resulting implications for other dietary needs and the technology and organization of procurement. People without access to large fish runs, for example, may show greater emphasis toward hunting to provide meat, resulting in greater mobility, fewer material goods, and a different technological elaboration, as well as various social accomodations to these features. The differential protein content or caloric productivity of various crops suitable to specific local temperatures would influence the relative importance of horticulture in relation to hunting, herding, or fishing in mixed economies. In more complex economic systems, the regional temperature variation in relation to facilities for storage, transportation, and distribution would be crucial to the resulting subsistence diversity and nature of economic interdependence. Such temperature distributions, moreover, would significantly influence the varying availability of, and requirements for fuels and building materials, with implications for procurement and distribution systems.

In addition to these problems and constraints posed by the extremes and spatial distribution of temperatures, the effects of the variation and predictability of temperature over time must be considered as well. Regular temperature changes may occur over various periods, from daily to seasonal or longer intervals, and with various amplitudes, from small to extreme fluctuations. With increasing magnitude of daily temperature changes, it might be expected that certain activities, for example those involving strenuous labor or prolonged exposure, would become increasingly confined to certain periods of the day. One result of such an increasing compartmentalization of the day might be the development of scheduling conflicts among various activities competing for the same periods. The resolution of such conflicts and the coordination of these activities may have significant implications for sociopolitical organization.

Just as daily temperature patterns may impose a structure on the schedule of activities, so too would the nature of seasonal temperature differences influence the rhythm and variability of seasonal occupations. Large seasonal changes may confine most productive subsistence activities to short periods, requiring techniques of labor mobilization and high rates of energy expenditure. The prospect of nonproductive seasons may require surplus production and techniques of food storage and distribution. The resulting seasonal cycle of activities may impose a seasonality of goals as well, so that models assuming maximization of energetic efficiency would work well to describe behavior in certain seasons, whereas other assumptions, such as prestige maximization, may be required to describe adequately behavior at other times. Great seasonal temperature discrepancies might similarly restrict the possibilities of travel necessary for economic and social interaction. Problems stemming from such a restriction might include an intolerable degree of isolation or a conflict in the timing of regional travel and local subsistence activities, requiring, perhaps, both technological and organizational solutions.

Less extreme seasonal temperature changes would present a different set of problems. Subsistence activities might not be confined to certain seasons, but would nevertheless vary in their nature and productivity. Subtle changes in temperature or resources may have to be monitored in order to assist the scheduling of subsistence activities according to expectations of returns. The less obvious seasonality and its very lack of an imposed rhythm may render the behavior of both resources and other groups and individuals less predictable, thereby complicating decision-making processes in general by obscuring the effects of any single choices.

Such uncertainty surrounding decision making would increase as the variance around the daily and seasonal temperature average increases. Periods of the day scheduled for productive activities, for example, might prove to be unsuitably harsh on any particular day, requiring delays and rescheduling, and the predictability of any daily or seasonal activities encouraged by regular temperature fluctuations would decrease as these fluctuations become more erratic. The timing of first and last frost is critical to agricultural decisions. The onset of new pasture growth in the highlands is a vital consideration guiding decisions among pastoralists. Hunter–gatherers often must attempt to predict the timing of animal migrations or riverine freeze-up in planning their subsistence activities. Increasing temperature variance introduces correspondingly greater uncertainty and risk into these processes of decision making.

In such situations of uncertainty, the specific choices about the timing of activities may differ from those reached in more stable environments and, more important, the struture of decision making may be different as well. Situations of high risk may encourage goals of security over efficiency, generalist orientations over specialist ones, and mixed strategies over pure ones emphasizing single solutions. Repeated experience with the erratic occurrence of unfavorable extreme temperatures may encourage a conservative approach geared to the least favorable possible conditions. The applicability to human behavior of Liebig's "Law of the Minimum," suggesting that organisms adapt not to average environmental conditions but rather to the rarer, less favorable extremes, would derive precisely from this greater conservatism in the face of increased environmental uncertainty.

Paradoxically, increasingly erratic and variable environmental factors might also encourage greater behavioral experimentation and risk taking. If the aim in a particular context were the maximization of energetic return or profit, for example, the perception of the environment might stress the opportunities presented by the rare, extremely favorable conditions and anticipate the best possible outcome rather than the worst. High-yield crops with narrow temperature tolerances might be planted as a risk encouraged by occasional past successes.

It would seem, consequently, that variable environments would encourage similarly variable behavior, discussed here in terms of differing goals and perceptions, but ultimately deriving from differing past individual histories of reinforcement. Individual behavior may not be predictable without a knowledge of these histories, but the aggregate group behavior may be expected to show great heterogeneity unless limited by the organization of decision making by consensus, delegation of responsibility, or control of power. If individual behavior is, in fact, so determined by some higher level group organization, it may be that a mixed group strategy that includes both conservative and risk-taking approaches would be expected. What must be emphasized is that both extremes—stressing security and stressing efficiency—would be intermittently reinforced in a variable environment. As long as the decision strategies attain some minimum of security to allow the group's persistence, the total behavioral mix may be reinforced sufficiently to continue.

2.1.2. Rainfall

As is true with temperature, rainfall may be a source of problems owing to its extremes, its spatial distribution, or its pattern of temporal variation. Seen purely as a physical factor in the environment, abundant rain may require techniques for providing shelter for people, hearths, activities, and food stores. The greater the overall precipitation, in fact, the more elaborate such techniques may be and the more difficult food preservation. In conjunction with moderately warm temperatures, high-rainfall environments are potentially destructive, through erosion and decay, of much of human material culture. Elaboration of structures or their constant replacement may constitute a significant demand on labor. Abundant rainfall may also constrain or raise the energy costs of travel over marshy or flooded landscapes. A complex vegetation, which is often encouraged by high average precipitation in areas of sufficient warmth, would pose problems to foragers and farmers similar to those discussed in the context of high-temperature environments above. In addition, however, high-rainfall environments pose additional problems to farmers as a result of their land-clearance activities. The impact of erosion on cleared fields could be great, causing the destruction of crops, terraces, and channels and the removal of fertile topsoil. Moreover, heavy rains may more easily impoverish cleared land through the leaching of minerals and nutrients. The need for compensatory techniques of conservation and fertilization may increase as average yearly rainfall becomes greater.

Arid environments, on the other hand, support less vegetation, and thus little food for animal resources or humans. Artificial water control through wells, irrigation canals, or pipelines may be necessary for survival, and such facilities may anchor populations to their vicinity. Alternatively, natural water concentrations such as springs and temporary waterholes may provide a spatial focus of habitation, with considerable human mobility necessary to adjust to their changing yields in water or associated plants and animals. Erosion is a potential problem, especially that caused by wind, due to the lack of vegetation and the soil aridity.

The spatial distribution of rainfall may show greater local variation than does that of temperature. Hills and mountains may impose rainshadows in otherwise wet environments. Neighboring sections of the desert may show quite different rainfall patterns in any given year. Boundaries between regions based on rainfall may be abrupt in areas with great topographical variation or gradual when land gradients are gentle. In the latter situation, decisions regarding the system of land use may be more difficult. For example, Porter (1965) has suggested that among the Kamba of East Africa, moisture-requiring crops are often overextended into areas too dry to support them, precisely because of the lack of clear environmental boundaries in the local gentle topography.

Seasonality of rainfall is, of course, another major source of problems. As is true of temperature patterns, pronounced and regular seasonality of rainfall may confer the mixed blessings of a predictability in the appropriate scheduling of seasonal activities, together with the possibility of competition for time among a variety of activities deemed suitable for the same season. As the seasonal rainfall becomes more equitable or the patterns less regular, greater uncertainty is introduced into many decisions. The suitable timing of field clearing by burning, of planting, and of harvests, as well as of traveling, feasts, and communal work projects becomes less predictable. Unanticipated droughts or torrents may require short-term corrective measures anywhere, but an environment with a frequent but erratic occurrences of such extremes may require long-term, anticipatory technological and sociopolitical adjustments.

2.1.3. Other Physical Factors

A variety of other features of the natural environment may be sources of problems for human adaptation. Differences among soils in texture and fertility have vital implications for drainage and water retention, crop productivity, techniques of soil preparation, and duration of cultivation. The spatial distribution of such soils, moreover, affects the overall complexity of horticultural practices in any region. Winds, storms, tides, waves, and currents may provide differing degrees of stress according to their intensity, frequency, and regularity. River floods may vary in their timing and magnitude, and in the predictability of these features. In each case, the specific problems posed by any single situation or event may be quite different, but the general patterns of distribution and predictability in time and space may require similar accomodations or solutions.

2.1.4. Composite Situations

Real environments, of course, show combinations and interactions among the various factors isolated above. Since humans must cope with the total environment with multiple, perhaps contradictory solutions, it may be useful to discuss briefly the outstanding problems of various biomes. Here, too, gross simplification is required to reduce large areas to apparently homogeneous provinces, but by focusing on the general features of such areas, it may be easier to account for patterns of similarities and differences in cultural behavior as problem solving.

Tundras. High-latitude tundras contain a number of extreme physical conditions that present unique problems to the inhabitants. Groups such as the Chipewyan of the Canadian Barren-Grounds survive because they have devised solutions to these problems. Temperatures are extreme and seasonality is pronounced, with occurrences of below $-60°F$ during the long winters and above $80°F$ during the brief summers. Precipitation is generally low, but so is evapotranspiration, allowing long-term accumulation of snow. Summer melting coupled with permafrost leads to widespread flooded and marshy conditions. Obstacles to travel are consequently formidable, both in winter due to crusted snow and in summer due to water accumulation.

The asymmetrical continental climate permits only a short growing season, and vegetation is further limited by the permafrost soils. Trees are absent or rare and stunted, and both floral and faunal diversity are low. Potential animal resources are highly mobile and show great temporal changes in local abundance due to migration, hibernation, and longer-term population cycles.

The Chipewyan and other groups exploiting tundras, therefore, must deal with environments demonstrating severe temporal and spatial fluctuations. The scarcity of trees imposes problems of finding fuel, construction materials, protection from the wind, and camouflage from game. Human mobility is necessary, yet hampered by the seasonal conditions. There are few alternative resources, and these show spatiotemporal unpredictability that must be anticipated. Despite the paucity of animal species, there may be periodic large aggregations of individual animals, especially caribou, so that techniques must be found for taking advantage of this temporary abundance. Storage of food is facilitated by the long duration of subzero temperatures, but stationary food caches may be difficult to incorporate into the nomadic and changing patterns of settlement. Reindeer domestication, as practiced by groups like the Chukchi of Siberia, permits a mobility of the food stores in the form of the herds, but presents new problems of trying to maintain herd size in the face of environmental fluctuations. Seasonal provision of fodder through gathering or exchange requires measures to incorporate these activities into the yearly cycle.

Boreal Forests.   Subarctic coniferous forests show many problems similar to those of the tundras, including low temperatures, pronounced seasonality, and population oscillations of animal resources. Trees are often dense, but vegetational diversity is nevertheless quite low, and little is available for human use. Animal diversity may be higher than in the tundra, but these resources are usually more scattered and in smaller groups, permitting less intensive harvesting. Animals may be less mobile in the forest, but they may also be less visible. Winter travel is hindered by snow accumulation, which may be deeper and softer than on the tundra.

Temperate Forests.   Mixed and deciduous forests occur at sufficiently low latitudes that growing seasons tend to be long despite pronounced seasonality. Accordingly, vegetational abundance and diversity are greater than in more northerly regions. Moreover, the richer understory tends to include more plants suitable for exploitation by animals and humans. Both plants and animals tend to show scattered distributions in small aggregations, although the greater heterogeneity and patchiness of these forests may allow greater spatial clumping of resources than is true of coniferous forests. Visibility for hunting is limited by the trees and underbrush, but unlike the northern forests, this limitation is seasonal, declining as the leaves drop in fall. Such forests are sufficiently far south that farming is practicable, but the trees pose problems of land clearance. Although browse is abundant, the lack of large natural grazing areas limits the size of domestic ungulate herds to that supportable on small natural pastures or cultivated feed crops.

Tropical Forests.   Forests in the Tropics and Subtropics vary substantially from one area to another but are generally characterized by relatively even, high average temperatures and high precipitation; rainfall may or may not be strongly seasonal. Vegetational productivity and diversity are quite high as are growth and decay rates. Only a small percentage of the vegetation is suitable for human exploitation, and this tends to occur scattered throughout the forest. Animal resources are difficult to locate, in part because of the poor visibility afforded by the dense vegetation, and in part because of the scattered distribution of the animal biomass, which is largely in the upper stories of the forest. Agriculture can be highly productive, but necessitates clearance (in which the use of fire may be hampered by the high precipitation) and intensive weeding. Soils tend to be thin and fragile, easily leached and exhausted. The lack of large natural grazing areas limits the type and size of easily maintained domestic animal herds. The twin hazards of insects and bacteria take heavy tolls by the destruction of foods and material culture.

Grasslands.   The outstanding physical characteristics of temperate and sub-tropical grasslands is their relatively high aridity. Temperatures may show intense seasonal differences or more uniform relatively high averages. Water itself may become a critical resource by virtue of its limited distribution. The general lack of trees may pose problems similar to those of tundras, but gallery forests and groves are more abundant in grasslands, depending on the local distribution of water. Except for the concentrations around river courses and water holes, vegetational diversity may be relatively low, with much of it not useful to humans. The abundance of graze, on the other hand, can support high animal biomasses, often in the form of large herds. Agriculture can be highly productive owing to the frequently rich and deep soils, but this economic activity faces special problems of grass clearance and water shortages. Overexploitation in marginal areas may easily lead to extreme wind erosion and desertification. Herds of domesticated animals can be maintained readily, although high mobility and flexibility of the herds may be necessary, especially in semiarid regions, to take advantage of water and grazing conditions. Local overgrazing can have long-term destructive effects by increasing local erosion and moisture loss.

Deserts.   The hazards of desert life are well known and hinge on the relative scarcity of water. Precipitation may be virtually nonexistent, and yet, occasionally torrential. Permanent water holes are rare and form a vital focus of life where they occur. Temperatures may show large diurnal variation, with both extremes of hot and cold encouraging inactivity and necessitating shelter. Vegetation is scant, often subterranean, and may be highly seasonal and spatially variable, in accordance with varying rainfall patterns. Concentrations of food plants may occur in favored areas, but these locations may change from year to year. Animal biomass is quite low and is usually in the form of small, solitary, and secretive species. Occasionally, herds of larger game may pass through desert regions, but only seasonally and rarely reliably. Maintenance of domesticated plants and animals requires techniques—often energy intensive—of insuring access to adequate water (and food in the case of animals). Travel and visibility may be easy due to lack of vegetational obstacles, but at the same time, fuel is scarce, cover for stalking game is lacking, and travel must be structured according to the availability of water. Sand deserts, furthermore, may pose problems to foot travel equal to those of snow, marshes, or underbrush.

Each of these major biomes presents a unique set of problems through its physical and biotic characteristics. In addition, they provide differing contexts for the solution of other problems of survival. Problems deriving from the structure and distribution of population and from competition and other forms of population interaction will require different solutions in different habitats. The means for solutions available in tundras will differ greatly from those in forests. Such differences must be kept in mind when examining these other types of problems.

2.2. Demographic Problems

Demographic problems may be discussed briefly in terms of overpopulation, underpopulation, and population distribution. Whereas the first topic has received a good deal of anthropological attention, the others have received much less. It should be noted that both concepts of ''over-'' and ''underpopulation'' imply some reference value and the problems resulting from a discrepancy from this standard. In fact, a number of such reference values might be suggested for any population, depending on the criteria used, and the problems of deviation would differ accordingly.

2.2.1. Overpopulation

Overpopulation is usually considered in reference to some concept of carrying capacity, and many instances of culture change have been viewed as responses to the problems resulting from exceeding this capacity (Cohen 1977). It is generally realized, however, that there can be several levels of carrying capacity in a given area, depending on the subsistence technology and temporal frame of reference. Critical to the concept in addition to productivity are work effort and level of needs and expectations (Sahlins 1972). Overpopulation poses subsistence problems, then, when productivity falls in relation to needs or wants, when population or demands rise in relation to productivity, or when work effort begins to increase. These three events may be perceived and dealt with differently.

Falling productivity may result in periodic or general food shortages, posing problems of production, storage, and distribution requiring technological or organizational solution. Expansion of productive efforts through use of new land and resources, development of new techniques, and increase in labor, as well as the development and augmentation of technological means and sociopolitical networks of preservation, sharing, and distribution may all be seen as valid solutions when problems are perceived in terms of declining yields. If, on the other hand, emphasis is placed on the increase in population or its demands, then solutions may be aimed at this side of the imbalance between population and resources, focusing on limiting population or lowering expectations. Such solutions are being attempted currently in much of the industrialized world through legislation and education. Finally, if overpopulation is viewed in terms of its excessive demands on work effort, solutions may be taken in the direction of technological innovations designed to lower this effort. Any specific case of overpopulation in relation to resources, of course, may be perceived in all three ways, and may involve responses of all types simultaneously, depending on the means available.

Overpopulation need not be defined, however, solely by reference to resources and productive effort. Population may become too large in relation to a number of mechanisms of coordination and social interaction as well. Means of decision making, conflict resolution, and role identification may have maximum optimal population sizes that, if exceeded, strain these means and lead to conflict or ambiguity. Distribution systems of resources and information may require alternative forms depending on the population size involved. The specific habitat becomes crucial to an examination of overpopulation, consequently, not only in terms of its potential for resource productivity but also through its spatial characteristics affecting the distribution of such interaction networks.

2.2.2. Underpopulation

Underpopulation is a problem relatively neglected in the anthropological literature, except for extreme situations such as those arising from initial outside contact. Too few mouths to feed would hardly seem to be a problem, but a lack of labor might definitely be problematic in some situations. Some tasks, such as game drives or weir building, require moderately large work forces to be done at all. Other activities become more efficient as the labor pool increases because of the potential for division of labor. Overall subsistence security may rise as the number of producers increases, especially if they are spatially dispersed in such activities as hunting, herding, or working widely separate plots of land, thereby subject to differing environmental conditions.

A relative labor shortage might, consequently, pose problems of subsistence inefficiency and insecurity. It might also prevent the accumulation of surpluses deemed necessary to social and ritual feasting or distribution. If the social structure and prestige system of a group is based largely on the ability to mobilize labor and production, then underpopulation poses real problems of group organization. In addition, underpopulation may threaten group survival through a shortage of marriage partners. It has been well demonstrated through simulation that, given stochastic variation in the age–sex structure of populations, small groups of hunter–gatherers have certain minimum sizes of mating networks necessary for insuring mates and that, furthermore, marriage rules can profoundly affect the necessary network size (Wobst 1974). Endogamous small-scale horticultural groups or even larger societies with sufficiently restrictive marriage rules could face severe demographic and social problems in a situation of a shortage of eligible marriage partners. Needless to say, such a shortage can be created not only by overall underpopulation or restrictive marriage rules (including both pre- and proscriptions of partners and amounts of accompanying wealth or service), but also by cultural practices that cause relative underpopulation of certain age-sex classes (such as preferential female infanticide or warfare causing mainly young male deaths).

2.2.3. Population Distribution

Population distribution per se is not a problem, but the specific pattern of distribution of any one group may be problematic in a number of contexts. Dispersal for subsistence reasons may hamper communication, exchange, and interaction necessary for social and political purposes. Dispersal due to personal and political rivalries and warfare may hinder efficient subsistence cooperation. Aggregation for temporary economic activities or permanent utilization of economies of scale may strain sociopolitical means of conflict resolution, whereas aggregation for rituals, councils, or defense may lead to overexploitation of local resources. The distribution of resources and the barriers to travel of specific habitats and seasons must be examined in relation to the great variety of needs for population communication and interaction. Low population densities in regions with poor travel conditions threaten the very existence of social groups and require great energy expenditure for their maintenance. Linear environments such as narrow valleys and coastal plains will impose different communication costs than will similar habitats with a different geometric configuration (Wobst 1976). Patchy population distributions may pose obstacles to labor mobilization as well as to intercommunication. Increasingly large human aggregations may require increasingly complex methods of food distribution. No problem can be considered adequately without attention to the spatial distribution of the population involved.

2.3. Problems of Competition

The discussion of demographic problems focused essentially on perceived imbalances between supply and demand—for resources, labor, or space. The resulting problems and possible solutions were considered only in terms of single, isolated units of perception and decision making, for example, individual families or homogeneous and totally integrated social groups. Such units would have communal perceptions and would take collective action in problem solving. Such units are, of course, idealized and represent only one end of the spectrum of cultural integration and isolation. At the other extreme, one might focus on the differences among individuals and groups, that is, differences in their perception, experience, access to information and resources, goals, and influence in decision making. In other words, one might emphasize the heterogeneity within, and the differences between, societies because no group is uniform or isolated, nor are any two societies alike. Once such differences are stressed, once distinctions are made in the decision-making process between self and others, between "us" and "them," then the problems of imbalance of supply and demand take on new meaning and the range of potential solutions broadens. Supply shortages can then be viewed as scarcity of resources for which the excessive demand can take the form of competition.

No individuals or societies exist in a vacuum, but rather must cope with the presence of other groups constituting the social landscape. With an emphasis on the "social environment," such other groups might be viewed as concentrations of labor and material, of demand, and of potentially interfering activities and structures. Other groups, consequently, may be simultaneously resources for exploitation, competitors, and physical obstacles. As both resources and obstacles, they may be evaluated in terms similar to those used for elements of the natural environment. Their exploitation or avoidance, for example, must take into account their size and spatial distribution. The costs of their exploitation, whether by raiding for slaves or foods, or by exchange mechanisms, may be weighed against the risks and the costs of alternatives.

It is as potential competitors with rival demands, however, that other groups become new factors in the environment. Competition can take several forms. It may consist only of interference, by which the physical presence or activities of other groups indirectly hinders resource exploitation. Clearance of forests, fencing of grasslands, damming and pollution of rivers, and construction of roads or pipelines are all forms of such indirect competition between complex societies and smaller-scale groups of hunter–gatherers and horticulturalists. Competition may, on the other hand, take the form of exploitation, the direct rivalry of demands for resources. The greater these demands and the more important the resources are thought to be, the more intense is the competition and the more crucial are the solutions.

Solutions to the problems of competition may be reached by a number of means. Perhaps the most common of these are, as mentioned earlier, a variety of methods of avoidance. Just as many aspects of organic evolution seem to have the effect of avoiding competition, so too, can much of human behavior be viewed in terms of similar effects. Each means, of course, will entail different costs and subsequent problems. Productivity may be increased through technological innovation or through increased productive effort. The former may increase the demand for particular materials and special knowledge, whereas the latter must be compromised with other energy demands and the inherent limits of the energy budget. On the other hand, demands might be lowered, for example, through population regulation or reduced per capita utilization. Again, however, there are limits imposed by other needs for labor and marriage partners.

Competition might also be avoided through changes in the nature of demands. A commonly observed biological response to competition is character displacement, in which niche overlap is reduced. Behavioral differentiation and specialization may have the same effects. The possibility of such differentiation depends in part on the environmental and technological heterogeneity or complexity, allowing greater variety in the definition and division of niche dimensions. Tundras and deserts, for example, currently allow fewer human niches than do structurally more complex environments. A problem with increasing specialization may be an increasing risk of overexploitation or resource failure, requiring solutions to increase security perhaps through growing interdependence of the specialized groups. An additional problem with greater specialization might be a greater differentiation of perceptions and goals, which may increase social differentiation and increase the intensity of competition in other areas. The management of both competition and interdependence poses additional organizational problems.

Still another way of avoiding competition might be to change location. Rather than reducing overlapping demands through differentiation of activities, spatial overlap in the demands may be reduced through dispersal and migration, solutions which must evaluate the availability of refuges, the costs of moves, and the potential risks of relative isolation.

Competition, of course, may not be avoided at all, but rather might result in direct confrontation through warfare or its threat. Such a solution might be one of the only options available in a situation with little possibility of differentiation of activities or few refuges. Conflict, may on the other hand, be an attractive solution even when many alternatives are available, since its benefits frequently seem to include, in addition to resource acquisition or removal of competitors, other reinforcements such as prestige allotment or the enhancement of the power or authority of a decision-making elite. These benefits would have to be weighed against the costs of mortality, labor, and organization involved in both offensive raids and defensive aggregations.

In summary, individuals and societies face general problems in exploiting the natural environment, insuring population continuity and social interaction, and coping with the presence of others. Specific groups will face different combinations of such problems, both simultaneously and consecutively. Perceived potential solutions may be abundant or limited, and each has associated with it a different set of costs, risks, benefits, and subsequent problems. Understanding specific solutions taken may require a focus on the distribution of benefits in relation to decision making and on the sequence of effects in terms of reinforcement schedules.

Chapter 4

Feeding Strategies

1. PROBLEMS

Coping for survival includes, most obviously, obtaining adequate food. Feeding behavior has long been a focus both of biological ecology and, under the heading of "subsistence," of anthropology. In addition, since human-environmental interaction is clearest and most direct in the procurement of food, studies in ecological anthropology have emphasized this aspect of behavior as well. Precisely because human ecological relationships are so obvious in the pursuit of food, however, ecological anthropology too often appears to be limited to the study of these activities, with the result that this approach becomes overly simplistic, materialistic, and reductionist. It need not be. Food procurement is simply one (albeit vital) aspect of human behavior. Just as food is necessary for survival, so survival is necessary for any other activity. On these grounds alone, one might be justified in assigning research priority to subsistence. One might even trace the causal relationships from subsistence to other aspects of behavior, without assuming its complete independence and causal priority. If human behavior is to be viewed in systemic terms, then subsistence activities provide one point at which to enter the system for study.

Feeding strategies will be viewed here as the set of solutions to a number of basic problems. These problems involve (1) insuring sufficient energy intake for survival; (2) insuring sufficient nutritional intake for survival; (3) insuring sufficient regularity of these intakes for survival; and (4) insuring sufficient intake of higher levels or of other resources deemed necessary.

Solutions to these problems require decisions about *which* resources to utilize, *how much* of each, and *how many* overall to exploit. Other decisions intricately related to these, including *how* and *when* to exploit them, will be considered in Chapter 5 as part of procurement strategies.

64

2. GOALS

2.1. Efficiency

Ecological studies of nonhuman feeding strategies have given great emphasis to efficiency of exploitation as a major factor determining resource selection (Schoener 1971). Cost-benefit ratios of various resources seem to provide one useful measure of the probability of the inclusion of the resources in diets, with low-cost, high-benefit foods ranking first. Efficiency has similarly been stressed in the study of human food selection, and a variety of models have been developed to analyze feeding strategies from this perspective (Keene 1979; Smith 1979). It must be realized, however, that efficiency can be calculated in various ways depending on the currencies or measures utilized and that the models and their predictions will differ accordingly.

Efficiency is a *ratio,* an expression of output per unit input. The measures of output and input, however, can vary greatly. Several measures have been proposed in the literature of biological ecology, and several additional such measures may be relevant to the study of human behavior. Output is most commonly expressed in terms of energy or calories, but other possible measures of output include weight, protein, other nutrients (such as fat, water, vitamins, and minerals), and nonfoods (such as raw materials, manufactures, labor, mates, land, and even decisions and "prestige"). The importance of these various measures of output to particular decisions depends on the requirements and perceived needs of each specific situation. Since the production of all these categories of output characterizes all human feeding strategies, it is the relative proportion of each that will vary among situations. The factors that determine the demand for each must be examined in order to ascertain the importance of each in the decision processes. Calories, protein, and other nutrients are required for growth, reproduction, and simple metabolic maintenance. Additional caloric requirements are imposed by various work levels demanded by goals quite unrelated to biological survival. Output by weight rather than by calories may be an important consideration in decisions related to transportation, exchange, or sharing. Raw materials, manufactures, or prestige become important output measures only when they are culturally defined and requirements imposed.

Just as output can be measured in a variety of ways, so too can input. Again, energy is the most common measure used in ecological studies, but a critical distinction must be made between total energy input and human energy (or labor) input. Many technological and institutional developments can be viewed as shifting the input from human energy to other sources, often with an absolute increase in input energy. Another measure of significance is time, which has been stressed in the literature of both biology and anthropology (Schoener 1971; Smith 1979). Energy and time are not the only possible measures, however. Output per unit area or per unit money are also important (and often quite contradictory) measures considered in specific decisions. The relative importance of these various measures of input depends on the availability of each currency (and assessments of what is in short supply), the variety of perceived potential uses for each, and the magnitude of demands placed on each. Smith (1979) has suggested that it should be possible to assess when energy is in short supply for a population. Similarly, it should be possible to determine the relative scarcity of time, land, or money for one population in relation to another and, thus, to estimate the relative importance of these measures to each.

Efficiency, consequently, is an expression of output per input, which might take the form of calories per calories but which might also be expressed as pounds per hour, grams protein per acre, decisions per month, or "prestige points" per dollar. Different kinds of efficiency should be expected to be significant in different situations, and it is the task of ecological analysis not to assume a priori the importance of any one measure but to determine the relative structure of supply and demand of the various input and output measures so that the role of these different expressions of efficiency in decision making may be estimated.

Attention must also be given to the techniques of measuring each of the different types of input and output. Ecological studies tend to use continuous scales such as calories, minutes, acres, or grams and to assume that such scales are adequate assessments of the factors so measured. In the empirical world, on the other hand, such factors are distributed discontinuously, in packages of individual animals or plants, individual bundles of labor, episodes and trips, days, and garden plots or other units of landholding. Such naturally and culturally structured parcels may, in fact, be the important units in decision making, the role of which may be obscured by a conversion to continuous scales of measurement. The search time for two different species of prey by a hunter, for example, might be found to differ by a factor of 4, with important implications for their respective roles in a hunting economy assumed on this basis. If, however, the actual search times involved are 1 and 4 minutes, the difference between the two might be regarded as negligible, with both animals considered as requiring a "brief search." Conversely, the absolute distances to two different food locales (nut groves or pastures, for example) may differ only slightly in terms of miles, but that differences might be translated into a distinction between a day trip and an overnight trip for exploitation, with important behavioral implications for their relative utilization (Lee 1969). The natural and cultural packages of the different inputs and outputs must be considered in examining the decision-making process.

2.1.1. Time Efficiency

Efficient production per unit of time invested in one goal that guides many choices in a wide variety of settings, yet the importance of time costs in decision making varies substantially among individuals and cultures. The differential importance of such costs (in comparison to the costs in labor or land) should be partially explicable through an examination of time as a potentially limited resource. Greater emphasis on time efficiency should characterize those situations in which there are greater limits on production time. Patterns in the emphasis on time efficiency should reflect patterns in the general distribution of such limits.

Production time may be limited by a number of factors. Necessary productive resources may be available only briefly so that their exploitation is constrained, not by considerations of labor or area, but by this period of availability. The shorter this period, the greater the time efficiency must be for adequate production. Similarly, necessary productive capital or labor may show limited temporal availability because of other demands. The strength and elasticity of these demands would determine the necessity for time efficiency in production.

The clearest and most predictable occurrences of limited production time are in those environments with significant seasonality. Hunter–gatherers typically show seasonal activity changes, the magnitude of which varies directly with the intensity of environmental seasonality. In addition to changes in the *type* of activity, however, these seasonal rounds show significant fluctuations in the *intensity* of productive activities as well.

At middle and high latitudes (and altitudes), the critical factor in determining this seasonality is temperature. With increasing latitude, there is a decreasing length of the warm, productive season, so that foragers frequently must compress many of their productive activities into increasingly short time periods. The Tlingit Indians of coastal southeastern Alaska, for example, spent 96% of their total yearly food-gathering time in the 8-month period of March through October; in other words, most of their food-gathering activities were confined to the warmer 67% of the year (Oberg 1973:77). The Round Lake Ojibwa of Ontario accomplished 68% of their total yearly food production by weight (which included fish for sale) during the 6 months from May through October (Rogers 1962). Salmon runs along the Pacific coast of North America decrease in duration with increasing latitude, and Schalk (1977) has emphasized the increasing production and storage labor requirements of salmon specialization as the runs become briefer. Similarly, other migratory resources, such as waterfowl or caribou may require bursts of labor in order for people to take advantage of their short-term availability (Gubser 1965; Honigmann 1961). Such temperature-imposed limits to production time consequently may lead to an emphasis on time-efficiency at the expense of labor costs.

It is often difficult, however, to separate the characteristics of time costs from those of labor; a savings of one usually accomplishes a savings of the other. "Man-days," which are frequently used as a cost measure, tend to combine the two, with implicit assumptions about the constancy of effort expended per day or the uniformity of work-day length. A goal of time efficiency, however, would lead, in certain situations, to behavior quite different from that aimed at the efficient use of labor. In order to take greatest advantage of limited time, it may be necessary to expend large amounts of labor, that is, to work hard for a short period. If yields are sufficiently high, this period of activity might, indeed, be quite labor efficient as well, but it might not. What should be important is the yield per unit of time regardless of the labor productivity.

Time efficiency both differs among resources and varies for a single resource according to the level of its exploitation. As the need for time efficiency becomes increasingly important, so should those resources that are most susceptible to an increased intensity of exploitation in a short period without significant decline in productivity. Concentrated or aggregated resources provide one example of this potential for short-term intensification. As more people are mobilized to intercept mammal herds, bird flocks, or fish schools, or to gather nut or wild rice crops, they are frequently rewarded by larger harvests within the same limited time period. The daily yield from hunting migrating caribou can be increased greatly with an increase in the number of cooperating hunters; the yield from hunting the more solitary moose is much less expandable in response to increased labor input. Similarly, the daily yield from exploiting pike or grouse is much less responsive to added labor inputs than is that from salmon or geese.

The latitudinal trends in the relative importance of gathering, fishing, and hunting in the economies of hunter–gatherers may reflect, in part, the relative importance of time efficiency as expressed in the local environments. In general, plant gathering is most important below 40 degrees north latitude, fishing more so between 40 degrees and 60 degrees north, and hunting most important above 60 degrees north (Lee 1968: 43). Obviously, these trends depend to a great extent on the varying relative abundance of plants, fish, and game. But, if the need for time efficiency increases with latitude, then there should be a latitudinal gradient of increasing exploitation of clustered resources. Between 40 degrees and 60 degrees north latitude occur many of the anadromous fish that show huge annual runs, whereas north of this area fish are not only increasingly scarce but more dispersed as well. By contrast, the major game animals between 40 degrees and 60 degrees north latitude are the relative solitary deer, moose, and woodland caribou, whereas north of 60 degrees north these are replaced by the more gregarious barren-ground caribou (Fig. 4.1). An emphasis on time efficiency alone might dictate a shift an emphasis from fish to game as one moves north-ward. Even those "Eskimos who in the Far North had the best fishing opportunity made relatively little use of fish, and one of the reasons was that they could not afford to spend much time fishing. Time thus spent can be occupied with work that yields better results" (Rostlund 1952: 147).

A similar limitation of the productive time for foraging populations in lower latitudes due to the seasonality of rainfall does not seem to be as significant. In semiarid regions, productive activities may be easiest during the rainy months

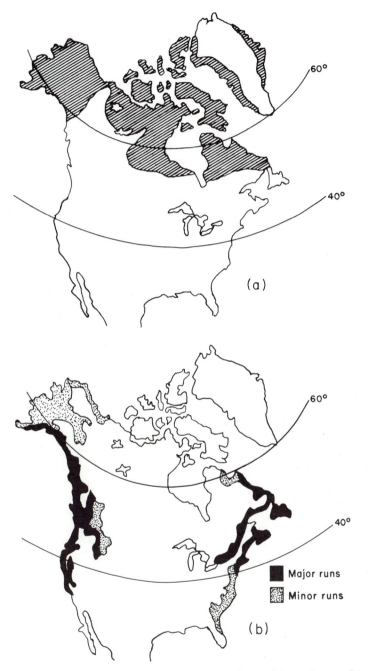

Fig. 4.1. Latitudinal distribution of (a) barren-ground caribou and (b) anadromous fish.

and the early portion of the dry season, whereas the productive potential of the environment may be harder to exploit as dry season progresses. One major difference, however, between low-latitude regions and those of higher latitudes is that food storage is more difficult in the former, warmer climates. As a result, it becomes less feasible to intensify production in one season for use at other times of the year. Without some means to spread out a seasonal surplus production, time efficiency of production during the good season has no benefits. At low latitudes, consequently, time efficiency should be stressed primarily when there is a unique storage potential offered by a resource, or when there exist cultural mechanisms of banking the surplus for later dividends. Since such mechanisms often involve exchange with other populations having a different subsistence technology, using a goal of time efficiency to cope with seasonally productive differences may lead to greater economic interdependence on a regional scale.

For example, the G/Wi and !Kung San of Botswana inhabit regions of pronounced seasonal rainfall. Among both groups, hunting contributes less than half the diet, and although there are marked seasonal fluctuations in the intensity of hunting, with some meat being dried for later consumption, the dried meat will last only a few days in the hot climate (Lee 1968, 1979; Silberbauer 1972; Tanaka 1976). The changing intensity of hunting activities, as a result, is not likely to be due to a strategy of time efficiency at the expense of labor. The seasonality of the Kalahari (and of other arid regions) does not represent such a clear distinction between productive and unproductive periods as is true farther north. Most dry environments contain numerous species of plants that have evolved mechanisms to survive seasonal droughts. Such adaptations provide humans with a natural system of storage of which they can take advantage. The !Kung environment, for example, contains abundant mongongo nuts that remain edible on the ground for up to 12 months after ripening (Lee 1968:33). Similarly, *Bauhinia* beans can be gathered by both G/Wi and !Kung long after ripening, whereas numerous roots are available year-round (Tanaka 1976:109; Yellen and Lee 1976:38). In fact, the G/Wi do take advantage of the ease of natural preservation of the beans by concentrating on gathering a surplus for storage despite the low returns of gathering and transporting beans still in their inedible pods and despite the fact that many other plants are abundant at this time (Tanaka 1976:107). In this case the G/Wi seem to stress time efficiency over that of labor.

In humid areas, by contrast, most productive activities may be conducted more easily during the drier seasons because of the difficulties of movement in the rainy months. Again, however, since storage is difficult, time efficiency may offer few benefits worth the high labor costs of intensification unless some method of banking a surplus is possible. The nethunting Pygmies have such a method through their relationship with Bantu agriculturalists (Tanno 1976). They regularly exchange meat obtained from hunting with the villagers for cassava, plantain banana, and rice. Some of this meat is, in fact, smoked, but most is provided fresh during the main hunting season, which coincides with the dry season of December through February. Farm products are received, in turn, throughout the year but mostly during the rainy season when the Pygmies reside near the villages. Thus, there is a delayed return on their surplus hunting. In order to obtain this surplus, the Pygmies intensify their hunting during the dry season, striving to obtain high yields during this brief period. During the rainy season, nethunting is undertaken about once every 3 days, whereas during the dry season, this frequency is increased to every day. Tanno (1976:120) has estimated that half or more of the total meat captured at this time goes to the villagers.

Similarly, horticulturalists may face situations of limited production time in which an emphasis on time efficiency would be advantageous. Growing seasons decrease in duration with increasing latitude or altitude and with decreasing length of rainy season. Such limited growing seasons can have major significance for choices of crops and techniques. In the Sudan, for example, sesame is often substituted for dura as a primary crop in areas of regularly short wet seasons because sesame matures several months sooner than dura does (Graham 1969:427). Similarly, in North Thailand the more rapid-growing varieties of rice are regularly planted in the fields watered by rainfall because of the risks of drought, even though the yields per acre from these varieties are lower than those of the slower-growing varieties (Moerman 1968:155). By contrast, dry seasons that are too brief may indirectly impose time efficiency on the choice of crops. The brief dry season in equatorial Amazonia may limit the effectiveness of field cleaning and burning and thus encourage the planting of manioc instead of the more demanding maize (Harris 1971:495).

Even in situations in which water is artificially provided through irrigation, there may be time limits on productivity that influence crop choices. The irrigation systems described by Moerman (1968) in north Thailand serve a series of fields in sequence, with those being served last called "semi-irrigated" because they receive significantly less water over a shorter period of time. These semi-irrigated fields are not only watered later, but they are also drained earlier than the "Great Field," which is closer to the water source. As a result, "the semi-irrigated field is planted in faster-maturing varieties of rice which, although sown after the seed in the Great Field, ripen earlier" (Moerman 1968:42).

Other opportunities and demands on labor can also encourage time-efficient crop choices. Despite their lower productivity per acre, the faster-growing varieties of rice are being planted increasingly even on the Great Field. This change in crop selection is associated with the growth of commercial tractor agriculture at some distance from the village. The earlier harvest of the Great Field that is now possible enables farmers to travel to the commercial fields in time to harvest those crops (Moerman 1968:152). The resulting low yields per acre are compensated for by the increase in land cultivated, and land is plentiful in the region (Moerman 1968:81). Of course, other opportunities and demands may be nonagricultural as well. Netting, in summarizing a study of Central Thailand, points out that people may well choose a system of shifting agriculture, which is efficient in terms of neither labor nor land use, in order to have more time to devote to hunting, fishing, and collecting (Netting 1974:39). Among the Yanomamo of Amazonia, "maize is sometimes used as an 'emergency' crop because it is easily transported and produces a return in a short time" (Chagnon 1973:141). In this case, the emphasis on time efficiency is encouraged by the threats of raids and warfare necessitating frequent movements.

2.1.2. Labor Efficiency

Like time, labor may be scarce in relation to the demands placed on it. If so, then a goal of labor efficiency or "Least Effort" may guide decisions about productive activities. The greater the relative labor shortage, the more important this goal should be. A number of special circumstances may lead to a relative scarcity of labor in relation to specific tasks. Certain families may be too small because of demographic accidents or because of family strategies unrelated to productive activities. Women's labor may be relatively scarce because of selective female infanticide or high bridewealth; the availability of men's labor may be limited by high mortality through accident or warfare. Depopulation through epidemics and outside contacts can cause a labor shortage in relation to the demands of former, traditional activities. A population dispersed in order to exploit generally scattered resources may find it difficult to gather sufficient labor together for particular activities. The development of a nonproductive subgroup, such as craft specialists, can increase the demands on a shrinking labor pool.

A more important impetus to labor efficiency other than such particular limits on labor, however, would seem to be the existence of other demands for its uses. The wide applicability of the "Law of Least Effort" suggests that these demands virtually always outstrip the supply. People tend to work no harder than they have to at production unless constrained by overriding shortages of time, land, or money. These other demands on time available for one productive activity may be posed by different activities including wage earning, manufacturing, trading, fighting, gossiping, celebrating, traveling, sleeping, or simply relaxing. From an evolutionary point of view it might be argued that labor efficiency is ultimately most adaptive since energy saved in productive activities can be used for other behavior that may enhance fitness (Smith 1979). Yet any labor saved in production might also be used for activities that decrease fitness, a situation that an evolutionary framework could not predict. The importance of labor efficiency in productive decisions depends on the perceived alternative uses of labor and the priorities of the decision maker. It may be useful to assume the widespread importance of labor efficiency, but one should not fall into the trap of assuming a priori that any saved labor will be used to enhance fitness, and thus, that labor efficiency must be most important. One of the problems encountered by the application of principles of evolutionary ecology to human behavior is the widespread occurrence of seemingly maladaptive behavior. Although one solution to this problem might be to seek underlying, "latent" adaptive functions of such behavior, a decision-making framework simply can recognize that certain choices can be short-sighted and create as many problems as they solve.

Labor efficiency, consequently, is an important objective of productive decisions, perhaps the most important unless scarcity of time, land, or money encourages people to work harder (for less benefit) than they otherwise want to. It may be useful to assume labor efficiency as a major decision objective when neither land nor time seem to be limited. Ease of collection or net yields for labor do, in fact, appear to be widespread criteria for resource selection. Hunter-gatherers, for example, commonly prefer large game over small and clustered resources over dispersed ones, in part because of the possibility of larger payoffs for the effort of exploiting them (Jochim 1976:17–18). Highly mobile and unpredictable animals rarely dominate their subsistence economies because of the high procurement costs. Ease of collecting is also an important criterion for choices of plants gathered. The Batak of the Philippines prefer wild kudot yams over abagan yams because the former give higher yields for labor invested (Eder 1978:61). *Bauhinia esculenta* beans, although considered tastier, are less important to the G/Wi San of Botswana that are the more easily obtained *B. macrantha* (Tanaka 1976:107).

Similarly, crop selection among horticulturalists frequently emphasizes yields per unit effort. In southeastern Nigeria, because of the attractions of trade and wage labor, "both men and women are on the whole devoting less time to farming and therefore tending to concentrate more on cassava since it is the easiest crop to plant and tend" (Morgan 1973:202). A comparison of groups in the New Guinea Highlands by Clarke (1966) revealed that those groups with lowest population density and most abundant land grew proportionally more *Xanthosoma* (taro kong) than did other groups at higher densities; it is no accident that *Xanthosoma* is almost six times more labor efficient than the sweet potato, the other major crop in the area (Rappaport 1968:260). The Yanomamo of Amazonia frequently plant newly established gardens in maize rather than plantains because the effort involved in transporting maize seeds is less than that required for plantain cuttings, which may weigh 10–15 pounds apiece (Chagnon 1973:141). In many areas of Africa, certain spiked varieties of millet are increasing in popularity at the expense of other varieties that are more susceptible to bird predation. This shift is a response to a shortage of labor: "Fewer children are available nowadays to scare away birds, owing to the demands of education" (Morgan 1969:262). Date palms are a crop favored for incorporation into the strenuous economy of Iranian pastoralists because they can produce up to 20,000 pounds of fruit for only 21 man-days of labor per year (Spooner 1972:259).

2.1.3. Land Efficiency

In a variety of situations, land that is available for productive exploitation may be sufficiently scarce that its most efficient utilization per unit area becomes a dominant goal of subsistence decisions. "Population pressure" on land and resources may be so intense that behavior that is quite expensive in terms of time and energy is practiced in an attempt to increase land efficiency. Dramatic changes in resources and the organization of production have been attributed to the increasing relative scarcity of land (e.g., Boserup 1965; Cohen 1977; Harris 1977; Spooner 1972). Unfortunately, too many of the proponents of population pressure as a prime mover of cultural change focus almost solely on population size or density as a primary measure of this pressure, with the result that population growth has emerged as an independent explanatory variable for much of cultural change.

Land efficiency, however, must be viewed in the broader context of the relationship of demands on land to land available. In this context, a greater emphasis on land efficiency may be the response to factors that either increase the relative demands or decrease the relative available land. Population increase certainly would raise the level of demands, but unless the land is simultaneously limited or circumscribed, a more efficient use of land is not necessarily to be expected (Carneiro 1970). Such circumscription may be due to natural factors, for example, through barriers of rough terrain, poor or marshy soils, or lack of adequate rainfall or water supplies. Obstacles may also be posed by social factors such as competing and potentially hostile or more powerful neighbors. Individual differences in land tenure may lead to relative circumscription for segments of the population. Circumscription may also result from a more voluntary limiting of the land exploited. For example, whenever there is some clustered resource or focused object of high demand, people may limit their activities to a rather small region around this focus and thus suffer a relative land shortage (Bronson 1972:214–215). Hunter–gatherers or pastoralists who become more sedentary by restricting their movements to the vicinity of farmers' villages, trading posts, or choice fishing spots may face land scarcity in their pursuit of wild resources or grazing. Farmers who preferentially locate and remain near cities, waterways for communication, or specialized coastal fishing settlements may similarly perceive a shortage of agricultural land. Demands on circumscribed land can be raised as well by factors other than population increase. The development of exchange relationships, increased ritual display, a group of elite consumers, or foreign market ties can all increase the level of demands for productive land. In addition, the growth of nonproductive uses for land—for example, as sacred or ceremonial areas or as boundaries or no-man's lands—will create a scarcity of land available for production.

In all these situations, if land is seen as scarce and options to exploit more land as limited, then land efficiency may guide resource selection. Foragers thus may come to emphasize more abundant resources such as small game or fish regardless of their ease of exploitation. Farmers may stress more productive crops per acre despite the necessity to work longer and harder to grow them. The instances of choosing manioc over maize in Amazonia (Chagnon 1973:141) and of sesame over millet in areas of poor soils in the Sudan (Graham 1969:420) reflect, in part, an emphasis on land efficiency. Among the New Guinea Highlanders studied by Clarke (1966), those groups with the highest population densities and the greatest scarcity of land depended to a much greater extent on sweet potatoes and banana than did the other groups, probably because of the high acreage yields of these crops.

It should be pointed out that just as costs in time and labor are often difficult to separate, so too are costs in labor and land. Frequently, land requires a significant labor input in order to be productive. Once a plot is thus improved, it may become a scarce commodity, even though land in general may be abundant. By stressing land efficiency in its exploitation, people may avoid the labor costs of improving additional land. For example, among the Yoruba of Nigeria the labor required for clearance of forest is quite high compared to that of their neighbors who clear savanna grasslands. As a result, the forest plots tend to be planted with a greater variety of crops than are savanna fields, so that productivity per acre in the forest is greater (Moss and Morgan 1977:24). Similarly, the labor costs of irrigation in northern Thailand are significant, so that the slow-growing, high-yielding rice varieties are preferentially planted on the irrigated fields to maximize their acreage productivity (Moerman 1968:152). With the development of much more irrigated land in conjunction with commercial cropping, however, this choice type of land has become more abundant and demands on time have become greater, leading to a substitution of less productive, faster-growing rices on the original fields.

Table 4.1 presents some figures from the literature on the efficiency of production of various types of resource-procurement activities. These figures utilize different scales of costs (time, energy, land) that could be compared to one another with appropriate assumptions and conversion factors (such as number of hours per work-day and uniformity of energy expenditure throughout the day and per acre). They point out three important factors about the study of efficiency in subsistence activities. First of all, there is a paucity of quantified studies, making comparison and generalization difficult. Second, there is a wide range of efficiency for a given activity like "hunting"—in these examples, from 20.60 pounds per man-hour for the Bisa to 0.06 pounds per man-hour for the Rofaifo.

TABLE 4.1

Production Efficiency of Various Activities

Activity	Efficiency		Area	Source
Time efficiency				
Land hunting	1.64	edible pounds/man-hr	Coastal Nicaragua	Nietschmann 1973
Turtling	1.78	edible pounds/man-hr	Coastal Nicaragua	Nietschmann 1973
Hunting (muzzle loader)	16.95	edible pounds/man-hr	Zambia	Marks 1976
Hunting (shotgun, rifle, & muzzle loader)	20.60	edible pounds/man-hr	Zambia	Marks 1976
Night mammal hunting	0.06	edible pounds/man-hr	New Guinea	Dwyer 1974
Flying fox hunting	0.29	edible pounds/man-hr	New Guinea	Dwyer 1974
Moose hunting	13.75	edible pounds/man-hr	Canadian forests	Feit 1973
Fishing	2.29	edible pounds/man-hr	Canadian forests	Feit 1973
Beaver hunting	1.38	edible pounds/man-hr	Canadian forests	Feit 1973
Small game trapping	0.69	edible pounds/man-hr	Canadian forests	Feit 1973
Hunting (net)	0.17	edible pounds/man-hr	Zaire	Harako 1976
Hunting (net)	1.01	edible pounds/man-hr	Zaire	Tanno 1976
Kodot yam gathering	4.07	edible pounds/man-hr	Philippines	Eder 1978
Abagan yam gathering	1.14	edible pounds/man-hr	Philippines	Eder 1978

Activity	Value	Units	Location	Reference
Shellfish gathering	0.92	edible pounds/man-hr	Philippines	Eder 1978
Taro agriculture	1.84	pounds/man-hour	Fiji	Rutz 1977
Manioc agriculture	0.90	pounds/man-hour	Fiji	Rutz 1977
Dry rice agriculture	5.50	pounds/man-hour	Philippines	Rappaport 1968

Energetic efficiency

Activity	Value	Units	Location	Reference
Turtling	5.50	cal/cal	Coastal Nicaragua	Moran 1979
Hunting	2.48–9.33	cal/cal	Amazonia	Moran 1979
Fishing	2.99	cal/cal	Amazonia	Moran 1979
Fishing	1.95	cal/cal	Amazonia	Moran 1979
Hunting	0.16	cal/cal	Amazonia	Moran 1979
Gathering	0.68		Amazonia	Moran 1979
Mixed swidden agriculture	15.90–16.50	cal/cal	New Guinea	Rappaport 1968
Rice swidden	10.00	cal/cal	Borneo	Rappaport 1968
Maize swidden	13.00–29.00	cal/cal	Yucatan	Rappaport 1968
Wet rice agriculture	53.50	cal/cal	Yucatan	Rappaport 1968
Swamp rice agriculture	11.00	cal/cal	Gambia	Rappaport 1968
Grain agriculture (Hoe)	10.70	cal/cal	Gambia	Rappaport 1968
Wet rice agriculture	14.00	cal/cal	Borneo	Rappaport 1968

No a priori general assumptions about the relative efficiency of hunting versus gathering can be made for a particular area until its specific resources and their attributes are examined in relation to the technology available. Third, the relative efficiency of procurement of different foods, when measured, does not serve as a reliable guide to the relative importance of these foods in the economy. All potential foods are not alike. A pound of pork is often more highly valued than a pound of yams; moose meat is usually preferred over the equivalent weight of fish. Resources are evaluated and ranked according to their contents, and some measures for these contents are essential. These measures of productivity would form the numerator in the estimation of efficiency.

2.1.4. Measures of Productivity

Efficiency is an expression of productivity per unit cost. As has been suggested, costs can be measured in terms of time, labor, and land (as well as money). It has been suggested also that productivity can and should be measured in a variety of ways. Like the measures of costs, the importance of the different productivity measures should depend on the relative availability of each and on the level of demands on each.

Ecological explanations of human behavior frequently have involved assumptions about the minimum requirements for calories, protein, or vitamins, the fulfillment of which in particular environments is problematic. Tropical forests have been described as posing problems of protein scarcity; arctic tundras may offer insufficient vitamin C or calcium; deserts are clearly characterized by limited availability of water. Various activities or the overemphasis of particular resources have also been discussed in terms of their implications for nutritional requirements: fishing may provide too little fat, root crops insufficient protein, or agriculture too little salt. Similarly, environments and economies have been portrayed as providing insufficient amounts of "essential" nonfood resources such as workable stone, firewood, and metal ores.

A major requirement of ecological research is the separation of the concept of "requirement" or "need" from that of "desire." Unfortunately, truly biological requirements are still poorly understood; recommended levels of intake are frequently generous guesses (McArthur 1974). In addition, although survival may depend on sufficient energy and nutrient intake, this "sufficiency" for survival varies among individuals and populations. Humans display an amazing array of dietary differences. Through trial and error and biological accomodation, various populations have attained strategies of food selection that succeed in permitting survival. Certain constraints may be placed on these strategies by biological requirements, but it would seem that desires and culturally determined demand levels may be more significant.

Although the most frequently used measure of productivity in the anthropological literature has been energy or calories, recent studies, attempting to simulate optimal human feeding strategies, present more sophisticated models of food choices aimed at satisfying biological needs for 10 different nutrients (calories, protein, vitamins, minerals) at lowest costs (Keene 1979; Reidhead 1977). Despite the difficulties of determining biological requirements, these models, which employ linear programming techniques, certainly represent an improvement over studies that stress only the relative caloric content of different foods. Costs are estimated as time (Reidhead 1977) or as time modified by some risk factor (Keene 1979) and, although neither study justifies adequately the use of this measure instead of labor or land, they do represent methodological advances as compared to earlier nonquantified studies. The linear programming approach provides for a simultaneous evaluation of all resources in terms of their contents for all 10 nutrients, as well as a specification of the mixture of resources that can satisfy the requirements at lowest costs.

In each case, the methodology is impressive in its potential for simulating the complexity of decisions, yet in each case, the model's predictions deviate from actually observed feeding strategies. These deviations may reflect, as the authors suggest, slight errors in estimation of resource attributes. They may, on the other hand, derive from a more basic inadequacy of the approach.

These models, like many other recent studies in ecological anthropology, attempt to produce the *effects* of optimal decision making using objective (etic) attributes that can be quantified. In so doing, they tend to ignore the *process* of decision making and the subjective (emic) attributes of actual significance to the people involved. In fact, even when realizing that people are poor processors of complex information, ecologists are using increasingly complicated mathematical techniques to handle all the data that *should* be relevant to optimal solutions. Optimal or near-optimal solutions to critical problems such as food choices are assumed to be adaptively necessary, yet the selective forces involved are not demonstrated. The relationship between the objectively necessary and the subjectively important, between the etic and the emic, is the greatest problem in ecological anthropology. It is precisely the same as the relationship between the reinforcers for behavior and the objective functions or effects of that behavior. Explanations of why people do what they do require interpretations of both subjective and objective causes and the links between them.

The discrepancies from the predictions of the linear programming models may be related, in part, to the differences between normal human decision-making processes and the procedures of linear programming. First of all, few people are aware of or are able to measure the nutrients used in the models. Counting calories and measuring vitamin C content are rather unique to western industrial society—even though calories and vitamins are essential for survival. Most people stress other resource attributes, especially weight or bulk and taste, in selecting resources. Ecologists must explore how choices based on these attributes may satisfy the needs for calories, vitamins, and other unrecognized nutrients. If these needs are satisfied, it may not be in the same manner or at the same costs as optimal solutions based on direct nutrient measurements.

Second, the subjective measurements of costs may differ quite radically from the objective scales of minutes, calories, or acres. A common observation among many groups is that time spent in communal labor is more enjoyable than is time spent alone. All "man-hours" are not equal. There is a subjective preference order distinct from the quantitative measures currently used in much of the literature. These preferences may yield a cost-ranking of foods quite unlike that predicted objectively. Decisions based on these costs may, consequently, differ considerably from those predicted. Again, ecologists must investigate the relationship between these costs and any proposed, optimal decisions.

Third, people do not tend to consider huge masses of information simultaneously in making choices; they simplify the procedure in two ways. On the one hand, they often restrict the information to that considered most relevant and ignore the rest (Dillon and Heady 1960). On the other hand, they tend to make evaluations sequentially and hierarchically rather than simultaneously, allowing a further restriction to the amount of information considered at any one time. The similarity of subjective classification schemes to monothetic and divisive mathematical techniques that progressively subdivide a group of objects according to single attributes suggests just this simplified, hierarchical approach (see Whallon 1972). The simplification procedures are indicated also by the frequently noted human tendency to categorize by means of binary oppositions, that is, by the presence or absence of a single attribute (Brown 1977; Greenberg 1969).

In terms of food selection, this simplified, hierarchical approach might take several forms. A hierarchy might be established, for example, according to a preference order based on taste or some other subjective measure of content. Thus, the !Kung eat as much meat as they can get and as many plants as they need to (Lee 1968:41). Similarly, rabbits and fish are considered second-class resources in comparison to caribou, moose, or beaver in the North American Subarctic (Nelson 1973; Smith 1978). In other words, resources are often classified *a priori* as preferred, back-up, or emergency foods, and this preference order may be distinct from considerations of cost or efficiency, providing a ranking that is imposed upon subsequent calculations.

Alternatively, a hierarchy might be established largely in terms of costs, with preference going to foods that are least expensive per unit weight. If land is short, those resources most productive of food bulk (of acceptable, but not necessarily preferred, taste) per acre may be given priority, and then other resources selected subsequent to this commitment on the basis of other demands or preferences.

Two problems with this approach, focused as it is on preferences and taste, are that (1) tastes seem to be quite variable cross-culturally and (2) choices based on taste would seem to be irrelevant to the biological needs for survival. The emphasis on taste preferences, however, is designed to make up for a lack of their consideration in much of the ecological literature, not to deny the importance of considerations of hours, acres, and kilograms. The latter are simply not the only factors examined. People may be committed or anchored by prior preference orders, and calculations would be modified accordingly. Furthermore, it is doubtful that tastes and preferences, however variable and capricious they seem, are totally unrelated to relevant biological and ecological factors.

For example, in an attempt to make ecological sense out of a diversity of practices, including food choices and taboos (as well as population dispersion, warfare, and cannibalism), much attention has been given to protein as a necessity in potentially short supply (Gross 1975; Harner 1977; Harris 1979; Ross 1979). These various studies identify a particular potential for protein scarcity in a given situation and seek to demonstrate that the ecologically most important effect of certain aspects of behavior is the alleviation of this scarcity. Support for these interpretations has been offered in the form of the almost universal preference for meat over plant foods, a preference that, while not instinctual, is "biologically and culturally conditioned" and makes good nutritional sense as well (Harris 1979:32–34).

Yet this general "Protein Hypothesis" faces a number of problems. Proteins per se are not recognized by most peoples of the world and thus are not considered in their evaluations. Furthermore, all meat is not preferred over all plants, and preference orders among animal foods do not correspond to protein contents. Certainly, high-quality protein is a requirement for survival, but since many peoples can give reasons for their food preferences, and since these reasons do not include the protein content of different foods, it becomes necessary to explore the link between stated preferences and nutritional consequences that include protein intake. One possible link between the two is the suggestion that, for lack of a better name, may be called the "Fat Hypothesis."

There are numerous examples of stated preferences for fat as a major attribute of food desirability. Animal foods are often clearly ranked according to fat content. This ranking is true of groups in northern latitudes such as the Copper Eskimo (Damas 1972:13), Nunamiut (Gubser 1965:299), Kutchin (Nelson 1973:142), Cree (Honigmann 1961:160), and Ojibwa (Rogers 1972:111). It is also characteristic of many groups in the Tropics and Subtropics, including the !Kung (Lee 1972:144), Pitjandjara (Tindale 1972:248), Wanindiljaugwa (Worsley 1961:170), Valley Bisa (Marks 1976:105, 205), Miskito (Nietschmann 1972:59), and Kalapalo (Basso 1973:25).

Equally impressive is the number of examples of food preference orders that, although not identifying fat as the important criterion, do generally correspond to a ranking by fat content. There are numerous statements in the literature to the effect that meat is the best or only true food (Denevan 1971:510; Gross 1975:532;

Nietschmann 1973:108; Tanaka 1976:113; Woodburn 1968a:195). Since animal flesh is generally fattier than plant materials (there are a number of important exceptions), the widespread preference for meat may reflect the simplified binary opposition:

Meat (fat) versus Plants (lean)

The importance of certain nuts (pinyon, acorns, mongongo, peanuts, *Pandanus*) and legumes may reflect a preference for the taste of these fattier plant foods as much as their abundance or ease of collection.

If fat is to be considered a link between the emic and etic, its relationship both to subjective preferences and to objective requirements must be demonstrated. In addition to the ethnographic statements identifying fat as a desirable food attribute, it is clear that fat content is intimately related to taste in general: "many of the substances responsible for the flavor and aroma of foods are fat soluable and are found associated with the fat in the diet" (Burton 1965:76). Moreover, "fat slows the emptying time of the stomach and decreases intestinal mobility. . . . Thus, fat-containing meals have a high satiety value; they 'stick' to the ribs longer" (Burton 1965:76). Consequently, tasty and filling foods frequently have high fat contents, and vice versa.

Just as fat can be directly correlated with subjective taste preferences, so too can it be linked to objective biological requirements. Certain fatty acids are essential in the diet, at least of infants, although the necessary levels are unclear (Burton 1965:75). Consumption of fatty foods encourages adequate levels of the fat-soluble vitamins A, D, E, and K, and vitamin D, in turn, facilitates the absorption of dietary calcium. Fat is the most concentrated form of energy, so that, all other factors held constant, fattier foods have higher energy yields per unit weight and per unit cost than other foods.

Finally, there is a strong association between fat content and protein content in most foods. Most natural foods with relatively high fat contents have high protein contents. Figure 4.2 and Table 4.2 compare a number of foods by their fat and protein contents. Notice that foods with more than 5 gm of fat per 100 gm edible portion also have 10 gm or more of raw protein. This relationship is unidirectional; there are numerous foods that are high in protein but low in fat. Thus, selection of fatty foods for their taste usually results in consumption of high protein foods as well.

In a brief dietary study among the Campa of eastern Peru, venison contributed 67% of the fat and 87% of the protein in the diet (Denevan 1971:513). Among the Aruni Enga of New Guinea, "fats are obtained largely from peanuts, fish, meat, and *Pandanus* nuts, as is protein" (Waddell 1972:127). Even the controversial Aztec sacrifices may have provided relatively large proportions of both fat and protein in the diets of those who ingested them (Harner 1977). Moreover, foods rich in both fat and protein would provide sufficient calories to spare the

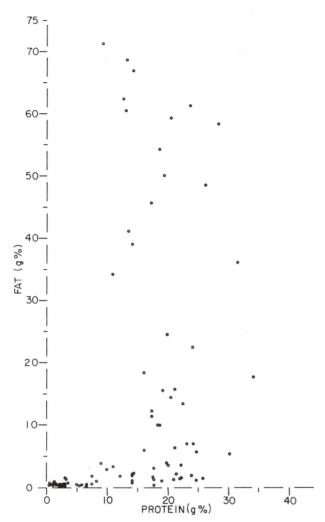

Fig. 4.2. Relationship between fat and protein contents of various foods.

protein from being metabolized as an energy source, leaving it free to be used for structural and functional needs. Adequate protein intake, consequently, may in part be an unrealized and unintended effect of food preferences based on fat. The value of focusing on fat rather than on protein is that it not only provides a link between motives and effects of food preferences, but also that it helps account for the preferences among animal foods that are equal in protein. Furthermore, it allows for the possibility that people will obtain inadequate protein despite the adaptive advantages of its dietary maximization.

TABLE 4.2

Fat and Protein Contents of Various Foods[a]

	Fat	Protein
Greens		
Hisbiscus leaves	.3	5.7
Sweet potato leaves	.7	3.6
Taro leaves	.8	3.0
Fruits		
Tsama melon	.1	.4
Banana	.2	1.1
Grewia berry	.2	5.4
Breadfruit	.3	1.7
Plantain	.4	1.1
Vegetable ivory fruit	.4	4.9
Blueberry	.5	.7
Mongongo fruit	.6	6.6
Mephate berry	.6	7.5
Blackberry	.9	1.2
Wild sour plum	1.3	3.1
Tubers		
White potato	.1	2.1
/Tan root	.1	2.2
Sha root	.1	3.0
Taro	.2	1.9
Xanthosoma	.2	1.9
Yam	.2	2.1
Manioc	.3	1.7
Sweet potato	.3	1.7
Kudot yam	.3	2.2
!Xwa root	.7	.6
Grains		
White rice	.4	6.7
Wild rice	.7	14.1
Barley	1.0	8.2

(*continued*)

Certainly, the preference for meat over plant food derives from many other factors as well. Animals are large food packages that may be more efficient to exploit in terms of time and labor costs, and big game hunting is often more efficient in these terms than is small game hunting. Among the Achuara of Amazonia the hunting of white-lipped peccary is 17.6 times more productive than small mammal hunting in terms of pounds of meat per man-hour (Nietschmann 1978:24). For the aboriginal Wabash Valley of Indiana, Reidhead

TABLE 4.2. *Continued*

	Fat	Protein
Rye	1.7	12.1
Brown rice	1.9	7.5
Wheat	2.2	14.0
Millet	2.9	9.9
Sorghum	3.3	11.0
Maize	3.9	8.9
Legumes		
Lentil	1.1	24.7
Bean	1.6	22.3
Soybean	17.7	34.1
Tsinbean	36.1	31.6
Peanut	48.7	26.2
Nuts		
Chestnut	1.5	2.9
Cashew	45.7	17.2
Beechnut	50.0	19.4
Almond	54.2	18.6
Mongongo nut	58.4	28.3
Walnut	59.3	20.5
Pinon nut	60.5	13.0
Butternut	61.2	23.7
Hazelnut	62.4	12.6
Brazilnut	66.9	14.3
Hickorynut	68.7	13.2
Pecan	71.2	9.2
Fish		
Cod	.3	17.6
Perch	1.0	19.0
Halibut	1.2	20.9
Cisco	2.3	17.7
Pacific herring	2.6	17.5
Catfish	3.1	17.6

(continued)

(1977) has estimated that deer hunting provided 2.6 pounds per man-hour, more than the hunting of turkey (1.5), beaver (1.3), opossum (1.1), raccoon (0.9), muskrat (0.4), and squirrel (0.4). Size, of course, is only one factor affecting exploitative efficiency, and big game may be relatively very expensive, depending on other attributes such as density, aggregation, wariness, and mobility. Clusters of small resources, in fact, may be more efficient to exploit than large resources. In addition, large animals are more suitable for widespread sharing,

TABLE 4.2. *Continued*

	Fat	Protein
Char	3.6	22.1
Pink salmon	3.7	20.0
Bream	4.0	19.7
Sturgeon	5.7	24.7
Whitefish	7.0	23.0
Lake trout	10.0	18.3
Shad	10.0	18.6
Atlantic herring	11.3	17.3
Atlantic salmon	13.4	22.5
Chinook salmon	15.6	19.1
Eel	18.3	15.9
Birds		
Ptarmigan	1.4	25.7
Loon	1.9	23.8
Grouse	5.3	30.1
Duck	15.8	21.2
Goose	22.4	24.0
Shellfish		
Clam	1.9	14.0
Mussel	2.2	14.4
Miscellaneous		
Green turtle	2.1	21.3
Muskrat	1.3	22.0
Rabbit	6.0	16.0
Hare	7.0	24.2
Deer	6.4	21.0
Whitelipped peccary	12.2	17.4
Caribou	14.4	20.5
Polar bear	24.5	19.1
Musk ox	34.2	10.8
Beaver	39.0	14.0
Seal	41.1	13.4

[a] After Watt and Merrill 1975.

and by being both more sharable and more dangerous, tend to be more prestigious to exploit than plants as well.

For a variety of reasons, consequently, a hierarchy of preferences based upon taste or size of individuals or clusters may be established that takes priority over the estimation of their efficiency of exploitation. Large, fatty animals may be ranked above more efficiently procured foods, and time or energy allotment structured accordingly. Among the Waswanipi Cree of Ontario, for example, the relative productivity of different food-getting activities as practiced is approximately

Moose hunting 13.75 pounds per man-day
Fishing 2.29
Beaver hunting 1.38 [Feit 1973:121]

Yet the relative contribution of each diet in terms of pounds (considering just these three resources) is:

Moose 51%
Fish 20%
Beaver 29%

Beaver are more important in the diet than their efficiency would warrant. Moreover, the relative time allotted in their procurement is:

Moose 11%
Fish 26%
Beaver 63%

Much more time is devoted to beaver exploitation than their efficiency would suggest. Beaver meat is very fatty and is considered very good eating.

In other words, the measures of productivity may be ranked according to preference and their efficiency of procurement considered sequentially. The most efficient procurement of fatty meat is given priority over that of lean meat in the decision-making process, as is that of big meat packages over small. The shift from the exploitation of the most preferred food to that of lower ranked food could then be stimulated by diminishing returns as the maximum sustainable yield is exceeded—a purely pragmatic concept useful in economics and general ecology (see Schoener 1971). The critical level of declining returns for human choices, however, is not necessarily as clear as the general ecological literature would assume. Since the preference order is not necessarily based on simple energetic efficiency, the shift is both qualitative and quantitative, from production of most desired foods to that of less attractive ones. Ten pounds of beaver meat per day may be preferred over 10 pounds of fish per day, but if beaver yields began to decrease, at some point activity would shift to fishing. If beaver hunting yielded only 6 pounds per day, whereas fishing produced 10, fishing might become preferable. The determination of this critical shifting point is largely unexplored in the literature of anthropology and ecology, although economics has approached the problem through the study of differential utility and decision-making. Certainly, more than simple energetics is involved.

Even if a particular preferred resource were infinitely exploitable and showed no tendency for diminishing returns with increased utilization, it is quite likely that shifts to less preferred resources would occur in subsistence economies. A desire for variety, for a diversity of foods, is widely documented in the ethnographic literature (see Jochim 1976:20–21). Although an argument could be made for the physiological benefits of mixing foods, and hence for the role of biological selection in shaping this tendency, what remains problematic for studies of feeding strategies is that a threshold of dietary monotony can be assumed but not specified. We have little idea about the degree of uniformity of the diet that is tolerable and about how this tolerance varies among biological populations and cultural groups. It should be noted that involvement with market economies allows a total specialization of activities without a necessary dietary specialization since the income from a single cash crop can be converted into a variety of foods for consumption.

If more than energy is involved in the assessment of different foods, so too is more than food involved in choices of food-getting activities. Any use of time, energy, or land may produce more than just food. Measures of productivity considered in decision making should include these other yields as well. A wide variety of demands exists for nonfood materials, some of which, for clothes, shelter, and tool manufacture, are intimately linked to survival. Such utilitarian materials—stones, metals, woods, fibers, skins, pelts, etc.—may be evaluated according to material properties amenable to measurement, such as durability, fracture characteristics, tensile strength, and insulating ability.

These attributes would allow ranking of materials and some estimation of differential productivity per unit cost. Again, however, it becomes difficult to predict when shifts from one resource to another would occur. Foreign metal implements have replaced those of native materials virtually everywhere, presumably because the former are mechanically much superior and more durable (and a source of prestige by virtue of their exoticness). It is more difficult to predict when a group might shift from the utilization of a mediocre but locally available stone to the expensive import of superior obsidian; that is, it is not easy to estimate just how superior the obsidian must be for its greater cost to be paid.

In the case of nonutilitarian demands such as those involved with adornment, ceremonialism, or prestation, the ranking of materials is symbolic and less amenable to translation into material terms. Certainly, ecological analysis can offer some suggestions about the differential occurrence of these activities since they are differentially reinforced in various contexts and since they comprise solutions of problems of different sorts. Population size and the degree of environmental, economic, and political complexity, for example, would affect the elaborateness of individual adornment and thus the strength of demands for the materials involved. The degree of subsistence insecurity might affect the scale and intensity of regional interaction and thus the intensity of certain aspects of ceremonialism and gift-giving and the demands for the necessary materials. In each case, although the relative *intensity* of demands may be suggested, the specific *objects* of these demands bear no necessary relationship to the material circumstances. Sahlins (1976:76) has emphasized the inability of ecological approaches to explain the content or form of various cultural practices, even when interpreting their general function. Any object of adornment could function to differentiate individuals and statuses if meaning is so assigned to the objects involved. Ecology cannot predict the objects chosen: the wearing of any designated symbol may be reinforced if it gains recognition of the individual or status position. Choices of materials may be initially accidental or arbitrary, but they subsequently impose demands that may be examined in a utilitarian framework. Once parrot feathers are deemed necessary, then the procurement of parrots may be organized quite rationally and efficiently.

In addition, it has been mentioned that communal labor is widely preferred over solitary work. One way in which to view this preference is that communal activities are potentially more efficient uses of time. Besides food they produce many intangible social benefits such as information, gossip, and psychological reinforcement. Similarly, wideranging nomadic activities like hunting may include bonuses in the form of information about resources or neighboring groups. All forms of productivity, both material and nonmaterial, may be taken into account in the decisions about time allotment, and therefore, would affect the food-selection process as well. The greatest time efficiency would be attained when time spent gives simultaneous yields of all measures of productivity.

The types of measures of productivity, consequently, are numerous and varied. Objective categories of nutritional requirements may be used to study diets or to predict optimal food mixtures for comparison, but the subjective measures used in the actual selection processes are quite different. Weight and taste are two of the most common to be mentioned, and some suggestions have been offered about how these relate to nutritional needs. In addition, dietary variety, nonfood materials, opportunities for socializing, and ancillary information gathered represent other possible scales for the evaluation of the efficiency of resource procurement. One other type of productivity, touched upon but not elaborated, is prestige.

Prestige, or high regard or influence, obviously derives from a number of factors and varies considerably cross-culturally in its nature. Some general principles that relate prestige to feeding strategies, however, may be suggested. A common route to prestige acquisition is the procurement and sharing of certain types of resources. Among most foraging and many mixed horticultural societies, for example, hunting, especially that of big game, is the source of most prestige (Gross 1975:532–533). This form of overt appreciation for hunting might be viewed as a reinforcement for a biologically necessary activity, shaped by selective forces to maintain the procurement of high quality protein. If this were the case, one would expect that the association between big game hunting and prestige would be variable: strongest in habitats of limited animal resources and weakest or at least quite variable where meat is abundant. Yet in the northern latitudes where virtually the only resources are animals, it is still big game hunting that is widely and strongly tied to prestige acquisition.

It would be convenient to be able to relegate prestige values to a secondary

position, ultimately dependent upon the material factors of biological requirements, but this would do injustice to the creativity of human survival techniques
and the latitude by which they survive. People are free to assign prestige to any
activity as long as they continue to meet survival needs. A finely engineered
system would certainly be designed so that prestige-seeking helps insure survival, but cultural systems are not necessarily so coherent.

If prestige values were indeed closely linked to survival benefits, for example,
one might expect that situations of real hardship such as drought would show an
intensification of prestige acquisition. There are a number of examples to the
contrary, however, in which sharing becomes less widespread, food acquisition
becomes more secretive, and even the hunting of the larger, more sharable
animals is avoided (Firth 1959:83–84; Holmberg 1950:60–62; Richards
1939:202; Turnbull 1965:120). If the prestige of sharing were strongly selected
in order best to maintain survival, the intensity of sharing should be greatest
during hard times. Yet among the Mbuti Pygmies the reverse seems to be true:
"Unless there is a general scarcity of meat, it was customary for meat to be
distributed among all members of a band" (Ichikawa 1978:177). And generally,
"sharing will break out not merely in bad times, but especially in good. The level
of generalized reciprocity peaks on the occasion of a windfall: now everyone can
cash in on the virtues of generosity" (Sahlins 1972:212).

Certainly, sharing contributes to survival and is commonly recognized as
doing so by the participants, but the ranking of shared goods according to
prestige value does not seem to involve survival benefits directly. Rather, the
most prestigious items often appear to be those for which there is highest demand. This demand, in turn, depends upon the rank order of food preferences
(headed by large fatty animals) and upon a number of other attributes such as
danger or difficulty of acquisition or geographical exoticness, which induces
scarcity. The desire for the production of prestige in food getting may lead to
costly activities and a decrease in energetic efficiency.

2.2. Security

Subsistence aimed at efficiency attempts to insure adequate levels of production at least cost. As often measured, efficiency may be virtually independent of
temporal context. A single communal kill by 12 men in 1 day might have the
same labor efficiency as six separate kills by 2 men, each in a different week.
The implications for survival of the two situations, however, are quite different.
If the people practice no food storage, then the second group has insured survival
for six times as long as the first. The difference is not in the cost of production,
but in its regularity. The second group has greater subsistence security. Security,
like time efficiency, is a ratio of production to time; but unlike efficiency, it is
elapsed time, not time expended in an activity, which is important.

There is no doubt that a concern for security underlies many subsistence practices cross-culturally, both among hunter–gatherers (Jochim 1976:16–17) and subsistence farmers (Bronson 1972:200; Johnson 1971; Wharton 1969). In fact, as Johnson (1972:151) has generalized, "traditional agriculturalists prefer costly 'security' strategies to strategies which might maximize their long-term earnings but which include unacceptable risks to survival." The widespread conservatism of subsistence economies may be traced to this emphasis on security and avoidance of risk taking, although such conservatism does not preclude cautious experimentation with new resources and techniques (Johnson 1972:151). Part of the problem with the "Green Revolution," the attempt to export Western crops and agricultural techniques to the Third World, has been, not native resistance to change, but a failure by Western scientists to recognize the emphasis given to security in peasant economies. "The peasant farmer's first goal is not to maximize his profits; it is to minimize his risks. Yet the Green Revolution crops perform to meet the Western commercial criteria of large production and high profits" (Wade 1974:1189–1191).

Insuring the regular availability of food can be problematic in two general types of situations. First of all, the potential environmental productivity may be *predictably variable* from one season or year to the next, so that periods of scarcity may be anticipated. A variety of strategies may be found to deal with such predictable insecurity, including the practice of food storage, wage labor, and migration to more favorable areas. In addition to these technological and organizational solutions, however, the actual selection of food resources may also reflect the need to overcome the seasonal shortages. During the productive seasons, for example, resources may be chosen as much for their time efficiency and storability as for other attributes. Root crops frequently may be planted rather than grains in part because of the ability of roots to remain preserved in natural storage underground. The Thompson Indians of British Columbia regularly obtained lean salmon from their upstream neighbors, the Shuswap, by exchanging fattier downriver salmon they had caught themselves; the fatty salmon were prized for their taste, while the lean fish could be stored for longer periods (Palmer 1975:219). During the harsh seasons, if sufficient foods have been stored, then taste preferences or a desire for variety may guide selection.

By contrast, variability in production may be quite *unpredictable* so that specific anticipatory solutions are difficult, and more general strategies of coping become necessary. Perhaps the most common of such strategies are (1) opportunism, the exploitation of wild resources as they are encountered—this frequently results in a utilization of resources according to their abundance, regardless of costs or taste preferences; (2) diversification, for example by planting a variety of crops, so that some will survive whatever the conditions; and (3) the emphasis of particular resources that appear most reliable in most situations.

These strategies may represent functional alternatives that are at least partially mutually exclusive. Thus, hunter–gatherers who devote their attention to relatively reliable fishing may be unable thereby to exploit diverse land resources. The Mkamba of Kenya, like many horticulturalists, plant a tremendous variety of crops in the most precarious agricultural land (Porter 1965); farmers of northern Thailand, on the other hand, solve their problems of (market) insecurity by specializing on what they perceive to be the most reliable strain of rice, to the amusement of the district official who diversifies his holdings in the same situation (Moermann 1968:69). The choice of alternatives in any situation would depend on the resource options available and the access to technology, labor, and information about the degree of uncertainty.

The importance of these strategies and of security as an economic goal would seem to depend on the degree of variability and unpredictability in the environment. People conditioned by frequent subsistence disasters would place greater emphasis on the relatively more rewarding practices aimed at minimizing risk. In order to assess the importance of such security measures among various groups, consequently, it would be necessary to determine the relative degree of risk in their environments. Unfortunately, much of the ecological literature treats risk as a relatively undifferentiated phenomenon and its minimization as equally significant in all situations. Every resource or environment poses risks to human exploitation; every group examined will have some strategies of coping with such risks. The risks will vary, however, in their nature and magnitude, and the coping devices will have to differ in kind and intensity as a result.

The analysis of environmental risks must specify the various dimensions of variability that appear relevant to people's decisions, the average frequency and amplitude of variation along these dimensions, and the range or degree of variance around these averages. Only by such attempts to operationalize the concept of risk may resources and environments be adequately compared and some expectations about the relative need for security generated. The three most general dimensions of variation relevant to food selection are (1) time; (2) space; and (3) abundance (see, for example, Dyson-Hudson and Smith 1978). People must cope with change and unpredictability along any or all these dimensions in determining their feeding strategies. An assessment of the general degree of risk confronting a group must involve an examination of the determinants of this variation, which may include factors of the physical environment, behavior of the resources themselves, and features of human exploitation.

2.2.1. Physical Environmental Risks

Rainfall is a critical factor influencing the availability of drinking water, the abundance and distribution of resources, and the timing of food-getting activities in many areas. The amount and the temporal and spatial distribution of rainfall, consequently, has important effects on the food-selection process, particularly in regions where rain is either quite scarce or quite abundant. In desert regions, for example, the uncertainty of rainfall is perhaps the single most important problem facing the inhabitants, yet such regions are not all alike and the specific nature of risks in food getting vary accordingly. In the Kalahari of southern Africa the major uncertainties involve the total amount from one year to the next and the geographical distribution. The yearly variation in the Dobe area is so great, for instance, that in a 46-year period of study, 12 years were characterized by severe drought with well below average rainfall (Lee 1972). The timing of these drought years was quite variable: although the average interval between droughts was about 4 years, the range was from 1 to 13 years. The geographical variation is similarly quite large, with significant differences among nearby areas during the same year and no consistent pattern in these differences from one year to the next (Lee 1972). This unpredictability in space and yearly abundance is partially compensated for by the presence of permanent waterholes in the !Kung region but not in the G/Wi area of the central Kalahari.

Cycles ↓ unpredictability [handwritten marginalia]

By contrast, the rains do show a fairly regular temporal distribution within the year, so that wet and dry seasons are rather reliable (see Fig. 4.3). For half of each year, as a result, the rainfall is predictable: the wet season may show rainfall in uncertain amounts and locations, but the dry season will be reliably dry. Since the relative abundance (however scarce) and distribution (either scattered or relatively concentrated around waterholes) of resources can be predicted for the dry season, appropriate strategies of exploitation for this season may be determined and will be reinforced quite regularly. The dry season represents a time of relative certainty in terms of the choices to be made: risk minimization should take precedence over efficiency or any other goals.

The Central and Western Deserts of Australia present somewhat of a contrast to the Kalahari. The average yearly rainfall is lower, only about half that of the Kalahari, and its variability from year to year is somewhat greater. More important, however, the rainfall patterns of the Australian Desert show much greater geographical and seasonal uncertainty. Aborigines of the Western Desert, for example, have been forced in the past to abandon temporarily most of their huge territories because of a virtual absence of rain throughout the area and seek other lands with local rains (Strehlow 1965). As one indication of this geographical variability, the average yearly totals of two weather stations about 470 miles apart may be compared (Fig. 4.4). The two records demonstrate little correspondence and, in fact, show a correlation coefficient of -0.11 (a coefficient of zero would suggest a complete lack of predictability). Records from two stations in the Kalahari region about 310 miles apart, by contrast, show a much greater pattern of correspondence and a correlation coefficient of $+0.73$. Longer records from more closely spaced stations would certainly make this comparison more valuable, but these figures are striking nevertheless. The Kalahari rainfall may not be very predictable from one place to another (Lee 1972:132), but that of the Australian Desert is much less so. More or less permanent waterholes scattered throughout much of this desert help provide a spatial security in the face of the uncertainty of the rains.

Adding to this geographical variability is the much greater seasonal uncertainty of the Australian Desert. Figure 4.5 presents the average monthly rainfall for Alice Springs and shows the lack of defined wet and dry seasons. Another way of determining seasonality is to examine for each month the probabilities of receiving no rain at all. Based on the same records, in every month, there is at least a 10% chance of no rainfall, with a range of up to 40% (Fig. 4.6A). By contrast, at Maun in the Kalahari, there is likely to be no rain in only 6 months of the year, and the range of probabilities is up to 100% (Fig. 4.6B).

Just these two examples suggest great differences between the Kalahari and the Australian Desert as human habitats—differences which rarely receive sufficient attention when the !Kung and Aboriginal groups are compared (Yellen 1977).

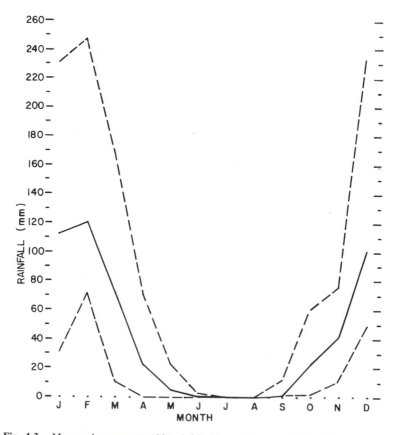

Fig. 4.3. Mean and extreme monthly rainfall, Maun, Botswana, 1951–1960. ———— indicates 10-year average monthly rainfall; ---- indicates highest and lowest recorded monthly rainfalls.

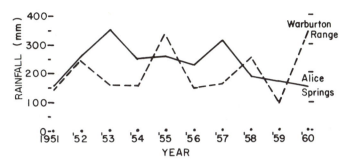

Fig. 4.4. Mean annual rainfall for two stations in the Australian Desert, 1951–1960.

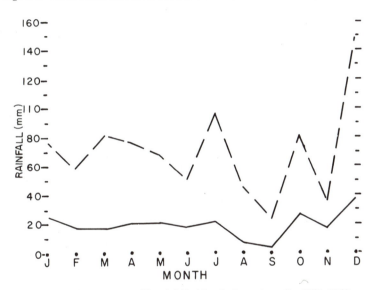

Fig. 4.5. Mean and extreme monthly rainfall, Alice Springs, Australia, 1951–1960. ———
indicates 10-year average monthly rainfall; – – – – indicates highest recorded monthly rainfall.

These differences have been stressed, however, by Gould (1969:268): "Since the
amount and distribution of rainfall is erratic from year to year, the movements of
the Aboriginal families are similarly erratic. They are not erratic in the sense of
being aimless, but rather because they do not follow a regular rhythm like the
seasonal movements of the Bushmen." The Aborigines are less able to predict
the abundance, timing, and location of water and food resources, and thus
encounter greater uncertainty in subsistence decisions. Security should represent
a more important goal guiding these decisions than it does among the !Kung. In
addition, just as there are significant differences within the Kalahari between the
habitats of the !Kung and G/Wi, so too are there differences between the Central

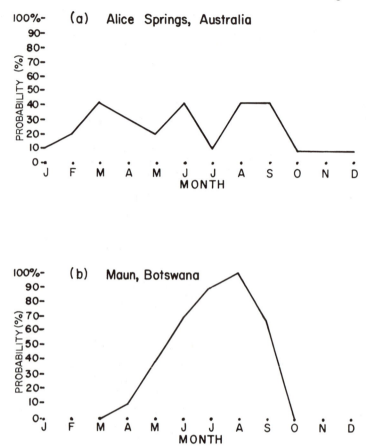

Fig. 4.6. Monthly probability of receiving no rain in the (a) Australian Desert and (b) Kalahari Desert.

and Western Deserts of Australia, with the latter characterized by less abundant and more variable rainfall and fewer permanent waterholes. The appropriate, successful strategies of food getting would differ accordingly (Gould 1979).

Rainfall distribution and reliability are obviously also of vital importance to horticulturalists and pastoralists. The choice of crops and farming techniques and of domestic animals and grazing strategies require a knowledge of both average rainfall and its distribution in time and space. In general, the practice of rainfall farming is regularly rewarded only in those areas receiving more than about 300 to 700 mm, depending on soils and crops (Graham 1969; Turton 1977). When annual averages exceed this minimum, crop-raising becomes more successful.

Pastoralism becomes more secure relative to horticulture, on the other hand, as average yearly rainfall decreases. As Netting (1977:42) generalizes, "the parts of East Africa where herding is dominant are generally those in which water is scarce and rain unpredictable, and thus where agriculture is at its least productive and dependable."

Regions with greater variability in precipitation, moreover, pose greater risks to these economies than do more regular and predictable areas. One method of assessing these risks is to map the rainfall reliability. Figure 4.7 presents such a map for a portion of East Africa: large portions of the region with an average of

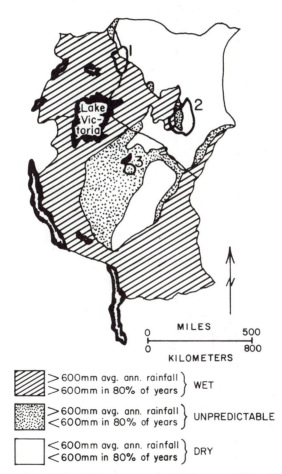

Fig. 4.7. Location of East African groups in relation to rainfall reliability. Group 1, Karamojong; Group 2, Kamba; Group 3, Barabaig.

greater than 600 mm of rainfall annually will receive less than this amount in four out of every five years. Clearly, cultivated plants represent a hazardous resource base in such areas, so that economies in these regions tend to be diversified. They combine pastoralism with horticulture and demonstrate great flexibility in the relative emphasis of each according to specific conditions of rainfall. Among the Karamojong, Kamba, and Barabaig, for example, who combine cattle pastoralism with the cultivation of sorghum, millet, and maize, the importance of crops varies considerably from year to year (Dyson-Hudson and Dyson-Hudson 1969; Klima 1970; Porter 1965). On a smaller scale, Porter (1965) has mapped the rainfall reliability according to plant-transpiration needs in two small areas of Kenya and has demonstrated the greater importance of crop cultivation as this reliability increases.

Rainfall unreliability in such marginal areas poses quite a different set of problems than those deriving from simple rainfall scarcity. If a farmer knows there is going to be little rainfall, then he can plant a drought-resistant crop as an appropriate strategy. If, on the other hand, rainfall has some (although limited) probability of being quite abundant, then planting a higher-yielding but less drought-resistant crop might be rewarded. The farmer might theoretically seek to maximize security, to maximize production, or to minimize regret, and uncertainty about the outcomes of these different strategies is greater. Gould (1963) has utilized a simplified game theoretic analysis to simulate crop choices in a situation of such rainfall uncertainty with the goal of production maximization. In his example, a mixed strategy of planting two crops in certain proportions is suggested. A goal of security maximization and a tendency toward sequential (as opposed to simultaneous) evaluation of alternatives, however, might lead to a very different solution, with the crop that is most productive in the driest years (in this example, hill rice) being planted in a much higher proportion. The more frequent the dry years, the more likely this strategy may be.

In contrast to these arid and semiarid regions, there are many areas of the world where rainfall reliability is problematic in a situation of overabundance. The equatorial zones of Amazonia, tropical Africa, and New Guinea, for example, are characterized by high precipitation and varying seasonality in its distribution. Since heavy rains make difficult such activities as forest clearance and planting, harvesting, food storage, and hunting–fishing, the predictability of rainfall would clearly affect the security of food getting. The Tropics are too often portrayed as stable environments lacking seasonality, and whereas this may be largely true of temperature patterns, it is not true of rainfall. Even close to the Equator there are definite wetter and drier seasons, and these become more clearly defined to the north and the south. Figure 4.8 presents average and extreme rainfall patterns for various stations in Amazonia, chosen to provide a north–south transect through this region. As these graphs indicate, there is considerable variability within this large area, so that discussions of "Amazonian"

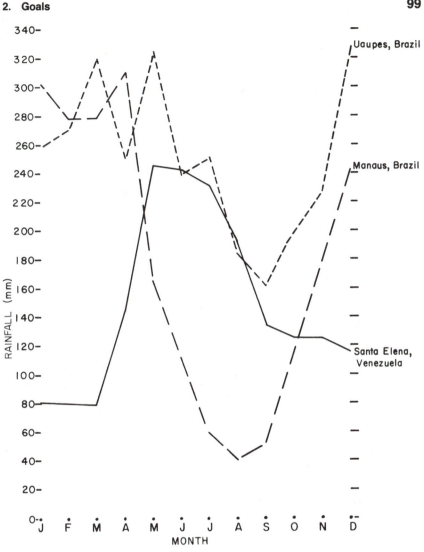

Fig. 4.8. Mean monthly rainfall in three stations in Amazonia, 1951–1960.

economies cannot ignore seasonality because of its weak expression in one small portion (Ross 1978:29).

The varying duration and reliability of the drier season within Amazonia may have important implications for food selection. As Harris (1971) suggests, maize cultivation requires more effective forest clearance than does manioc. Since short and unreliable dry seasons hinder effective clearance, the relative lack of seasonality close to the Equator may favor manioc cultivation. The inability to predict a sufficiently dry period renders maize cultivation too insecure.

Rainfall, of course, is not the only feature of the physical environment that may threaten people with insecurity. Temperature regimes may be equally significant at higher latitudes and altitudes. With increasing distance from the Equator and with increasing elevation, not only do temperatures decrease, but also the seasonal temperature differences increase. Seasonality of temperature also becomes greater with increasing distance from coastlines. One effect of such geographical gradients is a decrease in length of growing season in the same directions. Availability of wild plant foods and the success of cultivated crops would vary accordingly. Here, again, the distinction between simply short growing seasons and ones of unpredictable duration is useful. If one can anticipate a regularly short growing season, the choice of appropriate crops is rather simple. The planting of sweet potatoes in the New Guinea Highlands, of potatoes in the Andes, and of barley in the higher reaches of the Zagros is reliably reinforced by successful harvests.

In regions where the growing season is more unpredictable in duration, however, the choices again become more difficult. In the Lower Chibut Valley of western Argentina, for instance, the growing season is short and "the farmer never knows when the frosts will strike" (Williams 1977:67). This variability of frosts poses great risks to susceptible crops, and although there has been some experimentation with (and governmental encouragement of) the growing of "intensive" crops like fruit and vegetables, the farmers stress the more frost-resistant, secure crops of alfalfa and potatoes. That farming is not the only activity threatened by unpredictable temperatures, incidentally, is indicated by the numerous accounts of the difficulties encountered by Canadian and Alaskan Indian foragers in predicting the timing of freeze-up and spring thaw, and hence in choosing subsistence activities and their timing (Nelson 1973; Rogers 1972).

In addition to rainfall and temperature, there are many other environmental features, the distribution of which can be variable and pose risks to subsistence economies. River floods, whether they are considered a threat to crops as among the Nuer (Evans-Pritchard 1940) or necessary for irrigation as along the Egyptian Nile (Butzer 1976) may vary greatly in timing or magnitude, with differing problems accordingly. Storms may pose greater risks to coastal than to inland communities. Market prices may fluctuate widely or remain relatively stable. Raids and warfare may be rather predictably scheduled (Rappaport 1968) or more erratic (Chagnon 1977). As the uncertainty of these factors increases, risks increase, and food selection should give greater emphasis to security. Since any group faces multiple risks, the total constellation of these factors must be evaluated. The Argentinian farmers mentioned earlier, for example, contend not only with frosts but also with droughts, floods, plagues, and fluctuating markets (Williams 1977).

2.2.2. Resource Risks

Various resources themselves may be characterized by differing degrees of risk, in part due to the influence of the environmental factors already discussed, and in part due to innate characteristics and the influence of topography, competitors, and predators. Two attributes of resources that greatly influence their relative reliability are abundance and mobility. Hunting is generally riskier than gathering, in part because of the lesser abundance and greater mobility of animals as compared to plants. With animals, both the search and the pursuit once encountered may have high probabilities of failure. With wild plants, however, only the search is risky; once encountered, success is virtually guaranteed. One advantage of cultivated plants over wild ones is a further reduction of risk through an elimination of the uncertainty of the search. Since fish and small game tend to be more abundant and spatially more predictable than large animals, the former tend to be less risky to exploit. Domesticated animals, like crops, are reliable in space but may pose risks in their productivity from year to year according to their tolerance of environmental fluctuations.

This varying reliability of different resources helps to explain food choices in situations in which efficiency alone does not suffice. Among the Bayano Cuna of Panama, for example, bananas and plantains have largely replaced maize and manioc, in part because the former have greater productive reliability (Bennett 1962:46). The importance of cassava in much of tropical Africa is largely due to the reliability of its yields over a wide range of conditions (Morgan 1969:263). Millet and sorghum tend to show more reliable yields than maize and other crops in semiarid regions of Africa (Porter 1965:410). The exploitation of small animals may give long-term yields more reliably than the hunting of big game because of the latter's susceptibility to overpredation and slower rebound capacity (Ross 1978:5). The greater importance of turtles over land animals in the economy of the Miskito of Nicaragua may be largely because of the greater reliability of turtle fishing, in which 73% of trips are successful, as compared to land hunting, in which only 54% of trips are successful (Nietschmann 1972:58). Among the Valley Bisa of Zambia the buffalo is the most reliable animal to pursue: 26% of stalking attempts resulted in a kill; other animals show a range of from 3% to 18%. It is this species, consequently, which is most often stalked when encountered. Buffalo is stalked 84% of the times it is encountered; for other animals this frequency of stalking ranges from 9% to 67% (Marks 1976:229).

Since resources clearly differ in terms of their contribution to subsistence security, analysis of feeding strategies requires evaluation of their relative reliability. Many hunter–gatherers, for example, emphasize resources that are clumped in time and space. Two of the most prominent of such resources are caribou and salmon, both of which show seasonal migrations in large aggregations. The use of each of these two resources, however, shows a different pattern of correlation with human population density. The greater the dependence on caribou, the lower the density of people, whereas for salmon, the ethnographic literature suggests a positive correlation between use of this resource and human population density (Burch 1972; Graburn and Strong 1972). These different patterns may be related to the differing reliability of the two resources.

Both salmon and caribou tend to show periodic fluctuations in overall abundance: caribou in cycles of 35–100 years, salmon in cycles of 4–11 years. Both may be taken by individuals with spears or more efficiently in some situations by groups using pounds or weirs. Both may be processed and preserved by freezing, drying, or smoking in their normal habitats. Both may occur in restricted locations such as mountain passes or pools, allowing some predictability of their capture. Nevertheless, the predictability of their location differs greatly. When caribou are quite abundant they may occur everywhere; otherwise they may show yearly or longer-term shifts of their migration routes and may disappear totally from one area. Salmon, on the other hand, are restricted to rivers; they return to the same place, often at the same time (within a few days) each year. Thus, salmon are a much more predictable, spatially stable resource. For both caribou and salmon, the pursuit time once they are located can be quite low, and thus they can contribute greatly to subsistence efficiency. By contrast, the search time and probability of failure for caribou is quite variable and can be quite high, whereas that for salmon is low, and therefore, the contribution of the two resources to subsistence security is vastly different.

The predictability of caribou alone depends on a large number of regional and local environmental factors, on the abundance of caribou relative to other resources, and on the demands placed upon the resource base. Caribou predictability and its determinants have been differently perceived. Local and short-term studies still stress the remarkably predictable migrations of large numbers of these animals (Binford 1978), whereas studies over longer time periods and larger regions increasingly emphasize their local temporal and spatial variability (Burch 1972). If some assessment of the role of caribou in subsistence economies is to be made, a means of determining their reliability must be devised. The concept of ''predictability'' must be operationalized so that caribou may be compared to other resources, and so that caribou in one area and time period may be compared to those in others.

Although such an operationalized measure of predictability has not been devised, some of the factors that must be incorporated into such a measure can be suggested as follows:

(1) If one examines a large enough area of caribou habitat, there are almost always some caribou present somewhere.

(2) If one examines an area over a long enough time period, fairly regular

cycles of caribou abundance become evident, with a frequency of from about 35 to 100 years.

(3) With smaller areas under study, the functional nature of each area with respect to caribou behavior is significant to their predictability. Some regions represent core areas virtually always occupied, whereas other regions are overflow zones, likely to have caribou only in times of regional population peaks. On a finer scale, caribou predictability varies among calving grounds, summer grazing areas, migration routes, and winter habitats.

(4) Not only the functional role of an area, but also numerous local environmental features are significant in determining caribou predictability. These features include the degree of topographic channeling of movement by barriers, the extent of snow and vegetation affecting the size of areas suitable for seasonal grazing and calving, the relative proximity of different seasonally suitable habitats, the frequency and distribution of disruptive fires, and the nature and relative abundance of competitors and predators.

(5) Predictability of caribou behavior appears different, too, according to the time period under consideration. Climatic variability, for example, can be measured in terms of daily fluctuations within seasons, differences from year to year in the timing of freeze or thaw, or yearly variations in the severity of winter. Caribou behavior would respond accordingly, on different time scales simultaneously.

(6) Predictability depends also on the stage within the long-term cycles of overall abundance. When caribou generally are abundant they are easier to approach, the timing of their movements is more regular, and their spatial predictability is greater than when the animals are rarer.

In general, then, caribou cannot be rated simply as "predictable" or "risky," nor can specific habitats. The temporal and spatial scale as well as the features of specific environments determine the relative predictability of this and other resources. For wild plant foods, the varying yields according to rainfall and the changing spatial distribution through time must be taken into account (see Thomas 1972:686). For domesticated plants one must look beyond average yields to the variance according to soils, rain, and frosts; the tolerance of disease; and the response to shortened fallow periods. Since an assessment of predictability is significant only in reference to human decision making, the relevant scales might be estimated by a consideration of the spatiotemporal capabilities of human information gathering and the social context and frequency of decisions.

3. DIFFERENTIAL OPTIONS

Attention has been devoted so far to the general influences of external environmental factors on the resource choices of entire groups. All groups are heterogeneous, however, composed of subgroups and individuals in differing circumstances and with differential access to labor, land, and resources. As a result, individuals will differ in their perception of needs, costs, and strategic options. As societies become more complex, the differences among individual choices may increase as well. Nevertheless, even the most egalitarian of hunter–gatherer societies show internal differences that affect feeding strategies. Access to resources may vary because of differing ties of kinship and friendship. The ability to mobilize labor and the levels of demand for resources will vary with family size and the proportion of productive members. Physical prowess and skill will affect costs and risks of various activities. Consistently successful hunters can build large networks of reciprocal relationships that enhance subsistence security, whereas regularly poor or lazy hunters may encounter some resentment and social exclusion, decreasing their options for reciprocal relationships. The poor hunter, in addition, may have greater difficulty finding a wife, which further jeopardizes his subsistence position.

The more sedentary hunter–gatherers such as those of the Northwest Coast, together with many horticulturalists, are characterized in part by greater emphasis on individual resource holdings. This situation leads to further differences in feeding strategies. Differential access to salmon spawning grounds, shellfish beds, or lands with the best soils or surest water supplies will engender differing perceptions of subsistence options. Larger or more productive holdings will affect not only the calculation of land costs, but also, by attracting disadvantaged individuals, the calculation of labor costs as well. The differential control over labor emerges as a major dimension of sociopolitical differentiation, and generosity from above replaces the natural environment as the direct reinforcer for much of subsistence behavior. Just as the more fortunate tend to have greater access to labor as well as to land and its resources, so too can they mobilize and concentrate greater capital as well. Such investments as sea-going canoes, rifles, outboard motors, and tractors are often options available only to a few, and such options can greatly enhance the potential efficiency and security of food getting. It is the rare individual among the Miskito of Nicaragua who can afford to maintain the equipment necessary for both turtle fishing and land hunting; most men are forced to concentrate on one or the other (Nietschmann 1973).

Because of their greater access to labor and capital, such individuals can increase their time efficiency enormously over that of poorer people. Moreover, their perception of risk and margin of security is quite different as well. It is the large landowner who can most afford to experiment with different crops and techniques and who can take risks with half his land and still produce sufficient food on the remaining half in case of drought. It is the owner of large herds who can attract the labor of others and thus split his herd to take advantage of varying grazing conditions, and who can suffer a 50% loss of his herd and still manage adequately (Dyson-Hudson 1972).

Such differences among individuals in a society must be taken into account when analyzing feeding strategies. They may not only help to account for significant intrasocietal dietary differences but would have implications for many other aspects of behavior requiring the expenditure of time and energy and the evaluation of risk. In addition, the individuals with greater access to resources may attain greater influence in decision making as well. If so, then their perceptions and goals may dominate the strategies of the entire society. Since, as is so often true, the interests of the elite are quite different from those of the majority, this concentration of decision-making power may lead to general patterns of behavior that are distinctly maladaptive for the bulk of the population. For anthropologists to expect and predict the appropriate behavior in terms of greatest efficiency or security for the society as a whole without considering the locus of decisions guiding this behavior is a sure guarantee that predictions will deviate widely from reality.

4. NICHE WIDTH AND DIETARY CHANGE

From the foregoing, it should be clear that niche width, when measured by the number of different resources exploited, is the result of the complex interaction of a number of factors. The most generally valid statement that can be made is that niche width tends to vary inversely with subsistence security. Wide niches or generalist orientations may be increasingly advantageous as security decreases. Diversification of crops or hunting prey allows a spreading of the risk; the failure of one resource will have less of an impact than it would in a more specialized economy. There are numerous examples in the literature of groups who begin to exploit a greater variety of resources (including the less preferred famine foods) in times of hardship. Such hardship may derive from droughts or other conditions that lower productivity, from increases in population that raise demands or from increasing environmental variability that increases uncertainty.

Before the equation of insecurity and generalist strategies becomes reified in the literature of ecology, however, some exceptions must be pointed out. Insecurity does not necessarily lead to wider niches, nor do wide niches necessarily derive from insecurity. Distinct seasonality may lead to the use of a sequence of different resources throughout the year. The result would be a variety of total resources exploited and hence a wide niche. Yet, if the seasonal changes are predictable, the subsistence security may be high. A sequence of rather specialized strategies may, consequently, add up to a diversified economy. Similarly, the simultaneous specialization by different individuals, each upon a different resource, may create a total economy that is quite diversified. Unless the society has insitutionalized means of distributing the benefits of this diversification, the position of any individual may be quite precarious.

On the other hand, when faced with uncertainty, an individual does not automatically diversify. On the contrary, those activities that are most risky and least often rewarded may be progressively eliminated until the remainder constitute a specialized strategy, focused on the most reliable returns. Thus, many groups in the Canadian Subarctic tend to narrow their focus to fish and hare in times of hardship (Rogers and Black 1976). The Miskito of Nicaragua have come to specialize on the reliable and highly preferred turtle and to decrease their use of less reliable fish (Nietschmann 1973). Horticulturalists may emphasize only the most reliable crops in times of drought. People may also deal with uncertainty by not altering their resource spectrum at all, but rather by taking greater measures to redistribute people or the resources that are obtained.

The role of niche width in security strategies, in fact, might be profitably viewed as inversely related to time and energy expenditures (McNaughton and Wolf 1970:131). In a situation of reduced food abundance, people could theoretically maintain their level of time and energy expenditures by becoming greater generalists, or could increase their expenditures to maintain a more specialized economy. On the other hand, when food resources become more abundant and secure, people could become more specialized and maintain their level of effort or continue a more generalized subsistence with a savings in time and energy. Human responses to insecurity are creative strategies, not automatic reactions.

Another point that must be raised with regard to niche width is that simple, quantified cross-cultural comparisons cannot be very informative. The demonstration, for example, that subarctic groups exploit fewer resources than do tropical populations reveals nothing about the security of each group relative to one another. Without a knowledge of the specific environmental parameters, the behavior of various resources, and the abundance and variety of potential resources in each area, niche width remains a meaningless number. If Group A utilizes 10 resources and Group B 20, one might be tempted to infer that Group B was more diversified in response to greater subsistence insecurity. If, however, Group A was exploiting 10 out of only 20 total available edible resources, whereas Group B used 20 out of 100 available, then the latter would be considered more specialized. Niche width must be considered in relation to the potential of the area.

In this context, the evaluation of instances of economic change or resource shifts must allow for the complexity of potentially relevant factors. Change may be internally or externally induced; may derive from alterations in means, goals, or rewards; and may occur rapidly or gradually over a short period or a long term. Shifts due to external factors in the natural environment are perhaps the easiest to comprehend. An increase in moose at the expense of caribou in the Canadian forests led to an entirely different set of costs, yields, and risks for these two species and a shift to the hunting of the increasingly abundant and reliable moose (Knight 1965). The decimation of particular crops by long-term droughts or climatic changes may encourage a shift to other, more successful crops. Any environmental change alters the context of decision making and the contingencies of reinforcement.

External factors of change can also be cultural. The introduction of maize to Africa or of sweet potatoes to the New Guinea Highlands increased the crop choices available and could lead to their adoption in some areas without any change in goals. The encroachment of outsiders on the land, on the other hand, can lead to a situation of land scarcity and an increased emphasis on land efficiency in resource choices. The decimation of the American bison necessitated a shift by the native Plains populations. The introduction of rifles, snowmobiles, boat motors, and metal axes changed the relative costs of the more susceptible resources. The development of external market or trade contacts can intensify the local demand for particular resources such as cash crops or raw materials. The introduction of stores and a cash economy, together with a variety of exotic goods, can stimulate new demands and induce people to work harder at the expense of labor efficiency in order to attain a higher level of production. Sedentary villagers, fixed markets, and trading posts may come to be perceived as more reliable sources of food than wild resources, and the economy may be altered in accordance with the demands of the villagers and traders.

Finally, economic shifts may be internally induced, that is, may result from activities of the group itself. Overkill of caribou by some Eskimo groups (Kemp 1971), of sea otters by Aleuts (Simenstad *et al.* 1978), and of big game in some parts of Amazonia (Ross 1978) would require a change in resource emphasis. Farmers who allow insufficient fallow time for their fields may need ultimately to plant different crops on the wornout soil. Forest clearance for agriculture may lead to the local disappearance of game animals, whereas abandonment of old fields may attract deer and other species. Overgrazing can lead to desertification and a loss of productive land, inducing a land shortage and perhaps a greater emphasis of land efficiency. Increasing sedentism in order to exploit gardens or fishing spots can lead to an increase in costs of mobile big game hunting. Overirrigation can induce salt buildup and a shift to more salt-tolerant crops (Jacobsen and Adams 1958). Internal changes can also increase the level and type of demands, for example, through population growth or decline or through the development of an elite. The resulting economic shifts in all these situations would be inexplicable if only external determinants were sought or if it were assumed that people were perfectly adapted in a state of balance with their resources.

5. DISCUSSION

A group's subsistence economy is the result of a complex set of decisions involving the evaluation of many different factors in light of a variety of goals. People try to simplify the decisions through the construction of hierarchies of preferences and dichotomous scales of measurement, but anthropologists should avoid the tendency toward further simplification in analyzing the resulting choices. Multiple currencies, multiple measures of productivity, and multiple goals are all involved, and an overemphasis on energetic efficiency in analysis will obscure the real complexity. Three examples will be discussed in order to suggest how some of these various factors interact.

5.1. The San of Botswana

Two different groups of Kalahari San that have been well studied show some interesting differences in their food economies: the !Kung of the northwest Kalahari (Lee 1969; 1972) and the G/Wi of the central Kalahari (Fig. 4.9; Silberbauer 1972; Tanaka 1969; 1976). Given the fact that, compared to the !Kung, the G/Wi have no overwhelmingly attractive plant like the mongongo nut (which is abundant, tasty, and clustered), but do have greater access to big game herds, one might expect that the G/Wi would obtain a greater portion of their diet from animals than do the !Kung. Apparently, however, just the reverse is true. Because the diets of the two groups were studied at different times of the year, specific comparison is difficult, but the available figures may be examined (Table 4.3).

The !Kung data come from the month of July, a period of transition between good and bad times—the end of the early dry season. It seems reasonable to expect that in other, more favorable months their proportional intake of the preferred meat may be even greater than the figure given. For the same month,

Fig. 4.9.   Location of !Kung and G/Wi San.

TABLE 4.3

San Dietary Components[a]

	!Kung		G/Wi	
Period of study	Meat[b]	Plants	Meat	Plants[c]
July	256	400	164	?
Sept.–March	?	?	141–147	ca. 800
Total year	?	?	155	?

[a] Edible portions in gm/person/day.

[b] Uncooked.

[c] Excluding those used mainly as water sources.

the G/Wi meat intake is considerably less in absolute terms and probably in relation to plant foods as well. The highest recorded meat intake among the G/Wi, in fact, is only 242 gm per person per day, and this is in January, during the wet season when the !Kung intake of meat is also probably higher. It appears as though the !Kung eat relatively more meat—certainly not less—then do the G/Wi.

In order to understand these differences, it may help to examine the relative subsistence security of the two groups. Both groups live in the dry Kalahari, but the G/Wi habitat receives less rainfall, which is more unpredictable in its timing and abundance. This pattern of precipitation together with the lack of permanent waterholes (which the !Kung possess) makes the G/Wi region poorer and less secure in terms of water distribution. As a result, G/Wi food resources are similarly less abundant and predictable. Plant foods are scarcer and more variable in spatial distribution depending on local rainfall occurrence. Moreover, the abundant, clustered, and long-lasting mongongo nut of the !Kung is lacking in this area. In addition, the permanent animal biomass is probably lower as a result, whereas the big game herds (lacking in the !Kung region) pass through only seasonally and are quite mobile. The consequent difference in hunting reliability is suggested by figures estimating hunting success among the two groups. Among the !Kung about one in four, or 25% of the hunts are successful. The similar figure for the G/Wi seems to lie somewhere between 2 and 11% (15 hunters over a period of 26 weeks made 63 kills; since they hunted singly or in pairs, with a frequency of from 3 to 7 times per week, the number of separate hunting episodes ranges from 585 to 2730, of which only 63, therefore, were successful).

The G/Wi environment poses more risks to subsistence than does that of the !Kung. As a result, the G/Wi may need to emphasize security in food getting to a greater extent than do the !Kung. Since hunting in general (and the G/Wi hunting in particular) is quite risky, it may play a smaller role in the G/Wi economy, despite the fact that attractive big game species are available.

This greater emphasis on security does not, however, seem to have led the G/Wi to become more generalized in their food getting. Although they identify fewer edible plants and animals in their poorer environment (129 for the G/Wi compared to 154 for the !Kung), the G/Wi regularly exploit a smaller fraction of these as staples: their staples constitute 22 species (17% of the total), whereas the !Kung utilize between 33 and 40 species regularly (21–26% of the total). Although the !Kung are highly focused on the use of mongongo nuts, they nevertheless have 23 regular staple plant foods; the G/Wi, lacking a single most important plant, have only 13 staple plant foods. The !Kung regularly hunt 10–17 different animals (19–31% of the total available species), but the G/Wi normally utilize only 9 species (18% of the total). Despite their environmental potential for greater subsistence insecurity, the G/Wi appear to have a narrower niche.

These differences in niche width may derive from a number of factors. Plant foods tend to be more reliable than animals, and the !Kung plant foods more so than those of the G/Wi. As a result, the !Kung may be able more easily to insure a regular food supply and thus to afford to devote more time and attention both to the riskier but preferred animal foods and to obtaining greater variety in their diet on a regular basis. The G/Wi, by contrast, may be seeking to increase their security by a more specialized exploitation of those few resources considered most reliable.

Factors other than security, of course, clearly enter into the food-selection process. In their poorer and less predictable environment, the G/Wi have to work harder at subsistence; they devote about twice as many hours per person per week as do the !Kung to the food quest. In consequence, the G/Wi may perceive time as scarce and, therefore, may seek the more time-efficient resources. By contrast, the !Kung may see land as a more restricted commodity: they cover much smaller territories in food getting, in part because they are relatively anchored to the vicinity of permanent waterholes for much of the year. Moreover, the !Kung population density is from two to five times greater than that of the G/Wi, so that the density of demands per unit area is higher.

No definitive explanations of the dietary differences between the !Kung and G/Wi are offered here, but the discussion serves to point out the complexity of factors involved. The !Kung may be more easily insuring a reliable food intake and thus be able to devote greater attention to more preferred animal foods and to greater dietary variety. Their higher density and more restricted movements may impose a relative land scarcity and emphasis on land efficiency. The G/Wi, on the other hand, may need to strive harder for subsistence security and for time efficiency in their harsher and less predictable environments. Even the comparison of two such similar groups is made difficult by differences in rainfall and water sources; in the nature, abundance, and distribution of food resources; and in population density.

5.2. Cree and Objibwa

The Round Lake Ojibwa (Rogers 1962) and the Mistassini Cree (Rogers 1963; 1972) have been the subjects of intensive subsistence studies. These two groups, Cree and Ojibwa, inhabit similar environments in the Canadian Boreal Forest and exploit identical sets of resources (Fig. 4.10). Despite virtually identical economies, the diets of the two groups for the period of September through May show some interesting differences (Table 4.4). The Ojibwa rely more heavily on small game, whereas the Cree give greater emphasis to fish.

The Cree environment is somewhat harsher and its resources are poorer in both abundance and variety (Rogers 1969). As a result, the Cree population density is

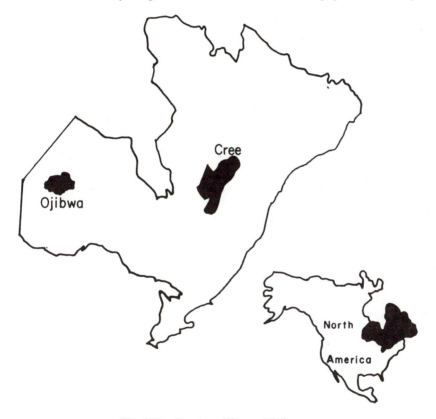

Fig. 4.10. Location of Cree and Ojibwa.

TABLE 4.4

Cree and Ojibwa Diets, September–May[a,b]

Food	Cree	Ojibwa
Big Game[c]	47%	42%
Beaver	18	17
Birds	4	5
Small Game	5	20
Fish	26	16

[a] After Rogers 1962; 1963.
[b] Figures represent percent contribution by weight.
[c] Moose, caribou, and bear.

much lower, only 0.59 people per 100 km², compared to 1.76 for the Ojibwa. Here again, two very similar groups differ in terms of relative subsistence security and availability of time and land. It may be expected that the Cree would devote more attention to obtaining security and, if their poorer environment necessitates, more time devoted to the food quest, that is, to an emphasis on time efficiency. The Ojibwa, on the other hand, with their more secure environment, may be able to devote more attention to efficiency, but given their higher population densities, that devotion is to an efficiency of land use rather than of time.

From figures presented by Feit (1973:120–124), it appears that fishing is much more time efficient than small game trapping, at least in the Cree habitat. Fish, moreover, are more reliable than small game. They are more spatially predictable and less subject to the cycles of abundance characterizing many northern animals. The Cree emphasis on fishing may be explicable in these terms. Small game, on the other hand, are more productive per unit area in this region (Jochim 1976:34), and if the Ojibwa stress land efficiency, then their greater use of small game becomes comprehensible as well.

5.3. The Batak of the Philippines

Even the economic changes of a single population may not be explicable if the analysis examines only energetic efficiency. The Batak of the Philippines are a group of foragers who have recently adopted both the practice of rice cultivation in swiddens and of copal collection for cash, which is largely exchanged for rice as well (Eder 1978). Currently the diet is composed of about 50% wild yams of two species and 50% rice from both swiddens and purchase. Eder analyzes the time efficiency of the major subsistence practices and concludes that these economic changes have reduced the efficiency of the group. Yet a number of additional factors should be considered in order to evaluate these changes.

Table 4.5 presents figures on the relative dietary contribution, time efficiency, and time expenditures for the four major dietary components: two types of wild yams and rice from two sources. The wild kudot yam is clearly the most efficient food source, but the wild yams together require 68 minutes to provide 1200 kcal, whereas 1200 kcal from rice of both sources requires only 63 minutes. In the current proportions, rice is, after all, more time efficient than are wild yams.

More important, Eder's conclusion that the addition of rice to the economy has reduced time efficiency is based on the assumption that copal rice has largely replaced kudot yams in tbe economy, at the current measures of efficiency. But abagan yams are also collected, and since their collection is so inefficient, it may be that this food needs to be included. That is, the efficiency of kudot yam collection might drop significantly if more were collected—the kudot yams are already currently scarce by the end of the season (Eder 1978:61). In addition, abagan and kudot yams have different, only partially overlapping seasons of availability: part of the year only abagan are available. In the past, without the present rice supplement to the diet, it may have been that a proportionally greater amount of abagan relative to kudot were collected by necessity, with the result being that yams collecting was formerly much less efficient that at present. If so, then the addition of rice to the diet may have improved overall time efficiency.

Furthermore, factors other than simply time efficiency may be relevant to the change. The encroachment of outsiders, and then the adoption of swiddening and assigning of individual copal lots have altered the nature of land access, so that land efficiency should be examined as well as time efficiency (the relative productivity per unit area of the yams, copal, and rice swiddens, however, are not presented). In addition, copal collection yields money, which can be converted not only into rice but also into other goods. Finally, the copal–rice complex includes the granting of credit at the stores, which may lead to greater subsistence security, since the natural environment does not advance credit. In this economic shift, as in the differences between similar groups, a complex set of factors is at work.

TABLE 4.5

Importance, Efficiency, and Cost of Batak Foods[a]

Food	Daily intake (kcal)	Time efficiency (kcal/hr)	Time expenditure (min/day)
Kudot yam	900	1739	31
Abagan yam	300	484	37
Copal rice	800	1012	47
Swidden rice	400	1500	16

[a] After Eder 1978.

Chapter 5

Procurement Strategies

1. PROBLEMS AND GOALS

The tasks of procuring resources encounter numerous problems and require many decisions about how to allocate effort and which tools and techniques to use to mediate and channel this effort. Essentially, people must make choices about *how, when,* and *where* to direct their procurement activities, and thus determine the nature of their technology and economy. Problems may be posed by the distribution of accessible land, resources, and raw materials; the temporal variability and predictability of these resources; and the conflicting demands on time and labor. Again, the two most prominent goals guiding the solutions to these problems are efficiency and security of procurement.

2. TECHNOLOGY

Technological choices and changes frequently can be understood by reference to their implications for procurement reliability and efficiency. Since tools and equipment channel and transmit human energy, their effects on energy budgets can be profound and direct. By technological harnessing of energy sources other than human effort, such budgets can be greatly expanded. By technological magnification of effort, the rate of work can be increased, leading to a great savings in time. By technological increase in the scope, intensity, effectiveness, or accuracy of directed effort, the productivity of land and the reliability of procurement can be expanded.

The general history of technological innovation records the desirability of this greater efficiency and reliability. Nevertheless, in every specific situation the complex of tools and implements reflects the solutions to problems peculiar to each context. Cross-cultural comparisons of technologies must examine the various problem contexts and the available means to solutions. Maximization of labor efficiency through the adoption of labor-saving devices is frequently an important consideration, but it cannot be assumed to be the overriding goal or effect of technological choices. It has proved valuable in modern contexts to view technological changes in part as directed toward saving whichever factors are relatively more scarce or expensive, be they labor, time, or land (Just *et al.* 1979). Moreover, every technological variant carries with it a number of constraints and secondary ramifications that can affect all other activities. Such effects would be important not only for other aspects of behavior, but also, if realized and anticipated, for the technological choices themselves.

2.1. Time Efficiency

Perhaps the majority of technological innovations can be viewed as measures to increase the direct time efficiency of procurement: they allow the performance of a task in a shorter time than was possible earlier. Snowmobiles and boat motors, for example, greatly decrease the travel time necessary for many economic pursuits. As technological devices become more complex, on the other hand, the total time costs of an activity may rise precipitously because of increased indirect costs. A remarkable feature of mechanization is the hugh costs in materials and time required for manufacture and maintenance. Such indirect costs, however, may not be an important consideration for the ultimate user who is intent upon time savings if they are not demands upon his time. Often, these costs are translated into other currencies, for example, money or goods for exchange, and although the production of these goods may require additional time expenditures, the relationship between the immediate time savings and these ultimate extra time costs may be so tenuous that they are not considered in the same context. People rarely compile extensive lists of total costs and benefits in making choices. In accord with both the tendency toward simplification and the importance of immediate reinforcers to conditioning and learning, it is common for only short-term, direct effects of choices to be considered, with the longer-term, indirect ramifications then to be viewed as secondary problems requiring additional solutions. Thus, it is the immediate savings in time that are usually most important in the adoption of new technologies.

The time efficiency of many devices can be well documented by a number of empirical comparisons. Among the Ye'kwana and Yanomamo of Amazonia, for example, the productivity of bow and arrow hunting by three hunters ranged from 0.25 to 0.92 kg of game per man-hour, whereas shotgun hunting by the same individuals produced from 0.61 to 2.88 kg per man-hour. On the average, the shotgun was found to be 231% more time efficient than the bow among these groups, a figure supported also by studies of other Amazonian peoples (Hames 1979:245). Although these firearms can be shown to be more efficient than simpler weapons, it is clear that there are large differences among firearms. The

Valley Bisa of southern Africa produced about 17 pounds of edible meat per man-hour of hunting using rather crude muzzle-loading guns, whereas the few hunters using shotguns and rifles could obtain meat at the rate of 108 pounds per man-hour of hunting (Marks 1976:203).

In agricultural activities, too, there are many examples of clear differences in the time efficiency of different technologies. Plowing using water buffaloes in Thailand can be done at the rate of about 0.01 hectares per man-day, whereas the use of tractors can increase this rate 300% to 0.03 hectares per man-day (Moerman 1968:171). Simply the type of draft animal is of great importance; horses, for example, can do field work at twice the rate of water buffaloes (Smil 1979:526). The raw material used for the tools may also be of significance, since experiments have shown that iron sickles can be used for reaping in half the time required with flint sickles (Steensberg 1943).

Many other examples could be amassed to demonstrate the great variation in time efficiency of different implements, but again it must be stressed that an understanding of technological choices and changes requires an examination of the specific context. Since there are, perhaps, infinite potential demands on people's time, it may well be that time efficiency in procurement is almost universally desirable to some extent. Nevertheless, certain contexts would seem to encourage relatively greater attention to this goal.

Time efficiency should be stressed in the selection of procurement technology, for example, when a resource is only briefly available. Migrating herds of caribou and other animals may cross a particular region quite rapidly; people along the migration routes may use fences and pounds to catch as many as possible during this brief period. The hunting technology of groups having a longer-term access to the game (for instance, in the winter or summer ranges) may be quite different—less time efficient but also perhaps less labor intensive. Similarly, the period of salmon availability in rivers generally decreases toward the north along the western coast of North America. Accordingly, there is a corresponding increase in the emphasis on time efficiency in fishing technology toward the north as well (Schalk 1977). Many other resources might also have a short period of availability: whales, migratory birds, nuts, wild grass seeds, grubs, or ripe grain crops. If such resources have been chosen for procurement, then it is likely that time efficiency will become a major determinant of technological development. Certain regions, such as migration corridors or areas characterized by great temporal variation in resources, will provide contexts for cultural evolution in which time-efficient technology will have a selective advantage. Moreover, since many of the resources that display such brief periods of availability are also spatially concentrated at these times, they are particularly rewarding to many of the time-efficient devices that enable mass harvesting.

Another context favoring time efficiency of procurement technology would be that in which the suitable conditions for the procurement activities are of brief duration. Development of efficient irrigation technology may be most favored along stretches of rivers having only short periods of high water. Areas where climatic conditions allow only a brief growing season may be especially suited to the development of time-efficient agricultural technology. Despite many disadvantages, tractors are used to cultivate fields in northern Thailand in those years when late rainfall does not allow enough time for the traditional techniques of plowing and transplanting (Moerman 1968:158). Steel axes and machetes have found acceptance in most tropical regions, but may have been most immediately desirable in areas where a short and unpredictable dry season made other techniques of field clearance particularly difficult. Peoples in the Subarctic and Arctic have embraced outboard motors because these devices decrease travel time so dramatically; it is to be expected that such machines would have been most readily accepted in regions where ice conditions rendered periods of open water least predictable and most brief. Groups depending for winter survival on foods frozen in the late fall should increasingly emphasize time efficiency in their food procurement as the period of both food abundance and suitably low temperatures decreases in duration.

Finally, time efficiency in procurement should receive greater emphasis as the culturally allotted time for procurement decreases. Irregular, unanticipated events such as funerals, visits, outbreaks of warfare, natural catastrophes, or disease epidemics could require the rapid accumulation of food for feasting. The Kaoka speakers of Guadalcanal, for example, resorted to the construction of a complex leaf fence to gather fish quickly for a feast, whereas they used spears and some nets at other times (Hogbin 1964). Other demands may be placed on a person's time by activities such as wage labor or communal or state-sponsored construction projects. If these are practiced alongside normal procurement activities, then a premium may be placed on the selection of time-efficient technologies in each activity. Time-efficient technology may evolve in direct relationship to the development of increasingly complex sociopolitical organization, the growth of supralocal demands on time, and the appearance of institutions capable of enforcing these demands. In addition, it may be that certain economic systems, because of the level of their time demands, provide a context of selective advantage for technological time efficiency. If, for example, agriculture in general tends to require more work than foraging, then one might expect that farmers would be more likely to accept time-efficient technological innovations than would be most hunters and gatherers. The evolution of technological efficiency, consequently, might partially reflect the upward spiral of time demands of the evolution of economic systems.

In summary, it can be shown that there are clear differences in the time efficiency of various technological devices. The selection of any particular implement that can perform the activity in a shorter time period should be encouraged by a relative scarcity of time available for procurement. By examining both the natural and cultural environments, it should be possible to identify contexts of time shortage, to pinpoint bottlenecks of time. In such contexts, where adequate time allocation is a real problem, technological solutions offering greater time efficiency would be especially rewarded, and hence, especially likely. Phrased in terms of cultural evolution, technological devices offering time efficiency will have a selective advantage in such environments, and there are good reasons for expecting the development and proliferation of such devices in these areas.

2.2. Labor Efficiency

Another form of procurement cost, in addition to time, is labor, and the wide acceptance and popularity of labor-saving devices attest to the general significance of labor efficiency in determining technology. Labor can be measured by kilocalories of work input for a particular activity, work that is channeled and amplified by technology. People, however, are capable of working at different levels of effort only up to some finite maximum; in the absence of technological assistance, work demands beyond this maximum rate require additional workers. Labor costs, consequently, have two components: individual exertion or work effort and number of laborers. Technology can increase labor efficiency by reducing either or both of these components.

Many devices can be demonstrated to reduce the effort of procurement. Some perform this by modifying the way in which this effort is applied, increasing the effectiveness toward the desired goal. Snowshoes, flint and steel firemakers, spear-throwers, steel axes, wheels, and levers fall into this category. Steel axes, for example, have been shown to be 300 to 500% more labor efficient than stone axes (Hames 1979:219). Other tools, by being more durable, have a longer lifespan and thus require less effort to repair and replace. Iron and steel implements, which have been readily accepted by most peoples, offer much greater durability than the native items they replace. Still other devices reduce labor by substituting other sources of power for human effort. Animal power in the form of domesticated livestock, wind power through sails and windmills, gravity through deadfall traps and gravity irrigation, water power through waterwheels, chemical power in the form of gunpowder, and fossil fuels through engines for boat motors, gasoline pumps, and snowmobiles have all been harnessed to reduce significantly the demands on human effort.

In many cases, these devices reduce work time as well as effort, but much of their significance derives from the easily perceived reduction in work they accomplish. In addition, many of them enhance labor efficiency not only by lowering the work effort of individuals but also by allowing a reduction in the number of workers for particular tasks. One irrigation pump can replace many individuals with buckets. One game fence can substitute for many hunters in directing animal drives. One boat motor can replace many oarsmen. These increase labor efficiency by requiring fewer laborers.

Again, the emphasis given to labor efficiency in technological choices depends on the particular situation. As in all aspects of technology, some major determinants include the relative access to materials, skill, and knowledge for manufacture, or to the finished products and the means to obtain them. In addition, however, there will be differing contexts of labor supply and demand, presenting various problems of labor allotment and distribution.

Although the minimization of effort seems to be one virtually universal goal of human decisions, there are some situations in which this goal should be of particular significance. Some environments require relatively greater labor input than others for the same economic activities. Hunters and gatherers may be forced by general resource scarcity in some areas to work relatively harder in locating game or plant foods. The amount of work required of herders will vary with grazing conditions and water distribution. Agricultural effort is significantly affected by the local type of soils, weeds, and pests. Such situations of greater labor demands should be particularly reinforcing to attempts to increase labor efficiency. Gross *et al.* (1979), for example, have classified different regions of Amazonia according to their "resistance" to swidden farming. They found that those groups facing the greatest resistance—suffering the greatest labor demands—are precisely the groups who have adopted Western technology to the greatest extent.

In many economic complexes, moreover, there are certain activities that are especially strenuous or sufficiently frequent and repetitive that they place relatively excessive demands on labor. Gardening among the Tsembaga of New Guinea, for example, is composed of 12 major sets of activities, yet just one of these—weeding—accounts for over 30% of the total labor input (Rappaport 1971a:120). Such particularly demanding activities would be especially rewarding contexts for labor-efficient technological innovations. Not only may certain poor environments or strenuous activities provide contexts for labor efficiency, but so also may the limited work ability of certain subgroups of populations. Older men among the !Kung, for instance, are less capable of strenuous hunting activities then are the younger men. It is largely by these older men, consequently, that the more labor-efficient (but time-consuming) trapping technology is practiced (Lee 1979:208).

Another context promoting labor efficiency is a situation of relatively low density of the producing population. The process of colonizing empty lands has led to the development of similar frontier economies in many parts of the world (Thompson 1973). One underlying basis of these economic similarities is the common problem of labor shortages on the frontiers. A common element in the solutions to these problems has been an emphasis on labor efficiency in many activities. Much of the complex technological development characteristic of American agricultural history, for example, demonstrates this emphasis (Just *et al.* 1979).

In addition to such conditions of relatively low total population density, other situations may give rise to labor shortages through reductions in segments of the population. The development of complex economies with much specialization may lead to a decreasing relative size of the food-producing sector of the population, encouraging greater labor efficiency in production activities. In the American economy, for example, the percentage of farmers has declined over the last 70 years from 33 to about 2%, in part due to the demands and opportunities of other, nonagricultural activities (Just *et al.* 1979). Since such activities may include administrative duties or warfare, societies characterized by growing administrative elites or by frequent warfare would represent contexts for the increasing emphasis on labor efficiency in production.

One final situation in which labor efficiency may be stressed consists of those environments precluding the formation of necessary work groups. Dispersed settlement patterns and poor transportation facilities as well as low population density may prohibit activities requiring communal labor. Large work groups may be difficult to maintain in the absence of effective means for their coordination. If internal conflict or dispersed population limits the size of available work groups, then labor efficiency may guide the choice of technological solutions. Villagers in northern Thailand may come to accept a concrete dam to replace their cheaper wooden dam precisely because of the growing difficulties of organizing communal work groups to build and maintain the wooden dam (Moerman 1968:52). Such contexts should encourage labor efficiency in the technological choices.

2.3. Land Efficiency

Many technological devices raise the productivity of land. Some accomplish this by allowing a fuller exploitation of land already utilized. The carrying capacity of a habitat for hunter–gatherers, for example, can be raised through the use of traps and snares that allow greater spatial density of the hunting effort. Storage facilities allow temporary food surpluses to be spread out over time, thereby enriching the leaner periods of the year that, according to Liebig's Law of the Minimum, are most critical in determining the level of population supportable. Fishing habitats can be made more productive by equipment allowing greater harvesting of deeper waters. Agricultural fields can be rendered more productive through the use of fertilizers and tools such as hoes or plows that allow deeper and better mixing and aeration of soils. Mining becomes more productive as technology allows deeper excavation under the surface.

Other technological devices can increase land efficiency by expanding the areas that can be exploited. Arid regions can become productive for farmers and herders with the development of cisterns, wells, irrigation canals, or water pipelines. Dense forests become more accessible to agriculturalists through the use of tools for land clearance, such as machetes, axes, and bulldozers. Plows allow the cultivation of heavier soils. Steep slopes can be made suitable for cultivation by the construction of terrace-retaining walls. Digging equipment and pumps can open swampy land to agricultural production. Sea-going boats can expand fishing activities to offshore waters. Modern penetration and exploitation of the Far North is facilitated by a vast technological complex providing heat and insulation and allowing construction in permafrost conditions.

It should be possible to specify conditions in which such land efficiency in technological choices should be particularly reinforced. Rising populations, especially in circumscribed areas such as islands, should provide these conditions of reinforcement. The agricultural development of Japan, for example, in contrast to that of the United States, has given great emphasis to land efficiency (Just *et al.* 1979). Demands on productive lands may be increased by a number of factors in addition to absolute population growth, however. Growing devotion of land to the grazing of domestic animals can restrict the acreage given over to plant food production and stimulate greater efficiency on these remaining fields. Increasing involvement in market economies can lead to the production of cash crops for sale on large proportions of cropland, encouraging greater efficiency in subsistence production on the remaining acreage. Growing demands by an elite for luxury goods may lead to an increased production of food for exchange. Many of the early civilizations that are characterized by technological developments allowing greater land efficiency in production also depended largely upon food exports to obtain luxury goods and raw materials.

Land efficiency may be stimulated not only by rising demands but also by decreasing access to land. The expansion of neighboring populations, of elite landholdings, and of nonproductive uses of land will limit the land available for production to sectors of the population. Access to land may also be restricted by decreasing mobility as a result of ties to resource concentrations. Such concentrations may include storage caches, labor markets, and distribution centers in the form of forts, villages, and cities, or transportation routes like roads, rivers, coasts, and landing strips. All of these situations may provide contexts in which land efficiency will be rewarded and have a selective advantage.

2.4. Security

Technology can contribute significantly to subsistence security by increasing the reliability of procurement. In some instances, this reliability is attained at the expense of procurement efficiency. Rifles, for example, have proved to be more efficient than many traditional hunting weapons. Their noise, however, alerts game throughout a large region, with potentially detrimental effects on sub-sequent hunting success. In addition, when used for hunting of sea mammals in the water, rifles may allow more wounded animals to escape than do harpoons attached to lines (Kemp 1971:110). More important, efficiency may be sacrificed for security when the more efficient devices demand excessive inputs of time, labor, or money. The reluctance of agriculturalists in many developing countries to adopt more efficient Western technology derives in part from their lack of the necessary capital to obtain and maintain the equipment and in part from the fact that, even given the necessary capital, the possibility of failure after such a large initial investment would be so devastating that it outweighs the promise of higher average yields. Many problems with the Green Revolution reflect the greater emphasis given to security by Third World farmers in light of their relative inability to absorb losses (Wade 1974:1190).

Very often, on the other hand, technological devices can simultaneously in-crease both procurement efficiency and security, at least in the short run. Time-efficient implements, by shortening the procurement time, can take advantage of optimal situations and reduce vulnerability to variable weather conditions. Labor-efficient devices, by reducing the necessary work force, can reduce vul-nerability to variable labor conditions. Land-efficient technology, by expanding the variety of habitats and resources exploited, can reduce reliance on a few resources whose failure would be catastrophic. Fluctuations in natural factors can be dampened by devices that also happen to be more efficient in some ways as well. Irrigation complexes not only expand the agricultural land but also may provide more reliable water to crops than does local rainfall, even in areas with sufficient yearly averages. Dammed rivers can be made to flood more reliably than do untamed rivers with variable flood levels.

Various hunting devices also show parallel differences in efficiency and relia-bility. In a series of experiments, the bow and arrow was demonstrated both to extend the range of hunting over that of a spear with spear-thrower and to improve the reliability of hitting targets at a certain distance, in one case by over 500% (Browne 1940). Harako (1976) has compared different hunting imple-ments among the Mbuti Pygmies: nets were far superior to bows and arrows and spears in both average yield per day and frequency of successful hunts (see Table 5.1). Similarly, studies among the Valley Bisa of Zambia demonstrated that shotguns were both more productive and reliable than muzzle-loading guns (Marks 1977:32).

It should be realized, on the other hand, that if these more efficient (and more immediately reliable) devices are used to increase production rather than to reduce time or effort expended, then they can lead to long-term insecurity. Overhunting can reduce game populations. Overcultivation can lead to soil exhaustion. In such cases, yields will become increasingly variable and increas-ingly unreliable over the long run. Since these long-term effects, however, are

TABLE 5.1

Success of Mbuti Hunting Tools[a]

Hunting tools	Hunting episodes	Successful episodes	Success percentage
Nets	17	15	88%
Bow and arrow	29	15	52%
Spear	11	5	45%

[a] After Harako 1976: 53–70.

often difficult to anticipate and less important in reinforcing behavior than are immediate results, they may not be considered in technological choices. Rather, the growing unreliability frequently will be viewed as a new problem requiring solutions (perhaps in the form of technological change) instead of a component of the initial technological choice itself.

Contexts generally encouraging an emphasis on security in technological decisions would be those containing significant variability and risk in the natural and social environments. Natural factors to consider would include the severity and spatiotemporal distribution of droughts, frosts, storms, floods, crop pests, and animal parasites. Predictability of game behavior would vary according to type of game, its density, and habitat types, as well as various climatic factors. Labor supplies would vary in their predictability depending on population distribution, the threat and frequency of warfare, the nature of conflicting demands for labor, the reliability of transportation facilities, and the organizational capacities available for coordinating work groups.

All environments contain risks, but these will vary in their kind, intensity, and predictability, and thus will determine different contexts for technological choices. Perception of these risks, moreover, will vary among individuals, depending in part on the differential ability to absorb losses. Poorer individuals, with restricted access to resources and capital, will tend to stress security to a greater extent than will the wealthy, and thus will have different, more conservative technological strategies as a result. Such individuals can often afford neither the more efficient tools themselves nor their possible effects.

2.5. Technological Diversity

Technology represents an important means by which people solve innumerable problems of production and distribution. A society's total technological inventory depends in part on the problems it faces and the means available to their solution, yet technological diversity reflects not so much a diversity of problems as a diversity of solutions. Tools differ in their functional specificity and adaptability: multipurpose tools can be the equivalent of a great variety of more specialized implements. In many parts of Amazonia, for example, just three tools of Western economies—shotguns, steel axes, and machetes—have largely replaced a host of native implements (Hames 1979:247). In this instance, the problems have not decreased, but the number of solutions has been reduced.

Many specialized tools may be more efficient in their tasks than one multipurpose tool, but technological simplicity would often be less expensive than more diverse tool kits in terms of time and energy costs of manufacture and repair. If so, then situations in which time and labor efficiency were emphasized may lead to a low technological diversity. One clear example of the relationship between a need for labor efficiency and technological diversity is the commonly observed negative correlation between mobility and the extent of material culture. As people's mobility increases, the work of transporting goods also grows; as a result, highly mobile groups have relatively limited and multipurpose technology.

Technological diversity may also be restricted by limitations on the means available for solving problems. Through lack of access to raw materials; lack of sufficient time, capital, or labor; or lack of special knowledge, only limited technology may be possible, even though more complex solutions might be more efficient. Such limits may be imposed by factors in either the natural or social environments. In most societies, for instance, only a small proportion of individuals can afford the capital investments necessary for certain efficient but costly devices such as ocean-going fishing vessels or tractors. These wealthier individuals can also frequently maintain several technological complexes simultaneously (Nietschmann 1972:49) and can use their technological superiority to enhance their position of wealth by more efficient production; by exchanging the use of these devices for labor, goods, and money; and by their greater margin of security.

The greater security of relatively wealthy individuals derives not only from their larger holdings, but also from their diverse technological inventories. There is a very clear relationship between technological diversity and security of procurement. Just as a diversification of the resource base represents a common solution to subsistence insecurity, so too does technological diversification. The territory of the Chalkyitsik Kutchin, for example,

> is an ideal place to see a wide range of modern hunting methods, since moose are "scarce" here by comparison with much of interior Alaska. This means that the people have to use their abilities to the fullest to find and kill enough of them. In places where moose are abundant, they are so easily taken that the more difficult and subtle hunting techniques are never used. [Nelson 1973:85].

Similarly, commercial fishermen of Newfoundland coped with variability in catches by maintaining a wide variety of fishing gear (McCay 1978:405). Eskimos of Baffin Island adopted snowmobiles but often maintained dog teams in case of machine breakdown (Kemp 1971:111). The Ye'kwana of Amazonia have responded to unreliable supplies of ammunition for shotguns by maintaining their skill in archery (Hames 1979:247). Such technological diversity represents one more example of spreading the risk in contexts of insecurity.

2.6. Implications of Technology

Given the systems framework of an ecological approach, technology cannot be viewed simply as the materials facilitating certain kinds of behavior. Technology may constrain or affect behavior through its secondary implications as well. Dietary choices may require a certain procurement technology, for example, but specific technological devices may influence dietary composition in return. These implications of technology represent one form of feedback in cultural systems and must be considered in order to understand behavioral patterns.

Some devices make possible the exploitation of new resources, thereby both broadening the potential food base and changing the relative importance of different foods. By their possession of shotguns, boat motors, and headlamps, the Ye'kwana of Amazonia can hunt caimans, birds, and arboreal monkeys much more effectively than can the Yanomamo who lack these devices. Although caimans comprise only 2% of the Yanomamo kills by weight, they make up 30% of the Ye'kwana kills (Hames 1979:232). The Cree Indians of James Bay, Canada use nets of different mesh sizes, with the larger sizes selectively catching large, mature whitefish, while the smaller nets catch mature and immature whitefish and the smaller cisco. The small nets, consequently, yield a more diverse catch initially, but by removing immature whitefish, can lead to the local depletion of this species, with the result that continuing use of small nets becomes selective for small cisco only (Berkes 1977). The hunting methods of the Mbuti Pygmies are suited to different types of game: "spearing aims at large animals; netting, at terrestrial animals; and bow hunting at various kinds of medium- and small-sized animals" (Harako 1976:50). Moreover, nets appear to be more selective than bow and arrow: netting commonly yields 22 different animal species, whereas archery can be used to obtain 40 different kinds of animals. There are many other examples of the implications of technology on foods exploited. Sickles and grinding implements facilitate the regular harvesting of wild and cultivated grains. Harpoons and sea-going canoes allow the regular hunting of whales and other sea mammals. By altering the relative costs of procuring different foods, increasing the variety of accessible foods, and facilitating the overexploitation of certain resources, technology can profoundly affect dietary choices.

The degree of mobility and the choice of procurement locations can be influenced similarly by technology, with significant implications for both diet and land availability. Since big game often are highly mobile and show low population densities, devices that increase human mobility and enlarge hunting areas may permit greater specialization on these resources. Snowmobiles appear to enhance caribou hunting in the Arctic, for example, whereas boat motors in Amazonia and domesticated horses on the historic Great Plains allowed a similar specialization on the hunting of caiman and bison, respectively. Although allowing greater distance to be traveled, easier transportation devices may, paradoxically, decrease the area of exploitation. Because of the ease of riverine travel, the Ye'kwana now rarely exploit the interfluvial zones of the forest (Hames 1979). Similarly, Chipewyan hunting in the Canadian north has become increasingly restricted to waterways in summer, with the adoption of the canoe, and to areas around trails in winter, with the adoption of dog teams (Sharp 1977:38). "Corridors of exploitation" may develop along the routes most suitable for the available means of travel. Not only do these transportation devices allow a greater specialization, but they may also encourage a restricted access to other habitats and resources as well.

Greater ease of transportation may, by contrast, permit a greater economic diversification by allowing more rapid movement among different habitats. Various garden plots, suited to different crops, may be more easily tended by the same group. Hunting, fishing, and farming regions may be more easily integrated into the same economy by more efficient transporation devices. The implications of technology for dietary diversity and land-use patterns are not deterministic; technology is simply one important factor affecting the costs of procurement, thus influencing the choices of resources and areas exploited.

3. PROCUREMENT TECHNIQUES

Procurement strategies involve much more than the material implements utilized. Also significant are the organization of labor and the structure and directness of the relationship between people and their resources. The size of work groups, the division of labor, the intensity of procurement activities, and the degree of specialization and exchange are all part of the strategies for procurement.

3.1. Procurement Group Size

An important component of procurement strategies is the size of work groups, since this reflects the organization of labor inputs into various activities. Group size can range along a continuum from individuals to large communal work parties, and any point along this continuum will represent a compromise between opposing forces, a solution to multiple problems in procurement.

Larger work parties offer benefits in a number of situations. When time available for an activity is short as in the transplanting of rice seedlings in their land

(Moerman 1968:39), larger groups will increase time efficiency in procurement. The harvesting of crops, brief riverine fish runs, and short-term game migrations, for example, is often performed by cooperating groups, whereas the chores of weeding, lake fishing, and hunting animals present all year-round are commonly more solitary activities. Communal labor is also common when a particular activity requires large amounts of labor for each single performance, such as in the construction of fences, weirs, or houses. Such activities contrast with others like herding that demand much labor also but demand it through the repetition of tasks. Larger work groups also are advantageous in the performance of complex activities that may be more efficiently conducted through a division of labor not feasible for small groups and individuals. Game drives, for example, frequently entail a number of different roles, including drivers and corralers. Moreover, when an activity like hunting is relatively unreliable, larger groups may offer some security by decreasing the risk that animals will escape nets or corrals.

In all of these situations, larger work parties may offer benefits of increased efficiency or security. A common factor in all such situations is that the productivity of the activity can be increased by the addition of workers; productivity is responsive to additional labor. There are, in addition, other benefits of communal labor: social contacts, companionship, gossip, and information sharing. These may constitute rewards for working together even when the procurement activities themselves can be done individually. These benefits may explain why women often form groups to gather wild plants that are collected by the individuals working side-by-side. Besides companionship, working in groups can offer defensive security, perhaps an important consideration in contexts in which raids and conflict are frequent. Such benefits, essentially unrelated to subsistence, can be significant rewards for communal subsistence activities.

Despite the many advantages of communal labor, there are many instances in which it may not be beneficial or even feasible. Some activities, for example, may not respond to greater labor inputs with increased productivity. The hunting of solitary game is not nearly as responsive as that of herd animals, and, in fact, large parties of hunters may actually alert the game and decrease the probabilities of a kill. Moreover, the formation of a large work party requires sufficient availability of labor. In areas of low population density, large groups may not be possible, so that activities may need to be performed less efficiently or through the use of technological substitutes for human labor. Among the Chipewyan of the Canadian Barren-Grounds, games drives can be conducted by a few men who construct pounds as substitutes for additional hunters (Sharp 1977:39). Large groups may be prohibited, in addition, in situations discouraging cooperation. Such situations may develop when land or other resources are sufficiently scarce so as to engender competition and conflict. Especially in the absence of institutionalized authorities capable of managing conflict, increasing competition for scarce resources can lead to a greater individualization of procurement.

3.2. Division of Labor

A common feature of most societies is that there is a division of economic activities so that several economic roles are defined. Different individuals will interact with different aspects of the natural environment. As a broad generalization, the most common division of labor seen among hunters and gatherers is between men and women; men are usually the hunters, whereas women gather plants. This dichotomy in sexual economic roles seems to parallel several dichotomies observed in general ecological studies.

This division, for example, might be viewed in terms of differential mobility: men often travel 15 miles or more out from camp to hunt, whereas women exploit resources usually within a 5-mile radius. These different patterns of mobility have been formulated by Watanabe (1968) into the concept of differing "activity fields" of the sexes, arranged like concentric circular zones around camps. Men may be so much more mobile than women largely because women are allotted so many duties which restrict them to the camp: food preparation, shelter construction, and child care. Old men and young children are relatively less mobile also and so often perform the "female" activities. This differential mobility shows a correlation with the mobility of the resources focused on as well. The big game that forms the major prey of the hunters is usually quite mobile. By comparison, the females' resources, plants together with rodents and lizards, are either immobile or fairly restricted in their movement.

An additional dichotomy may be seen in the way in which the two groups allot their time in economic activities. In general, time spent in procuring resources can be divided into search time and pursuit and capture time. The ecologist MacArthur (1972) has suggested that birds that eat small, relatively stationary insects spend most of their time searching for these foods, whereas little time is necessary for their pursuit, capture, and ingestion. Lions, on the other hand, frequently have prey in sight and must spend most of their time pursuing and catching the prey. The birds may be characterized as "searchers," whereas lions are "pursuers." Such a distinction relates, in part, to the mobility of the resources: the foods of searchers are generally quite immobile, whereas those of pursuers are very mobile. This distinction might be applied to the two economic strategies of hunters and gatherers: men who hunt highly mobile big game spend much time in the pursuit; women, on the other hand, devote most of their time to searching for plants, and once located, these foods require little time to capture.

MacArthur (1972) has taken this division further into an analysis of general strategies of food selection. For birds that spend most of their time looking for food, it is adaptive to add any insects that are palatable to the diet, thereby reducing the search time. Searchers, consequently, tend to be generalists and have broad ecological niches. Lions, on the other hand, would benefit from concentrating on those prey species with the lowest necessary pursuit times (which depend on the abilities of the prey) and thus, pursuers should be specialists. These generalizations hold up to some degree for hunters and gatherers as well. Men tend to specialize in the hunting of a few species of animals, whereas the number of different plants collected by women is usually greater. The !Kung show this to a limited extent: of the 54 species of animals classified as edible, only 17 are hunted on a regular basis, whereas 85 species of plants were regularly eaten, although only 23 provided about 90% of the vegetable diet. The G/Wi have no one major plant food like the mongongo nut and so exploit a great variety of different plants.

This sexual division of labor also roughly parallels a differential emphasis on the two major goals of efficiency and security. Hunting is a high-risk activity; unsuccessful hunts are quite common. The gathering of plants very often provides the secure, everyday basis of the diet. On the other hand, hunting may be quite efficient: the food yield per kill can be very high, especially with big game such as bison or elephants, and even more so when such animals occur in large groups so that several may be killed at once. Plant collecting, by contrast, usually provides lower yields per trip, and even when its average time efficiency is higher than that of hunting (as among the !Kung: see Lee 1979:450), it rarely has the high potential payoffs that hunting promises. Plant gathering requires regular, repetitive labor investments, and tends to provide steady, reliable yields. Hunting, on the other hand, tends to be episodic, requiring temporary bursts of hard work for variable payoffs.

In brief, the division of labor serves to define two different ways of interacting with the natural environment. There is a sharp division between male and female roles, values, and behavior. It is almost as though there were two different economies or two different ecological niches. No other animal accomplishes such a division of labor: males and females of the same species may do different things, but this usually entails a subdivision of the exploitation of the same resources. Humans seem to be virtually unique in the degree of differentiation, and it is possible only through the pooling of these separate efforts, that is; through constant and institutionalized sharing. Males and females, through sharing, and often through pairing, can take advantage of both economic orientations, of both niches (Table 5.2).

There are problems, however, with this simplified picture of the sexual division of labor. The entire division stems ultimately from one obvious dichotomy in nature: the division into two biological sexes. This pattern of duality is used as a structuring principle that is imposed upon behavioral roles and upon natural resources. Yet such a clear dichotomy is not present in the variety of natural resources and tasks, and so one has to be defined or imposed. It is because of the variability in the definition of roles and resources that one may find deviations and exceptions from the simple generalizations about sex roles.

For example, big game and plants are only two categories of the various

TABLE 5.2

Hunter-Gatherer Division of Labor

Distinction	Men	Women
Resource category	Large animals	Plants
Time allotment	Pursuers	Searchers
Strategy	Specialists	Generalists
Goal	Efficiency	Security
Mobility	High	Low

resources used by people; many other classes of foods are important as well. There seems to be considerable variability among groups in the way in which these resources are assigned to one sex or another. As suggested earlier, one important dimension along which resources are classified and assigned is mobility. Plants are stationary and big game is usually quite mobile. In fact, it is possible to place these two resource classes at either end of a continuum of resource mobility, and to arrange other food groups in between. The result provides a scale by which it is possible to suggest the probability that men or women are responsible for their exploitation:

(Most mobile)	Big Game	Men
	Small Game	Men and Women
	Fish	Men and Women
	Insects	Women
	Shellfish	Women
(Least mobile)	Plants	Women

This scale of mobility seems to reflect the usual patterns of resource collection. There are, however, many other factors that must be considered.

(1) *Clumping of resources:* both sexes may cooperate to take advantage of big aggregations of foods that would normally be the domain of one sex. Frequently, for example, women will participate in game drives or collective hunts, usually as drivers rather than as capturers. In the Great Basin, men and women would often work together to drive katydids into diches; in this case, the women did the final collection of the insects trapped in ravines (Steward 1955).

(2) *Difficulty:* Men usually perform the more difficult work if such a distinction is made within a resource category. On the Andaman Islands, women gathered shellfish in shallow water, whereas men dove for those in deeper water. Among the Alacaluf and Tasmanians, on the other hand, women did the diving for the deepwater shellfish, whereas men came along to guard the women from enemies while they worked (Coon 1971). Furthermore, in many examples of the

collection of tree nuts and fruits, men did the climbing or the chores of knocking the fruits down, whereas women would normally collect the fruits so obtained.

(3) *Technology:* Often, a technological division is made within a resource category, with men using more tools, or more complicated tools, or tools more similar to hunting implements used for big game. In fishing, for example, men often utilize spears and arrows, or construct weirs and dams, whereas women use baskets and dipnets and collect impounded fish from the weirs.

Of all the resource classes, two stand out as being truly intermediate, in that both sexes are involved most frequently in their exploitation: fish and small game. For an understanding of why, in any one particular society, these resources are assigned to one sex or the other, it is necessary to examine the other demands on time. Some of these other demands are posed by the degree of importance of the more easily assigned resources such as big game and plants, and so the role of these resources in the diet must be examined. If a woman is fully occupied with plants, then fish and small game may be the responsibility of men. Of equal importance are nonsubsistence activities in determining the time demands on the two sexes. Women are responsible for child care universally. They also do most of the society's maintenance activities such as food preparation, cooking, loading, and skinworking. It is interesting that such maintenance activities seem to be most important in northern latitudes: Eskimo women do very little food getting (plants are virtually nonexistent) but perform tremendous amounts of maintenance tasks necessary for survival. Men, on the other hand, are responsible for raiding and warfare universally, and they are also usually the ones to engage in any trade and contact with outsiders.

In fact, it might be useful to visualize all activities as being weights on a balance, the fulcrum of which can change position according to the various weights in time and energy. Each sex is assigned one side of the balance, and food getting is placed in the center because it is participated in by both sexes. The intermediate categories, such as fish and small game, then, may fall to one side of the center or another, depending on the weights of other categories (Fig. 5.1). It need not be assumed that the ultimate balance is such that men and women work the same amount of time; it may be that women usually work harder and longer and receive fewer prestige rewards in the process.

The sexual division of labor among horticulturalists and groups with mixed economies follows many of the same principles observed among hunter-gatherers (see, for example, Basso 1973; Chagnon 1977; Dyson-Hudson 1972; Hogbin 1964; Middleton 1965; Newman 1965; Pospisil 1963; Rappaport 1968; Waddell 1972; Williams 1965). Men perform many of the field-clearance activities such as burning and felling trees and clearing of underbrush and are also responsible for constructing fences, laying out plot markers, building and maintaining ditches and retaining walls, and cultivating special cash crops or ceremo-

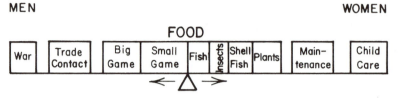

Fig. 5.1.   The balance of hunter–gatherer sexual division of labor.

nial plants. Women, on the other hand, tend to do most of the processing of crops after harvesting. Either or both of the sexes may be responsible for planting and harvesting, often with distinctions made according to the crop or technology involved. Domestic animals like pigs, which are often fed garden produce and remain in the settlement, are usually cared for by women, whereas cattle and other animals requiring movements to grazing lands are largely the responsibility of men. Women perform most of the duties of child care, food preparation, and the collection of firewood, water, and wild plants. Men do the hunting, the fighting, most of the fishing, house-building, and trading. In short, men perform most of the tasks requiring episodic bursts of energy, high mobility, and interaction with outsiders. Women, by contrast, do the daily, repetitive tasks providing many of the regular dietary staples, and confining most of their activities around the settlements.

If these distinctions seem familiar, it is because sex roles in more complex economies, including, until recently, that of the United States, tend to follow many of these general principles as well. Two major criteria distinguishing these economies, however, are the existence of wage labor and complex economic specialization. In fact, although the division of labor in simpler societies seems to provide both greater efficiency and security of subsistence, at the other extreme of social complexity, our considerable economic differentiation appears to have gained efficiency at the expense of security. Our economy is characterized by such an interdependence that one strike (by longshoremen, steelworkers, etc.) can disrupt the entire economy.

The differing effects of the division of labor upon economic stability and security derives from differences in the structure of energy flow in these two situations. Complex societies include many nonsubsistence specialists. Many people are distant in terms of energy flow from the environment and the production of food, leading to a great dependence of many on a few producers. There are, consequently, more links in the energy chain, with the implications that (1) there is greater energy loss as a result of the greater number of energy transfers; (2) there are more opportunities for disruption in the longer energy chains; and (3) there may be greater time lags in detecting disruption, causing greater difficulty in maintaining stability of energy flow. Moreover, the characteristic population nucleation (for both economic and political purposes) means that many people are spatially removed from the primary energy sources; the spatial channels of energy flow are also longer and more complex. Generally, the entire network of spatial relationships in complex societies is wider, which tends to increase susceptability to nonlocal perturbations. In addition, the individual differentiation in these societies includes a specialization of knowledge, capabilities, and access, leading to less individual flexibility and a greater interdependence. There is also a specialization of goals, views of the environment, and capacities for realizing the environmental and economic implications of individual actions. Rather, individual behavior is largely reinforced by factors unrelated to the direct environmental or economic effects of that behavior. This resulting greater diversity and complexity may foster a weakening of social cohesiveness, greater competitiveness, less sharing, greater dependence on specialized institutions for redistribution, and increased susceptibility to disruptions.

3.3. Domestication

One of the most important distinctions among types of procurement strategies is that between dependence upon wild resources and manipulation of domesticated resources. Agriculture has been called a "revolutionary" innovation in human history (Childe 1952), and even if its initial development was not as rapid as this term suggests, its ramifications certainly have been significant. Plant domestication has entirely altered the relationship between humans and their environment. The nature of these alterations can best be understood by a comparison of agriculture and hunting and gathering as contrasting general strategies of procurement. The focus will be on the structure and function of energy flow as these differ between the two.

The general structure of hunting and gathering is such that the economy may have coevolved with the natural system; it may be stable and efficient to the extent that the total system is mature. The natural environment provides many channels of energy flow, often with no one channel containing any great amount of energy; any concentration of energy is largely provided by the environment. The people exploit a relatively small percentage of the biomass, and the amount of energy harvested and available at any one time is rarely sufficient to allow damage to the environment to any extent. With agriculture, on the other hand, people concentrate energy in space and into fewer channels. They simplify the energy structure to increase the flow in some channels and must spend energy to remove selectively nonuseful biomass like weeds and to replace it with useful biomass, which may include more storable foods. The useful channels are tapped at low trophic levels, closer to the beginnings of the natural flow of energy, but the simplification causes the loss of many features of natural stability, and thus, additional energy input is necessary to create artificial stability.

In terms of energy flow, a major hunter–gatherer cost is human labor; agriculture may also include animal labor, machinery, and fossil fuels. A major component of hunter–gatherer labor costs is movement—procurers move to their energy sources. Consequently, the spatial distribution of resources is important in determining costs for hunter–gatherers. Agriculturalists, on the other hand, try to move their energy sources to themselves and concentrate the sources in space. Thus, they may be more tied to these energy sources and must expend energy to maintain and defend them. Moreover, agriculture runs the risk of possibly providing too little protein and also causing the destruction of natural protein sources such as wild game. This may encourage the keeping of domestic animals, which are additional work to feed. In addition, the greater manipulation of the environment involved in agriculture may risk unforeseen long-term changes, decreasing the stability of the ecosystem.

Using an agricultural strategy, gross productivity can be *much* higher than with hunting and gathering. Agriculture also requires more labor input, more time input, but less land input. Consequently, time and labor efficiency may be either higher or lower than that for hunting and gathering, depending on the particular context of each, but land efficiency of agriculture is certainly much higher. The development and emphasis of agriculture as the primary strategy, as a result, seems to be directly related to the relative scarcity of land (see, for example, Binford 1968; Cohen 1977). Agriculture, however, is practicable only in some parts of the world. It is not a viable option in the coldest and driest regions. In both of these types of areas, herding has provided an adaptable alternative to agriculture.

3.4. Intensification

The basic requirements of agriculture are sufficient soil fertility and adequate water supplies. In many regions, the agricultural strategies as practiced depend largely on natural processes to fulfill these requirements. The varied forms of swidden or slash-and-burn farming, widespread in forest regions, rely on the natural restoration of soil fertility in exhausted plots during a period of abandonment and subsequent clearing. Since the process of accumulation of nutrients may be slow, this fallow period may be as long as 25 years, after which time the forest that has developed again will be cleared by burning and cutting. Natural water supplies may be provided in areas with high water table, such as humid valley bottom lands, along regularly flooding rivers like the Nile, or in regions with sufficient rainfall. Unfortunately, each of these rather simple systems has some restrictions or inherent problems. Areas of high water table are usually quite limited. Rainfall or floodwater farming require sufficiently dependable rains and floods; droughts, torrential downpours, and excessive floods may be constant threats. Swidden farming depends on the availability of adequate land so that 75% or more can lie fallow at any one time.

Because of these restrictions and problems, in many situations the agricultural strategy is *intensified*—that is, is modified by the investment of additional labor, time, and materials—in order to increase gross productivity of the cultivated land. Fallow periods may be progressively shortened so that bushes or only grasses develop on the plots. Clearing of this vegetation and working the soil may require tools more effective than digging sticks, such as hoes or plows. Fallow periods may be dispensed with altogether, in which case, soil fertility will have to be restored artificially through manuring, the addition of chemical fertilizers, or crop rotation. As the fallow periods are shortened, larger areas can be brought into simultaneous cultivation, increasing the areal productivity. The amount and reliability of water supplies and the extent of their distribution can be increased through irrigation by wells, canals, or pipelines; through the creation of raised fields in marshy areas; or even through the excavation of fields down to the water table. In addition, productivity can be increased by the construction of ditches or mounds to facilitate drainage, the building of terraces on slopes to prevent erosion, and technological innovations to allow more complete harvests.

All these techniques of intensification impose additional costs in capital, labor, and time. Their effects are an increase in gross productivity, an increase in land efficiency of production, and, in some cases, an increase in security against floods, droughts, frost, and erosion. The introduction of such techniques must be seen, not as the inevitable progress of economic development, but rather as the attempts to solve particular problems facing production.

The contexts of agricultural intensification have been much discussed (Boserup 1965; Harris 1977; Netting 1974; Smith 1972; Spooner 1972). These techniques require additional labor and time, and may, despite increased gross productivity, actually lead to decreased time and labor efficiency in some cases (but see Bronson 1972). As a result, there is general agreement that intensification is often adopted only when land efficiency becomes a primary goal of procurement, that is, when productivity per unit land must be raised, even at the expense of more work and potentially lowered productivity per unit time or labor. The major general context of reinforcing agricultural intensification, therefore, is a situation of scarcity of productive land relative to the demands placed upon it.

The most commonly cited example of this situation is that of increasing population pressure through reproduction or in-migration (Barlett 1976; Boserup 1965; Brown and Podolefsky 1976; Clarke 1966; Dumond 1961; Geertz 1963; Harris 1977; Netting 1969). If access to productive land does not increase along with population growth, then relative land shortage can become a critical problem. Intensification of production is one solution to this problem (others might include out-migration, population control, or land conquest). It must be stressed, however, that demands on land may be increased by processes other than population growth. Domestic animals such as the pigs kept by many New Guinea peoples may place enormous demands on agricultural produce as the herds grow (Waddell 1972:210). The development of an elite (and of nonsubsistence specialists) imposes demands for their upkeep and sumptuary displays. Involvement with trade networks and markets for cash crops may introduce large external demands into the local system.

Even if demand levels remain constant, moreover, the amount of available land may decrease, creating contexts similarly encouraging intensification. Environmental change such as increasing desertification can take some land out of production or force population redistributions. An increased allocation of land to nonproductive uses can also cause a decline in productive land. In addition, an increased population concentration—in urban areas, along transportation routes—can reduce the per capita area within a given radius and effectively raise local population densities.

Intensification, thus, is a process of increasing productivity and land efficiency in response to relatively larger demands. It requires greater time, labor, and capital but is reinforced by the increased yields. It is a process, moreover, not limited to agriculture. Fishermen in Newfoundland attempted to solve the problem of declining catches by several techniques of intensification, including investment in more elaborate longliner fishing technology (McCay 1978). Turtle fishermen in Nicaragua responded to increased market demands for turtles by specializing on a few species, devoting more time to their capture, and traveling farther in the fishing trips (Nietschmann 1972). Mbuti nethunters increased the size of hunting groups and the frequency of hunts in response to the growing demands of commercial meat traders (Hart 1978).

Intensification may have a number of secondary problems and effects. Because such intensification is more demanding of time, it often leads to greater economic specialization, with the attendant risks of overdependence on a limited set of resources. The greater efficiency of production may, therefore, lead to greater insecurity should these resources fail. Furthermore, intensification has the potential for long-term overexploitation of soils or game, resulting in future declining yields requiring additional adjustments, often in the form of still greater intensification. Another major implication of intensification is its potential for the concentration of production and thus the concentration of access to productive resources into the hands of a few people. Often only a wealthier minority of individuals in a group can afford the tools or materials necessary to intensify production. Consequently, they may be able to increase their yields still further above those of other people, to enlarge the differences in wealth between themselves and others and increase their share of the productive resources of the group. To the extent that wealth may be transformed into prestige and power, this differential intensification can contribute to social and political differentiation.

3.5. Procurement by Exchange

Procurement need not always be direct. On the contrary, at least some goods are procured through exchange or purchase in virtually every society. Trade and exchange occur through a number of different processes, involve a wide variety of goods, and serve various purposes in addition to that of obtaining materials. The focus here, however, will be on exchange solely as a means of procurement, as an alternative to direct individual production.

One great advantage of procurement by exchange is that it increases the resource options available. Purchase or exchange can provide resources not accessible locally. If these include food resources, then the consequent expansion of the food base can increase subsistence security. If the resources include items of Western technology or raw materials such as metals, then exchange may increase procurement efficiency. The goods themselves, therefore, can often provide sufficient reinforcement for exchange behavior when direct procurement is not possible.

On the other hand, the processes of exchange as well as the foods, may prove to be rewarding in many situations. Stores, trading posts, and villages are fixed locations that offer the concentrated production of a number of individuals. As a result, they represent aggregations of resources that are spatially stable and less likely to vary significantly through time than are either natural resource clusters or individual harvests. Procurement through exchange should be relatively quite reliable in terms of resource location and abundance. Furthermore, if the exchange includes delayed reciprocity or credit, temporal variations in production may be dampened. Procurement may be subject, however, to significant cost fluctuations with variations in exchange rates or with shifting interpersonal or intervillage relations. Exchange networks expand procurement beyond the local natural and social systems; dependence upon exchange thus increases the number of potentially uncontrollable factors affecting procurement.

Exchange behavior may also have important implications for procurement efficiency. The availability of goods through trade or purchase may allow individual specialization on the production of one local resource. Intensification of one productive activity may be easier or less costly than the performance of several activities necessary to provide all the required resources. Specialization, for example, may reduce the variety of tools that an individual must own and maintain. It may also allow an individual to focus activities in one area, reducing travel and transportation costs. The development of exchange relationships, consequently, can lead to an increased procurement efficiency for all involved.

By contrast, exchange processes may develop as a necessary result of intensification and specialization. If a situation of relative land scarcity, for example, leads to the intensification of agricultural production, and therefore to the specialization upon certain techniques and crops, then dietary variety may become too restricted. The need for other foods, together with the relative ease of further intensification to produce a surplus, may encourage the development of exchange relationships as a strategy for procurement. The mutual feedback between exchange and intensification is well demonstrated by the evolution of complex economic systems.

4. PROCUREMENT LOCATIONS

The choice of locations for hunting or farming is an important component of procurement strategies. People distribute their activities differentially across the landscape, and the resulting patterns of land use reflect a number of decisions about the allocation of effort. Choices of locations must take into account a variety of factors, both natural and social, and represent the outcome of an informal estimation of costs, benefits, and constraints.

4.1. Resource Requirements

Resources themselves have varying requirements or behavior patterns that must be considered for successful procurement. The locations of game, fish, and wild plants can often be predicted with remarkable reliability on the basis of a knowledge of these requirements. In relatively uniform habitats some resources may be widely distributed, so that there are few restrictions on the locations of their procurement. Many plants show this pattern of dispersion, as do some animals. The Mbuti Pygmies, for example, appear to select the areas for net-hunting almost randomly because their major prey, the duiker, is so evenly dispersed throughout the forest (Ichikawa 1978:171).

Many habitats are quite patchy, however, and some plants and most animals show very uneven patterns of distribution. These patterns may vary seasonally and depend of factors of topography, climate, vegetation, and water distribution. During the dry season in most arid environments, the location of both plants and animals may be predicted according to the distribution of water sources, and human procurement activities will be concentrated in these areas (Lee 1969). In the Brooks Mountains of northern Alaska, caribou are naturally concentrated in narrow passes during the spring and fall migrations (Gubser 1965). Salmon may be seasonally concentrated in gravel spawning beds of rivers (Watanabe 1968). Estimation of resource locations may be more difficult in marine environments, which are more complex because of the additional dimension of depth, but a knowledge of fish behavior together with observations of tides and lunar phases may allow rather accurate prediction (Cordell 1974).

Numerous ethnographic studies emphasize the detailed knowledge of animal behavior and plant requirements possessed by hunters and gatherers (Lee 1979; Marks 1976; Nelson 1973). This knowledge is often coded in terms of a variety of environmental factors such as snow or wind conditions, the position of the moon or tides, and stages of vegetational growth. These factors can serve as cues for initiating particular procurement activities in certain regions. Land-use decisions are based largely on this accumulated environmental knowledge but may be modified by new information as well. Two episodes of successful fishing may be sufficient for a location to be added to the inventory of potential fishing spots (Cordell 1974:388). News about successful harvesting may lead to a convergence of people around fishing locations (Berkes 1977), concentrations of caterpillars (Silberbauer 1972), nut groves (Steward 1955), and game herds (Burch 1972). Information networks monitoring current conditions are as important to the choice of exploitation areas as is the knowledge learned through teaching and past experience.

Agriculturalists and pastoralists similarly have a detailed knowledge of the requirements of their domesticated plants and animals, and this knowledge is used to help select field locations and grazing areas. The Pokot of East Africa choose garden areas at different elevations according to the different crop requirements for temperature and rainfall, with the result that a distinct altitudinal zonation of crops and gardens develops. Bananas, which demand the most water, are planted at the highest elevations, whereas more drought-resistant crops like sorghum may be planted at lower altitudes (Porter 1965). The Waimaro of Fiji seek rich, black forest soils for growing the demanding kava plants, dry and well-drained soils of moderate fertility on sunlit slopes for their yams, and fertile clay soils that need not be well-drained for growing taro; areas for planting manioc, which is the least demanding of their cultivated plants, can be chosen after land is allocated to the other crops (Rutz 1977). The Karimojong of East Africa select grazing lands according to the seasonally shifting factors of rainfall, storms, and water supplies, grass abundance and quality, soil conditions for movement, cattle disease distribution, location and intensity of agricultural labor demands, and the threat of cattle raids or government confiscation (Dyson-Hudson 1972). Again, both the accumulation of past knowledge and the sharing of present experience contribute to the selection of agricultural plots and grazing locations.

4.2. Technological Requirements

The areas chosen for exploitation depend as much upon the tools and techniques of procurement as upon the resources obtained. Swidden farmers without hoes or plows may prefer dense forests because of the ease of clearing by fire and of working the soil with digging sticks. Farmers who possess plows, on the other hand, may select open grasslands in order to avoid obstacles of tree stumps as well as to provide graze for the draft animals pulling the plows (Boserup 1965). Irrigation farming encourages the selection of plots closest to existing rivers, especially along stretches of sufficient stream gradient and elevation so that gravity will do much of the work of water transport. Fishing with spears, harpoons, arrows, weirs, and dipnets requires stretches of rivers where the water is relatively clear and shallow. Larger nets, by contrast, require rather high and murky water as occurs in major rivers and restricted pools (Kroeber and Barrett 1960; Post 1938). The contrasting fishing technologies of the Haida and Tlingit of northwestern North America led them to select different regions of their rivers for exploitation (Langdon 1979).

Specific hunting techniques also affect the types of locations selected for procurement. The Valley Bisa of Zambia preferentially directed their hunting efforts to more open habitats, not only because these areas had higher game densities, but also because their stalking techniques were more successful in these habitats (Marks 1977:21). River fords, box canyons, peninsulas jutting out into lakes, cliffs, and arroyos are frequently chosen by hunters of big game herds because such areas facilitate certain driving techniques. Transportation devices may also influence hunting locations. As mentioned earlier, the use of canoes, outboard motors, dog teams, and snowmobiles may lead to the development of exploitation corridors along the routes suitable for travel.

4.3. Proximity to Other Activities

The requirements of resources and technology help to define *general* types of locations suitable for exploitation. Topographic features, streambed characteristics, vegetational habitats, and soil types may all be chosen according to a knowledge of the resources and the techniques to procure them. The choice of *specific* locations to exploit, however—the decision about what region of forest soils, which stretch of the river—requires consideration of a third set of factors: the distribution of other activities. Travel requires time and effort; distance is an important determinant of procurement costs. Savings would be considerable if all procurement activities could be concentrated in the same area as they may at shopping centers in the suburban landscape. In most environments, however, they cannot be so clustered. People must travel among locations in the course of procurement activities. The widespread preferences for saving time and energy will, nevertheless, lead to some attempts to minimize travel and concentrate activities in space. As time and energy become increasingly scarce, such concentration will become more advantageous; as land becomes increasingly scarce, concentration may become necessary.

Settlement locations represent fixed points on the landscape that anchor the calculation of land proximity and travel costs. Ignoring natural variation in soil types and resource abundance, procurement costs increase with distance from the settlement. As a result, many activities are "pulled" toward settlements: if all other factors are equal, procurement locations closest to villages and camps would be cheapest to exploit. Yet as the radius of travel out from a settlement decreases, the available land becomes increasingly scarce. Potential farmland within 2 km of a village constitutes 12.56 km^2; within a radius of 1 km, however, only 3.14 km^2 are available. Consequently, as travel costs become of greater importance in the land-use decisions, accessible land becomes less abundant and land efficiency will increasingly be stressed in procurement.

As a result of these distance effects upon travel costs and land availability, a common pattern of agricultural land use is a *gradient* of crops and cultivation intensity around settlements (Chisholm 1968; Hurst 1972; Morrill and Dormitzer 1979). Land closest to villages, being most scarce, is cultivated with crops and techniques requiring the largest labor inputs and the most constant care in order to achieve the greatest land productivity. Land at greater distances tends to be devoted to more extensive techniques and crops requiring fewer visits and less maintenance, since the land is more abundant and the travel costs are higher. Concentric rings of decreasing agricultural intensity become arranged outward around villages. Common practices in many areas, for example, are to maintain kitchen gardens of vegetables that are constantly tended around the houses, practice some form of relatively intensive cultivation of major staples in land close to the village, and plant swidden plots at greater distances in a variety of other crops (Clarke 1966; Pospisil 1963; Rutz 1977; Waddell 1972).

The choice of locations for growing particular crops, therefore, depends in part on the labor requirements of the crops and the techniques used in their cultivation. Labor is distributed differentially around settlements, with greatest intensity at the closest locations. The division of labor often reflects this differential distribution, with women responsible for the more constant labor of kitchen gardens close at hand, men in charge of the extensive plots farthest away, and both involved in the cultivation of the land at intermediate locations (see, for example, Waddell 1972:189). Hence, agriculturalists tend to show concentric activity zones of the two sexes just as hunter–gatherers do (Watanabe 1968), with women operating largely within an inner ring and men active in the more distant zones.

There are additional factors besides settlements which pull agricultural activity to their proximity. Permanent facilities such as wells or irrigation canals will provide more certain water supplies and concentrate agriculture in their vicinity. The location of other farmers' plots may encourage the choice of adjacent fields in order to facilitate the exchange of labor (Nietschmann 1973:144) or to decrease costs by allowing joint fence construction (Clarke 1966:354). As exchange and sale of crops become increasingly important, so too does the location of markets and transportation routes in choosing field locations.

A variety of such magnets exist that pull procurement locations to their vicinity, imposing conditions of relative scarcity on the land nearby. As such land becomes increasingly scarce, it may be that resources and techniques must be increasingly altered to suit the land. Swidden farmers and mobile hunters tend to select land to suit the requirements of their crops and prey. More sedentary hunters and more intensive cultivators, on the other hand, may increasingly select crops and game according to the accessible land. Furthermore, increasing land scarcity may disrupt patterns of intensity gradients. The most fertile soils may be farmed the most intensively regardless of their distance from settlements. Farmers with only small landholdings may intensify production even at considerable distances from the village (Morgan 1969:253–256).

In addition to the various factors exerting pulls on procurement activities, there are a number of other factors with the opposite effect: "pushing" production activities away. Prolonged settlement, for example, leads to local depletion of mobile or slowly renewable resources. Firewood may become increasingly scarce around camps and villages, requiring longer trips and camp relocations for its collection (Silberbauer 1972; Chagnon 1977). In the Canadian Subarctic there is a positive correlation between trapping productivity and distance of trapping areas from the settlement (Jarvenpa 1977; Savishinsky 1978). Hunting and fishing yields of the Miskito of Nicaragua show a tendency to increase with distance away from the village because of greater isolation from hunting pressure (Nietschmann 1973:172). Mbuti hunting is more productive far from the Bantu villages, and commercial meat traders will travel to the more distant Pygmy camps to gain access to their greater productivity (Hart 1978:336). Consequently, the seemingly paradoxical situation has developed that the more isolated Pygmy camps show the greatest involvement in commercial meat trade.

The increasing exploitation pressure on nearby lands can become so great that a shift in procurement locations becomes necessary. Over a period of three years Mbuti hunting success in more densely populated areas declined 32% (Hart 1978:347). The Ye'kwana and Yanomamo of Amazonia "have almost completely abandoned several once-rich hunting areas that are only an hour's walk from the village because of game depletion" (Hames 1979:248). The Cree around Fort George, Canada tend to fish a productive locale until catches decline, with the result that the preferred whitefish have virtually disappeared from the vicinity of the Fort (Berkes 1977). Declining soil fertility in nearby plots may lead to their abandonment by swidden farmers who base this decision upon decreases in crop yields or increases in the labor requirements of weeding (Netting 1974:26).

Procurement activities may also be repelled or pushed away from distance-minimizing configurations by competition and interference. Rutz (1977) has demonstrated how individual land-use decisions in a Fijian village must take into account the choices and activities of other farmers. Because landholdings may be quite fragmented and dispersed as a result of the processes of land acquisition and tenure, the individual farmer is not able to arrange his activities so as to minimize his movement costs. The uses to which his various plots are put, however, tend to conform to the principles of crop requirements and the relative distance of each plot from the village. As a consequence, although individual landholdings are widely distributed in a pattern deviating from that expected on the basis of distance minimization, the aggregate village pattern of land use shows the concentric zonation characterized by gradients of intensity and crops. Similarly, among the Tsembaga of New Guinea, patterns of land use depend in part upon the interaction among villagers (Rappaport 1968). As individual pig herds increase in size, so too does the frequency of garden invasions by the pigs and the frequency of disputes among farmers. The result is that individual gardens are progressively moved farther from the village center and from other gardens as the pig herds grow.

The ultimate strategies of land use for various activities, therefore, represent a compromise between the different forces pushing and pulling them, together with a consideration of the requirements of both resources and technology. One final factor that may influence land-use decisions deserves mention. The uncertainties involved in the exploitation of any one particular area, whether these be risks of drought, plant and animal diseases, or shifts in game, encourage a diversification of procurement locations—more so, the greater these risks. Traps and set-nets allow hunters and fishermen to spread out their spatial allocation of effort. Farmers may select several plots with different soils or with different microclimates in order to diversify in this way (Harris 1972:253). Pastoralists may split up their herds if possible so as to diversify the grazing areas used. All of these practices may obtain greater security of procurement at the expense of increased travel costs.

5. PROCUREMENT SCHEDULING

The timing of activities and their scheduling in relation to one another represent important aspects of procurement decisions. Again, a variety of natural and social factors are considered in these decisions, often sequentially rather than simultaneously, and often assigned varying importance depending on the context.

Many resources show seasonal changes that affect the timing of their procurement. In highly seasonal environments, wild plants tend to have only limited periods of availability (see Fig. 5.2). Wild animals may also show such extreme patterns of presence and absence (for example, migratory fish, game, or birds),

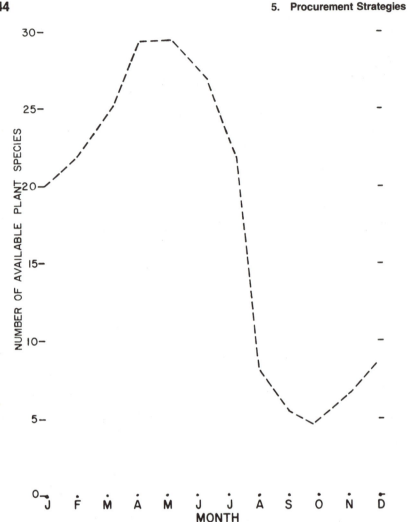

Fig. 5.2. Seasonal availability of plant foods among the G/Wi San (after Silberbauer 1972; reprinted with permission of M. Bicchieri).

but more often, animal resources are present year-round. Nevertheless, they frequently undergo changes in quality and behavior that render them more or less attractive to exploit. Hunters take these changes into account when scheduling their activities (see Jochim 1976:23–37). Variations in animal weight and fatness, mobility, aggregation, and in the condition of skins and antlers are all important in the timing of hunting and trapping. Seasons of procurement tend to be selected when the quality and weight of the prey is highest and when procurement is easiest.

Natural factors are critical in determining the timing of a variety of other activities as well. Neitschmann (1973) documents the importance of rainfall, winds, and currents to the seasonal pattern of hunting and fishing among the Miskito of Nicaragua. For many agriculturalists the scheduling of clearing, planting, and harvesting activities depends largely on the timing of the rains (Fig. 5.3). Social factors that affect the availability of resources or necessary labor or capital may be equally important in many situations. In northern Thailand, plow-

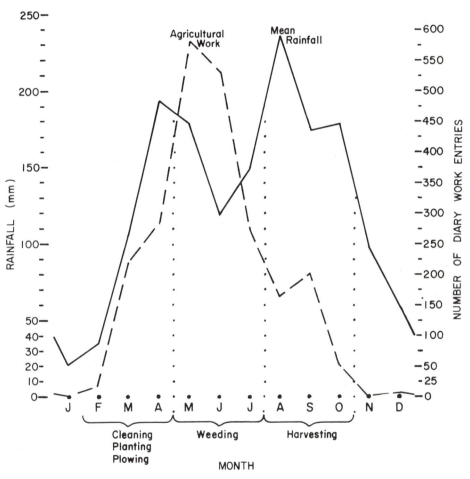

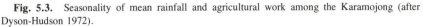

Fig. 5.3. Seasonality of mean rainfall and agricultural work among the Karamojong (after Dyson-Hudson 1972).

ing on distant fields is scheduled, not according to natural cycles, but according to the availability of tractors and the interests of their owners (Moerman 1968:65). A farmer must delay the harvest on these same fields until both his homefield rice has been gathered and his neighbors have completed the harvest on their distant plots which surround his, giving him access to this field by cart. For pastoral nomads of southeastern Turkey, "the migratory schedule is narrowly determined by the agricultural cycles of the villages through which they pass, and from which they secure grazing lands" (Bates 1972:49). It is likely that many hunter–gatherers, such as the Mbuti, who exchange labor or goods with sedentary groups, increasingly schedule their foraging activities around the work patterns and demands of the villagers (Tanno 1976:111).

The division of labor or specialization allows the simultaneous scheduling of several activities, such as hunting and gathering, herding and horticulture, or hunting and fishing. Figure 5.4 shows the timing of agricultural activities and hunting as performed by different specialized populations among the Bisa of Zambia. Frequently, however, such distinct subsistence activities may have such varying natural requirements that they may be performed sequentially, alternat-

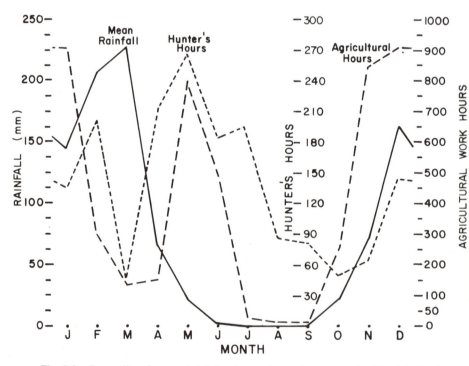

Fig. 5.4. Seasonality of mean rainfall, hunting, and agriculture among the Bisa (after Marks 1976).

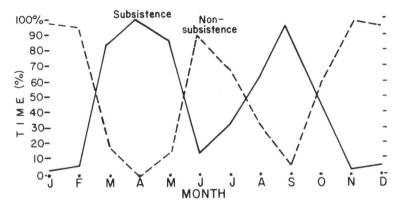

Fig. 5.5. Seasonality of subsistence and nonsubsistence activities among the Tlingit (after Oberg 1973).

ing with one another during the year (Bennett 1962:42). When conflicts do develop among activities, scheduling proceeds according to a hierarchy of resource importance. Thus, among hunter–gatherers the more variable and valued big game hunting is frequently scheduled first, and the procurement of the more stable and less valued small game or fish may then be scheduled subsequently. Moreover, the timing of nonprocurement activities such as tool repair, trading, or ceremonials is often determined after the subsistence activities are scheduled. Ceremonial activities among the Tlingit of the Northwest Coast occur largely in winter and midsummer, when few subsistence activities are conducted (Oberg 1973). Figure 5.5 demonstrates the distinct seasonal separation of subsistence and nonsubsistence activities among these people. A similar seasonal difference is shown by the Aruni of New Guinea, with more time devoted to subsistence activities in the dry season and more time to other activities such as church and council work and house construction in the wet season (Waddell 1972:89).

Some economic activities, however, may be more easily combined than others. Extensive swidden agriculture, for example, generally imposes very uneven work requirements throughout the year, and as a result, leaves much time available for other activities, both subsistence and nonsubsistence (Nietschmann 1973:233; Waddell 1972:218). More intensive agricultural techniques, by contrast, require both more work and more evenly distributed work during the year (Boserup 1965). Hence, as agriculture is intensified, it becomes more difficult to schedule other activities. In fact, any process of economic intensification, including commercial crop production and fishing for markets, will engender conflicts in timing of activities that require adjustments (see Nietschmann 1973:149). The frequency with which intensification and economic specialization are correlated reflects one adjustment to these scheduling difficulties.

Chapter 6

Settlement Strategies

Settlements can take many forms, from small, overnight camps to huge, permanent cities. They represent concentrations of many factors: labor, capital, information, and demand. The size, location, permanence, and composition of settlements reflect a number of decisions that determine the distribution of these factors in space. Both natural and social environments are important influences in these decisions.

1. SETTLEMENT PERMANENCE

Mobility is a strategy for redistributing people in the environment. Such redistribution may facilitate procurement and communication, help avoid risks and reduce stress, and allow the reorganization of residential composition. A strong association exists between procurement strategies and settlement mobility: hunter-gatherers and pastoralists depend largely upon the movement of people and their herds to resources, whereas agriculturalists attempt to concentrate their major resources around their settlements. Murdock (1969) has done a broad, cross-cultural study of the relationship between economy and settlement mobility. He classified 112 societies according to their dominant mode of subsistence and the permanence of their settlement, from fully sedentary to fully nomadic with no major fixed settlements. His results are summarized in Table 6.1. Clearly there are a number of other factors besides the general economic strategy that influence settlement mobility, for example, the kind of resources, their spatial distribution, the mixture of different economic forms, and a great variety of noneconomic factors. Nevertheless, a general patterned association does exist between economy and settlement. The key factor taken to explain this pattern is the efficiency of exploitation.

Lee's study of the !Kung San provides a neat model demonstrating the operation of this principle linking settlement and exploitation: "The Bushmen typi-

TABLE 6.1

Relationship between Economy and Mobility[a]

	Settlement mobility			
Economic focus	Nomadic	Seminomadic	Semisedentary	Sedentary
Gathering	8	6	3	3
Hunting	14	13	3	0
Fishing	4	11	4	22
Herding	10	6	5	0

[a] After Murdock 1969.

cally occupy a camp and eat their way out of it; when nuts are exhausted within a few miles the entire group moves camp to where water and nuts are still abundant'' (Lee 1969:51). Woodburn's (1968a) study of the Hadza of East Africa examines also the timing of, and reasons for, camp movements. In contrast to Lee, Woodburn thinks that too much emphasis is given to food shortages and food access, and there seems to be very little pattern to camp movements. Settlements are often shifted well before local foods are exhausted, frequently because some desired food is more abundant elsewhere. Other factors such as heavy rains, insects, rubbish accumulation, deaths, nightmares, and need to realign huts to validate interpersonal relationships also can cause camp movements. The importance of such factors cannot be denied, but camp moves must and do take into account local food resources, and the range of variation in the timing of such moves may be expected to reflect resource availability. Woodburn does, in fact, state that, ''more often than not a move does improve access to food supplies'' (1968a:203).

A great importance of local food abundance to camp movements is demonstrated by other studies of hunter–gatherer societies. Among the Birhor of India, 136 household moves were observed over a period of 14 months. Of this number, 12 moves were due to noneconomic factors and 124 were aimed at improving hunting or gathering conditions. That is, 91% of the moves were due to these economic considerations (Williams 1974:74). Hunter–gatherers do not need to exhaust local resources before they move. They need just deplete them enough so that it becomes more efficient to move camp to more productive areas.

Many factors influence the procurement efficiency and therefore the pattern of camp movements (Jochim 1976:47–63). These include the distribution of habitats and resources, the intensity of harvesting, and the costs and means of travel. Hunter–gatherers like the Ainu of Japan can remain quite sedentary because of the close packing of many resources in their environment (Watanabe 1968, 1972). The Mbuti Pygmies are relatively sedentary during the rainy season due to the discomfort of traveling, the villagers' demands for labor during this season, and the concentrated agricultural foods available in the villages (Tanno 1976:126). By contrast, when Mbuti hunting is intensified, the more rapid depletion of local resources requires a greater mobility involving longer and more frequent moves (Hart 1978:341).

Just as mobility is characteristic of most hunter–gatherers, sedentism is usually associated with agriculturalists. Cultivation involves the investment of time and energy in fixed locations; as these investments increase, so too does the necessity for maintaining proximity to protect the fields. With increasingly intensified agriculture, the investments increase, the work load becomes spread more evenly throughout the year, and residence becomes permanent.

Extensive swidden agriculture, however, depends upon the impermanence of fields, each of which receives relatively small investments of time and energy. As a result, swidden farmers tend to have much greater residential mobility than groups practicing more intensive systems. Part of the stereotype of swidden agriculturalists, in fact, includes a pattern of shifting of both fields and settlements. Much work has been devoted to investigating the specific relationship between settlement permanence and swidden agriculture (Brookfield and Brown 1963; Carneiro 1961; Conklin 1961; Dumond 1961). Carneiro, for example, constructed a mathematical model to express the relationship between land exhaustion and land needs for a given community, and then for more general, low average conditions. His results suggest that a community of 500 can remain in one spot in most cases, and that if villages are shifted, this is not required by the agricultural system. Incorporated into these calculations is not a minimization of effort but rather a low fixed figure, either a 3- or 5-mile radius of distance traveled from the village. If people truly aimed at minimizing travel, then movement of the village might be necessary.

It seems to be characteristic of human decision making that multiple, often conflicting goals must be reconciled, with the result being that any extreme manifestation, such as absolute maximizing or minimizing is rarely achieved. In decision-making theory, this process of reconciliation is often taken into account by a variety of "satisficing" approaches, in which certain ranges of values for different variables are designated as acceptable, and a decision is satisfactory if variables are kept in these ranges In this light, then, slash-and-burn agriculture can often permit permanence of residence with a satisfactory, low level of energy expenditure in certain regions. Specific factors of the habitat as well as varying cultural values about conflicting goals can alter the range of output deemed satisfactory.

Among the local factors that are important are the amount of available land and the fallow period allowed, the climate, soil types, vegetational cover, and the types of crops and their demands on the soil (Harris 1972:251–252). A number of other factors, however, must also be considered. Swidden farmers often depend upon hunting and fishing to supplement their crops; permanence of settlement can lead to the problem of local exhaustion of game or fish, which then may be solved by a shifting of settlement (Gross 1975; Werner 1978). Mobility is also a method of avoidance, and settlement shifts may be common in regions where warfare is frequent (Chagnon 1977).

Mobility of settlement, consequently, is a strategy used in a variety of situations. It is possible only when sufficient land is available for movement and is common when resources are mobile or shifting in distribution. There are, nevertheless, alternative strategies to that of shifting residence in such situations. Rather than having all the consumers move to the resources, for example, only the procurers may move, while the rest of the population remains sedentary (see, for example, Binford 1980). Hunters or herders may be absent for weeks of extensive travel, returning later with game or herds to the base camp or village. The distances and costs of these moves must be compared to the costs and benefits of moving the entire group. Aids to mobility may, in fact, cause greater settlement permanence: devices such as snowmobiles may allow such large areas to be exploited by hunters that the rest of the population can remain fully sedentary. When, however, residential mobility is practiced, it imposes constraints on other aspects of behavior. Most notably, settlement mobility limits the amount of equipment and other material items transported and restricts the size of co-resident groups. Conversely, when settlements, possessions, and investments in fixed locations are small, mobility represents a feasible strategy of coping with problems.

2. SETTLEMENT LOCATION

The placement of settlements can be viewed as a strategy for attaining economic, social, and political ends. The distribution of settlements represents the arrangement of consumers or demand, producers or labor, and technology or capital, in relation to the resources exploited. Settlement patterns also structure the relationship of people to one another in terms of competition, cooperation, and communication. The arrangement and accessibility of resources and other people, consequently, are critical factors in determining settlement location. Since large, permanent settlements, which represent considerable investments of materials and energy in one location, are so expensive to move, they cannot be responsive to many changes in the arrangement of these factors. The greater the mobility and impermanence of settlements, therefore, the more likely it is that their location can adjust to the distribution of resources.

Considerations solely of efficiency of access, travel, and procurement should result in attempts to minimize distances between resources and settlements. This general objective of distance minimization should pull settlements to particular resource locations (Jochim 1976:50–63). At the same time, considerations of security may distort this pattern, pushing settlements away from the least-cost configurations. The location of settlements reflects a compromise between the various pushes and pulls between security and efficiency goals.

If the inhabitants of a settlement are engaged in the procurement of just a single resource, then efficiency of travel would be greatest when the settlement is located at the source of the resource. The closest approximation to this simple situation would be provided by specialized settlements: acorn-gathering camps situated in oak groves, quarry sites at rock outcrops, and salt-making villages on extinct estuaries. Such settlements are uncommon and are either extremely short-term or else highly dependent upon others in a complex set of economic exchanges. More commonly, people locate their settlements in relation to several resources. If these resources have distributions that overlap or are in close proximity, then procurement effort can be minimized by locating the settlements in the region of overlap or juxtaposition. A common example is the situation of villages on river terraces, providing access to both agricultural land and riverine resources. An important implication of this strategy of settlement location is that settlements may become clustered and land become scarce, even when each single resource is widely available. Because of the manner in which settlement locations are chosen, carrying capacity may be much lower than that predictable from the individual resource densities.

More frequently, all the resources to be procured are not overlapping or adjacent in their distributions. This situation is characteristic of environments with great spatiotemporal variability and thus becomes more common with increasing distance from the equator (Binford 1980). Such resource distributions also characterize diversified economies that rely on many different resources, increasing the probability that all of them will not be available in one location. In addition, this problem of differential resource distributions may increase in importance with settlement permanence, since prolonged occupation may lead to local exhaustion of at least some resources. In all these situations, determining the location of settlements becomes problematic and requires the evaluation of the different resources and the assignment of differential importance to each in determining settlement placement.

The qualities of resources that are significant in these evaluations include their value, their reliability, their transportability, and the labor demands of their procurement. If two resources are virtually identical in these characteristics, then settlements may be placed halfway between their areas of occurrence. The Pitjandjara of Australia, for example, situate their camps to balance the pulls of standing water, firewood, and plant resources (Tindale 1972: Fig. 6-6). Most resources, however, are sufficiently different that they will exert different pulls on settlements. In evaluating these pulls, people tend to establish hierarchies of resources ranked according to various criteria, the most important of which is resource mobility.

Fixed resources are more important to settlement decisions than are mobile ones. Fixed resources are predictable in space and thus more reliable to procure. Consequently, hunter–gatherers tend to locate their camps where water, firewood, and plant foods are available and to exploit these resources within a small radius of camp. Mobile game animals, by contrast, rarely determine the specific camp locations, although ideally, hunting areas will also be accessible from settlements and hunting activities will be conducted over a wider area from camps. Fish are mobile but confined to streams, lakes, and seas, and so rather spatially predictable and of considerable importance to settlement decisions. As a result, hunter–gatherers demonstrate a hierarchical nesting of their activities in space around their camps, with procurement of the most reliable and fixed resources nearby and exploitation of more mobile and unreliable resources at greater distances. It is usually the more fixed resources that determine specific placement of the camps. Similar patterns occur among horticulturalists as well. Villages will be situated in close proximity to the fixed agricultural land, whereas the distribution of game or grazing land is less critical to specific settlement location. The more mobile hunting or herding activities occur at greater distances from the villages.

This focus on resource mobility establishes a direct relationship between human spatial arrangements and the spatial behavior of their resources. What this relationship essentially reflects are the costs and benefits involved in exploiting specific *locations* (rather than resources). If people attempt to minimize travel costs, then the locations that are most often visited should be situated closest at hand. Locations with fixed resources such as plant foods may be more frequently visited than any particular locale in hunting areas, even if meat provides most of the diet. Garden plots will be traveled to more often than any portion of hunting regions in the forest beyond.

By examining this spatial pattern of labor investments, the location of settlements in relation to different fixed resources may be examined as well. Agricultural plots around a village may be cultivated with a variety of techniques. The more intensive techniques require both more total labor and more regular labor inputs for weeding or other maintenance activities. As a result, settlements should be placed so as to minimize the distance to the most intensively cultivated plots. If only certain soils are suitable for intensification, then settlement may be placed adjacent to these soils. In the previous discussion of land-use patterns, it was suggested that, given a fixed settlement, the most intensive economic activities should be located in the closest areas. Now the same pattern may be formulated in another way: given fixed locations of intensive activities (due to soils or the presence of irrigation canals, for example), settlement should be pulled to their proximity for greatest efficiency of procurement. The result of both of these processes is a hierarchical nesting of activities in space similar to that of hunter-gatherers: concentric zones of decreasing intensity of labor investment with greater distance from the settlement. The most proximate zone may have the greatest investment of capital (requiring maintenance and protection), require the most frequent labor investments, and provide the most reliable yields.

Settlements may also be pulled by considerations of efficiency to locations other than natural resource patches. Markets in cities, villages, or posts represent sources of many goods that may exert strong attraction on settlement location. As labor markets, too, such fixed spots may pull settlements to their proximity. Transportation routes like roads, rivers, coasts, and landing strips may pull settlements to cluster along their length, providing easy access to markets and resource areas. Proximity to other settlements may be desired also for the ease of interaction and communication. Finally, efficiency of administration and control may encourage centralized elites to pull other settlements close to their centers.

The interaction of many of these factors may be seen in operation among the inhabitants of the Ituri Forest in central Africa. Bantu villages, which were formerly dispersed for subsistence reasons around the edges of the region, are now concentrated along the newly constructed roads (Tanno 1976:123). Nethunting Pygmy base camps have been pulled to the vicinity of these villages as the Pygmy–Bantu exchange of labor and goods has increased in importance. Because it facilitates their control over the Pygmies, the Bantu encourage this location of the Pygmy base camps. The Pygmies locate their more temporary hunting camps, on the other hand, out in the forest away from the villages, in order to escape the Bantu influence and to improve access to hunting areas. These hunting camps are spaced according to economic factors. Hunting is conducted within a radius of 3–4 km around the camp, and when this area has been exploited, camps are pulled to the center of the nearest unexploited region, about 5–8 km away (Tanno 1976:124).

In addition to these various pulls for the efficiency of movement, other forces operate on settlements to push them away from the most efficient locations. These pushes derive largely from factors affecting security. Despite all their possible attractions, for example, other settlements may represent potential risks. The competition of other villages for resources may dictate a wider spacing of villages than would be warranted by resource distributions alone. If competition takes the form of conflict, then distance from other villages may become a primary influence on settlement location. Similarly, transportation routes facilitate not only access to resources and markets, but also attacks by neighbors. Settlements may avoid rivers or roads because of the risk of attack (Butt 1970). Furthermore, settlements may be located to provide access to a diversity of resources or markets, with the result that, although security is increased thereby, travel costs are increased as well. The context of security must be examined in order to evaluate the importance of these factors on settlement location.

3. SETTLEMENT SIZE

If settlement location can be analyzed in terms of the shifting pushes and pulls of resources and other factors, then the size of settlements should reflect the strength of the forces of attraction. People should be clustered into larger settlements as the forces pulling them to these locations increase in intensity. Extremely clustered resources will attract population aggregation. One would expect larger settlements, consequently, in more heterogeneous environments, and smaller, more dispersed settlements in more homogeneous environments (Horn 1968). This environmental heterogeneity may take the form of an uneven and limited distribution of waterholes, fishing spots, nut groves, mountain passes, or fertile soil: in each case, the few rich locations promote population aggregation. The uneven distribution of resources encourages an uneven distribution of people, because such population clustering reduces the travel distance required for procurement. Settlement patterns can change with alterations in the environment or in the resources selected for procurement. The appearance of trading posts or villages introduces new, clustered resources into hunter-gatherer environments, promoting concentration in these locations. A shift to the exploitation of rather uniformly distributed resources like furbearers or rubber trees can encourage greater dispersal of the population (Murphy and Steward 1956).

Agriculture as a procurement strategy tends to concentrate resources in space, thereby creating environmental heterogeneity. As a result, farming populations may be more concentrated into larger settlements than hunter-gatherers. Average settlements of swidden farmers, for example, range in size between 50 and 250 people (Harris 1972), whereas hunter-gatherer camps are generally much smaller. More intensive agricultural techniques can concentrate resources to a greater extent and, therefore, can support larger populations in a small area. Consequently, larger towns and cities are virtually always dependent upon intensive agriculture of some sort. Paradoxically, however, intensive farming does not always lead to larger settlements; it may encourage population dispersal. Since intensive garden plots require heavy and frequent work inputs, the individual farmer may save effort in traveling if his house is close to his plot. Moreover, because agricultural intensification often develops in a context of relative land scarcity, competition for land may encourage a proximity of settlement and plots, so that the farmer can adequately defend his gardens. These factors of maintenance and defense of land lead to a common pattern of dispersed residences for intensive agriculturalists, so that each farmer can reduce the distance between house and garden. Thus, the relationship between economic intensity and settlement nucleation is complex (Netting 1974; Smith 1972; Waddell 1972). Intensive agriculture, by concentrating resources to a large extent, can facilitate population nucleation. At the same time, intensively cultivated plots require much attention in frequent visits so that even small distances can impose great travel costs, with the result that farmers will save energy and time by dispersing residences among the gardens.

This complex and contradictory relationship between agricultural intensity and settlement demonstrates the inadequacy of resource distribution alone in determining settlement size. Many other factors are important as well. The nucleation or dispersal of people in settlements affects not just the distance between people and resources but also the distance between people and other people. This interpersonal distance can be an important component of many aspects of behavior. Cooperative work groups are easier to mobilize in large settlements representing concentrations of labor. Consequently, contexts favoring large work parties may favor large settlements. Nethunting among the Mbuti Pygmies in a communal endeavor, with the size of the catch directly related to the number of hunters involved (Tanno 1976). Bowhunting, by contrast, is usually a solitary activity, and as a result, camps of the Pygmy archers are generally smaller than those of nethunters (Bicchieri 1969; Harako 1976; Turnbull 1968). Similarly, caribou and bison drives and whaling expeditions require cooperative effort so that the camps of the hunters at the time of these hunts are usually larger than those at other seasons. Swidden agriculture may require large work parties for some activities such as initial forest clearance and thus will encourage a degree of settlement nucleation (Waddell 1972). Intensive agriculture may promote dispersal in many situations, but if it involves communal endeavors such as canal construction, larger settlements may be one means by which the labor may be assured (Netting 1974:34).

Fighting in the form of either offensive raids or defense is another type of activity that may be more successful or efficient with large work groups. As a result, population nucleation is a common response to the threat of conflict (Netting 1969; Smith 1972; Thompson 1973). Among the Hehe of southern Tanzania, small dispersed settlements were characteristic in regions influenced by colonial peace keeping, whereas larger nucleated communities were typical in areas outside this influence where raiding was common (Winans 1965). "Safety in numbers" may be an important consideration in settlement decisions.

"Security in numbers" may be provided by large settlements even in the absence of cooperative exploitation or defense. Large populations may allow the simultaneous exploitation of a number of scattered resources, thereby increasing resource diversity and potential subsistence security (Netting 1974:35). In some areas of the Ituri Forest, Pygmy archer camps are as large as those of nethunters, in part because the simultaneous hunting by many individuals helps insure that some meat will be brought into camp (Ichikawa 1978:138-139). For the advantages of these larger groups to be realized, reliable systems of sharing and redistribution must be maintained.

By reducing interpersonal distances, larger settlements offer other advantages as well. Interaction is necessary and desirable for a variety of purposes, including communication and information sharing, obtaining mates, and maintaining alliances. The cost of all of these activities will be lowered as the interacting populations aggregate in fewer settlements. Counterbalancing these benefits are the greater costs of coordinating and integrating these aggregations. Potential competition and conflict increase in larger settlements. Many hunter–gatherers show a pattern of periodic group fission and dispersal as a response to growing conflict within large groupings, although alternative means of resolving disputes may be provided within the context of strongly developed kinship organization and ceremonialism or by outside mediators (Ichikawa 1978:178). Disputes may take the form of arguments, fights or, more subtly, accusations of witchcraft (Rogers 1969). The size of farming villages, too, seems to be limited, in part, by the lack of effective means of conflict resolution (Harris 1972). The emergence of formalized authorities capable of mediation and adjudication would allow greater population nucleation and might also encourage it for greater ease of administration (Netting 1969:105).

As a result of the complexity of factors involved, predicting the size of settlements is extremely difficult. Some cross-cultural patterns exist, however, that reflect patterns in the general contexts of settlement decisions. Natural resource clustering promotes population clustering, especially among hunter–gatherers who do little to alter natural resource distributions. Thus, relatively homogeneous environments such as tropical rainforests may show smaller, more dispersed populations than do more heterogeneous environments. If environmental patchiness generally increases with distance from the Equator, then there may exist latitudinal trends of northward-increasing hunter–gatherer nucleation, at least seasonally. Agriculturalists create resource patches and so tend to show somewhat larger settlements than those of hunter–gatherers. Increasing population density seems to favor nucleation through a number of processes: (1) it favors the dependence upon agriculture (and thus the concentration of resources) over the less land-efficient hunting and gathering, (2) it encourages agricultural intensification that facilitates the support of larger settlements, (3) it might create land scarcity and increase the needs for defense against raids, (4) it might encourage economic diversification and the frequency of necessary interaction for sharing and redistribution, and (5) it might increase the potential frequency of interpersonal encounters and decrease the effectiveness of avoidance for conflict resolution, thus promoting the development of institutionalized mediators, which then would allow the peaceful formation of larger settlements. At the same time, however, increasingly intensive agriculture may encourage individual farmers to disperse their residences among the plots for greater efficiency in tending and protecting the crops. As a result of these opposing responses to agricultural intensification, there may be no apparent relationship in some areas between population density and settlement nucleation (Brown and Podolefsky 1976:221).

The settlement patterns of particular groups reflect a compromise between these various advantages and disadvantages to nucleation. Population may be both clustered and dispersed but on different scales. Farmers may concentrate around good soils or for purposes of defense, but within these concentrations, they may be relatively dispersed among their own fields. Such compromises may be simultaneous, as among the camel pastoralists studied by Sweet (1965). The groups, or tribal sections, of these people emerge as compromise units of intermediate size, balancing the need for small groups with great mobility to take advantage of changing grazing lands, against that large enough groups for necessary defense and subsistence security (Fig. 6.1).

Compromises may also be sequential, in that settlement size changes through time on a regular basis. This pattern is most often seen among hunter–gatherers with a seasonal round of fission and fusion, although agriculturalists may demonstrate this pattern as well. Rappaport (1968) described the Tsembaga settlement pattern as "pulsating" between a nucleated village and dispersed homesteads. In this case, growth of pig herds led to an increase in garden invasions and consequent disputes between individuals. In the absence of effective mechanisms to mediate these disputes, people moved out from the village center, decreasing the chances for pigs to invade other gardens. At some point, the population became so dispersed that daily interaction became difficult and the very existence of a

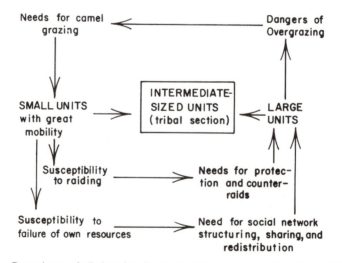

Fig. 6.1. Determinants of tribal section size among camel pastoralists (after Sweet 1965).

socially cohesive village became threatened. Since this threat coincided with excessive demands on women's labor to feed the growing pig herds, the pig festival was initiated and many pigs were slaughtered. People moved back to the village center in order to participate in the ceremonies and could now do so because the main source of disputes was eliminated.

4. SETTLEMENT COMPOSITION

The composition of settlements varies tremendously cross-culturally in terms of the stability of membership and the organization of component units. These aspects of settlement organization can be viewed as strategic responses to a variety of ecological problems. Even though specific problems may vary from one region to another, the general characteristics of these problems may by sufficiently similar so that similar organizational strategies provide satisfactory solutions. As a result, patterns in settlement composition develop despite the vast array of specific systems of social organization.

Insecurity, for example, is a characteristic of problems faced by every society. When this insecurity takes the form of unpredictability of resource locations or yields, a common coping strategy is to develop mechanisms for readjusting man–land relationships. Mobility is one such mechanism already discussed. Frequently correlated with settlement mobility is another coping strategy—the maintenance of flexibility of association.

Hunter–gatherers are largely dependent upon the natural distribution of resources and require mechanisms for adjusting population to this distribution as it varies. The resulting mobility of hunter–gatherers has long been recognized, but their flexibility of camp or band membership has only recently received attention. Traditional descriptions of such people emphasized the stability of membership and so could construct attractive models of exclusive bands with fixed territories arranged across the landscape. Radcliffe-Brown (1931), for example, described the local hordes of the Australian Aborigines as independent and autonomous units composed of the male (and unmarried female) members of a patriclan, their wives (obtained from other clans), and children, occupying discrete clan territories. Recent work, however, has shown this to be an unrealistic, idealized model that would probably be nonviable in practice.

Hiatt's (1968) studies, among others, have demonstrated that most stable residential groupings consisted of members of many patriclans, not one, and that not all the members of one patriclan lived together. In moving around to get resources, this residential group, therefore, did not restrict itself to the land of one patriclan but had access to the lands of all member patriclans; in addition, they could enter still other territories on invitation and did so often. Land claims and boundaries of the different patriclans were very weak; usually, only a few selected totemic sites were claimed, not a bounded area. An advantage to this system is that any co-residing group of people had access to a wide area; if the resources on the territory of any one patriclan failed, other regions could be exploited in an orderly manner.

For the Hadza of East Africa, another group of hunters and gatherers, Woodburn states: ''The use of the term territorial ownership, leadership, corporateness, and fixed membership, is inappropriate for Hadza residential entities, and I prefer to use the term 'camp,' meaning simply the set of persons who happen to be living together at one place at one time'' (Woodburn 1968b:103). This kind of flexibility of membership and variability in group size and location seems to be characteristic of most hunters and gatherers as they are studied in greater detail and over longer time periods. A premium seems to be placed on the ability to react to environmental changes, to redistribute people over the land and its resources. If so, then one might expect that such flexibility would show a positive correlation with environmental variability: the more unstable the environment, the greater the mobility and flexibility of size and membership of human groups. It has been suggested also that in such a case, one would observe greater cultural homogeneity over large areas in terms of such criteria as language, ritual, dress, and so forth. The maintenance of such a widespread group identity would allow participants widely separated to come together in times of economic necessity (Yellen and Harpending 1972).

The coast of Australia is a much richer and more predictable environment than the interior, and the inhabitants of these two areas show a number of differences (Yengoyan 1968). Local group exogamy occurred on the coast, whereas widespread marriage subsection systems existed in the interior. Moreover, rites of subincision and circumcision were widespread in the interior, but absent on the coast. The extension of section terms allowed movement of groups into larger territories, providing security in times of economic stress. The composition of local groups was highly variable in the interior and allowed a readjustment to environmental pressures through section terms and kinship. Survival in the interior, unlike the coast, required a means of linking groups and individuals through sections and subsections into a network that promoted small mobile groups to expand and contract under varying environmental conditions. Male initiation rites such as circumcision were mechanisms promoting social interaction and exchange. Yengoyan further suggests that the !Kung name relationships and the Netsilik Eskimo meat-sharing partnerships also had a similar function of linking together large groups, providing a form of economic and social security.

It may be argued, then, that populations in richer and more stable environments can be more settled and have a more constant size and membership. They also would have less of a need to maintain extensive areal relationships, and so one might expect to see greater local cultural differentiation. The Ainu of Japan are one group of hunters, fishers, and gatherers living in a relatively rich and stable environment. They live in permanent villages in narrow valleys and derive most of their diet from abundant salmon, deer, bears, and a variety of plants. One factor stressed by Watanabe (1972) that promotes their residential stability is the fact that a variety of rich habitats are located in close juxtaposition, so that many are exploitable from the village on the river terrace, whereas others may be reached by short-term hunting trips. The composition of these villages is also quite stable, and in fact, a fairly rigid hierarchy of group organization can be maintained. The village jointly owned and used the spawning grounds of salmon, and participated as a group in regular rituals. Neighboring villages, up to seven in number, were aggregated into larger groups whose only collective action was a bear ceremony. All of the settlements along a river formed a river group that regarded the river and its resources as its territory and had collective rituals only against natural catastrophes. In addition to its fairly rigid structure, it should be stressed that this framework of organization extended at most to include just the one river valley. If the salmon runs failed for one village, they usually failed for the whole river group, and few mechanisms existed to allow people to enter neighboring valleys. Of course, the essential point is that the salmon runs rarely, if ever, failed completely.

Pastoralists are similar to hunter–gatherers in their reliance upon mobility as a major means of coping with environmental variability and insecurity. As a result, they also tend to show great flexibility of association and maintain the social networks necessary for this flexibility (Goldschmidt 1965). Among the Pokot of East Africa, for example, both full-time farmers and full-time herders locate their settlements on elevated spurs of land, and use the same term—"korok"—to designate both this type of landscape feature and the social unit occupying it. The two groups differ, however, in the spatial extent and composition of these social units. Among farmers, the social unit may be confined to just one elevated spur, whereas the need for grazing regularly takes herders to several such places. Moreover, in farming koroks the lineage is localized, and a single korok rarely has more than four different lineages. Among herders, on the other hand, one lineage may be quite dispersed, and a single korok often contains as many as 30 different lineages. In order to adjust to the changing and uncertain distribution of resources, the herders maintain much greater flexibility in location and association (Porter 1965).

Farming populations, by contrast, demonstrate much greater stability of settlement composition related to the fixed location of their primary resources and the relative lack of mobility as a means of altering man–land relationships. Within this broad category of agriculturalists, however, a huge number of different economic and settlement strategies are practiced, and flexibility in group membership is demonstrated in some contexts. When land is abundant, allowing mobility for readjusting land, labor, and consumer relationships, bilateral kinship organization appears to be common. Such a flexible organization provides "a network of social ties radiating outward from each household, which facilitates residential mobility as an adjustment to microdifferentials in environmental conditions and economic difficulties'' (Netting 1974:31–32). As land or other resources become scarce, however, intensification of agricultural techniques tends to reduce residential mobility, strengthening the association with particular plots of land. Concomitantly, access to land becomes increasingly limited, flexibility of residence decreases, and bilateral kinship organization tends to be replaced by more exclusive and stable unilineal descent groups (Netting 1974:31–32). Since this increasing attachment to particular plots and the increased limitation of access to other areas prevents the redistribution of people as a means of dealing with insecurity or stress, other means may be necessary. It would seem that the movement of resources—through feasts, exchange, or redistribution—becomes more important as residential mobility decreases in frequency.

An advantage to stable, unilineal descent groups, in addition to the controlled access to resources they may provide, is that they offer an organized group that may be reliably mobilized as large work parties (Netting 1974:31). The need for large work groups has been discussed earlier as a factor contributing to settlement nucleation. Given a large settlement, cooperative work groups might be recruited in various ways, including through formalized partnerships, beer parties, or hired labor. Groups organized according to kinship, however, are one of the most common forms of communal labor parties, apparently because they are more reliable. Kinship has been called a ''social glue'' providing the cohesion necessary for social life. Descent and affiliation represent the major dimensions along which interpersonal relationships are structured. The resulting groups and networks so defined are the organizational solutions to a variety of simultaneous problems; they are the social units involved in strategies of procurement, settlement, and numerous maintenance and management activities. By formalizing relationships, kinship rules make group formation reliable and the members and their behavior predictable. The advantages to groups organized according to kinship and affiliation, consequently, derive from both their greater reliability and their utility in coping with a variety of problems, thereby avoiding the costs of reorganizing to solve each problem separately.

Contexts encouraging the formation of large work parties, therefore, frequently show institutionalized means of organizing such groups, most often in the form of kin groups and networks. Such contexts include economies based on extensive slash-and-burn agriculture in which forest clearance and field preparation often involve large groups. In this context, the extended family is a common residential and economic unit, large enough to provide the necessary work force. Groups moving into relatively empty land from high density areas have been observed, not only to adopt extensive farming techniques to suit the new abundance of land, but also to alter their family structure from nuclear to the larger extended families to suit the new labor needs (Netting 1965; Thompson 1973).

Extended families appear to represent a common organizational solution in many others contexts as well, most of which have in common high labor needs in the form of incompatible activities (Pasternak *et al.* 1976).

Family organization, for example, may vary within the same economy, depending on the distribution of resources and the resulting labor requirements. If resources are widely scattered, larger labor forces that can pool their produce may be necessary. Thus, Sahlins (1957) has demonstrated how the distribution of coconuts affects the family organization in the Fijian villages involved in cash economies based on copra production. Groups who must simultaneously exploit dispersed coconuts maintain extended families, whereas those with clustered holdings of coconuts are characterized by nuclear family organization.

Other contexts favoring the organization of large groups include situations in which labor is scarce (Reyna 1976), including frontier situations (Thompson 1973) and economies in which surplus production can be converted into prestige or authority, thus stimulating demand on production. Extended families, of course, represent only one possible solution to these demands on labor. Others include lineage organization, patron–client relationships, hired labor, and slavery. Each has its own characteristics (representing both advantages and secondary problems) that would be important in understanding both their pattern of occurrence and their implications for other aspects of behavior. In other contexts, by contrast, labor needs may be best filled by small groups. Nuclear families, for example, appear to provide labor forces suitable for the most efficient production in many intensive economies, especially where resources are uniformaly distributed (Murphy and Steward 1956; Waddell 1972). Despite the variety of ways in which groups may be organized and integrated, it is clear that the flexibility and organization of settlement composition is closely related to the context of labor demands and that the general characteristics of social organization may be related to the general properties of the problem contexts.

Chapter 7

Maintenance Strategies

Many aspects of behavior have been viewed as strategies for defining and procuring resources or for distributing people in relation to these resources, but a number of important factors have been omitted from discussion. In particular, it has been assumed that most strategies, once developed, will be carried out and proved successful. No mention has been made of unexpected environmental changes altering the resource configuration. No allowance has been made for an unanticipated lack of available means to the goals or to obstacles in the way of planned activities. Yet all of these factors form part of the context of decisions. If such decisions are viewed as compromises attempting to balance the allocation of effort among a variety of goals, then these factors represent perturbations or stresses threatening to disrupt this balance. Stresses can be of many types, but many seem to have the effect of causing imbalances between people and resources in both space and time. Maintenance activities consist of those strategies that anticipate or respond to these imbalances.

The major categories of behavior examined in this chapter are territoriality, exchange, and warfare. Obviously, each of these is a complex topic worthy of extensive treatment by itself. By viewing each as a type of maintenance strategy, however, it is hoped that at least a framework may be established in which these activities can be profitably investigated cross-culturally and related to other aspects of behavior. Each of these realms of behavior should be seen as multifunctional. Each is a potential solution to a variety of problems. Each involves relationships both among people and between people and resources. Both exchange and warfare, for example, can serve to obtain goods, obtain and maintain alliances (which are useful for obtaining goods, mates, labor, and access to land), and settle or avoid disputes. Given such complexity of possible effects of these activities, it is not surprising that generalizations about simple ecological functions of warfare (Vayda 1976) and exchange (Piddocke 1965) have been severely criticized (Hallpike 1973; Orans 1975). No simple patterns of correlation between warfare or exchange and certain environmental factors should be expected. Greater understanding of these activities could derive from an examination of their various attributes—spatial extent, number of people involved, organization, timing, frequency, and intensity (volume of goods or number of deaths)—as these vary with context. Rarely do we have, however, sufficient information to allow a detailed comparison among groups. This chapter, as a result, will not attempt any general "explanations" of warfare or exchange, but rather will try to suggest the various problem contexts in which each might represent a potential solution, and how each will vary with the specific characteristics of the contexts.

1. IMBALANCE OF DEMAND AND RESOURCES

Perhaps the most fundamental relationship examined in ecological studies is that between a population and its resources. The entire discussion about feeding, procurement, and settlement strategies has focused on this relationship. The current emphasis given in the literature to population pressure and energy flows reflects its importance. Survival depends upon a minimum balance between the resources available and a population's demands upon them. Yet both resources and demand fluctuate, so that their relationship may be quite variable. It is not surprising, consequently, that many activities serve to control or compensate for these fluctuations, to insure a spatiotemporal matching of demand and resources. Some of these activities are essentially anticipatory, in that they seek to avoid relative resource shortages. Others are more compensatory, redistributing either demand or resources in response to perceived imbalances. These will be examined in turn.

1.1. Anticipatory Strategies

1.1.1. Territoriality

Most anthropological studies focus on specific units or societies, but the question of how these units and their boundaries are defined is often not discussed. The definition of such units, however, is not only important and interesting in its own right but is also central to the ecological approach. Earlier the problem of ecosystem boundary definition was stressed. In order to measure energy flow, to trace exchanges of matter, or to examine regulatory mechanisms, one must set limits or boundaries. The problem is difficult for nonhuman ecosystems and perhaps more so for those containing humans.

Part of the problem derives from a commonly held intuitive model of human societies. As Leach states

> It is assumed that within a somewhat arbitrary geographical area a social system exists; the population involved in this system is of one culture; the social system is uniform [1964:60].

Or according to Sharp

> We Europeans come in with a conception of states with fixed boundaries . . . biased by the imposition of prefabricated constructs—the patriclan, the horde, and the band—which we go looking for [1968:159].

Each of these men goes on to emphasize that this model is not applicable to his area of study. What seems to emerge is the idea that units of interacting humans can be defined according to a number of criteria, and the resulting units rarely coincide with one another. An extreme case is depicted in these additional comments of Sharp:

> In studying the aboriginal population of Cape York Peninsula, I simply could not find a society. I would have to describe it in terms of an ego-centered *set* of societies; no one individual was the center of a system of networks that overlapped isotypically with anyone else's [1968:159].

These remarks pertain to Australian Aboriginal societies, which, of course, are characteristically fluid and flexible in composition, reflecting the reliance on mobility and changing associations as important settlement strategies providing necessary subsistence security. Nevertheless, even among sedentary and relatively complex agricultural societies, it is frequently possible to delineate different groups of interacting individuals depending on the criteria of interaction examined. Some possible criteria for defining such networks would include language, dialect, geographic area, kinship, subsistence techniques and cooperation, food-sharing, trade, ceremonial participation, and warfare alliances. If these criteria, in fact, define different units, then one must decide which to use as the focus of investigation.

All human groups, and hence, all anthropological studies, have some degree of geographic focus. Randomly wandering groups with no associations with a piece of land are unknown. Furthermore, ecosystems are not simply theoretical abstracts; they have their basis on the ground with a given set of producing plants that initiate the energy capture. As a result, the ecological approach tends to continue the practice of using a geographic focus as a major criterion for defining units of study. Specific problems may require other criteria, but the initial framework is usually in geographic terms.

Once such an orientation is accepted, however, the problem of determining the geographic boundaries is critical and involves a consideration of the general relationship between humans and space. Do individuals or groups define an area for exclusive use, and if so, how is this done? Is one area utilized by a constant, unchanging group of people, and if so, how is the group defined?

A major input into ecological anthropology consists of generalizations drawn from studies of animal behavior. Territorial behavior by other animals might be used to shed some light on the determinants and structure of human land use. Considerable debate has occurred in these studies over the definition and functions of territories. Some consider the hallmark of a territory to be its perimeter fixed by defense. Others stress the existence of aggressive defense in a floating area that moves with the animal. Finally, some ethologists do not consider defense or aggression to be critical at all; rather they emphasize habitual use of an area, which may or may not be defended. The application of any of these territorial concepts to humans is also debatable and depends not only on the definition but also on the quality and duration of field studies. It seems safe to say that humans, in general, do show some degree of territoriality, with a wide range of variation, from habitual use to strictly defined and defended perimeters. And to some extent the nature of such land relationships shows some correlation with factors in the natural and social environments.

The ethologist Klopfer (1969) has summarized some advantages derived from the maintenance of territories:

(1) An increase in the efficiency by which resources (food, shelter) are used as a result of restricting activities to a discrete and familiar area;
(2) Limitation in the intensity of competition for food or shelter since the number of territories will set a limit on the total population density;
(3) Reduction in predation both because territorial individuals are spaced apart and because they can more easily escape on familiar ground;
(4) Reduction on the time spent on aggression.

The ecologist Kummer (1971) has elaborated on this last point: a territory is a formalized relationship between animal and space. Once territories are fixed, movements become formalized and predictable, and conflict is minimized. Both men emphasize that territorial behavior can serve different functions among different species.

Active, constant defense of fixed boundaries seems to be rather rare among most animals. For those animals that maintain stable territories the usual pattern is to defend actively a central core area, while tolerating sporadic marginal intrusions. Furthermore, a system of marking or advertising—with urine, scents, or through display behavior—very commonly avoids open aggression, thereby saving energy for all concerned.

Unpredictability in the environment, primarily of food resources, tends to act against the formation of individual ranges and to favor larger group territories. An individual with a small territory could face the possibility of a total lack of food in a bad year, whereas with the larger area available, some food is sure to be found. In connection with this generalization, the ecologist Horn did a study of blackbirds that yielded some widely quoted (and apparently widely applicable) results:

If the food supply is evenly distributed in a stable pattern, it is advantageous for pairs to establish territories over which they have more or less exclusive control; if the food supply is both concentrated and shifting in location, it is of advantage for pairs to cluster together in a central location and perhaps forage in flocks [1968:684].

Not only blackbirds but nonhuman primates tend to show these patterns as well. In the forest, gorillas find their food (mainly leaves) rather widely available and evenly distributed, and their groups tend to be small and cohesive with evenly spaced territories. For chimpanzees, however, their food (mainly fruits) is often localized, and this location may change seasonally and annually; chimpanzees tend to show wider dispersal over relatively larger ranges with greater flexibility in group size. Furthermore, out in the savanna grasslands, the chimpanzees' food is even more uneven and unstable, and this seems to explain in part their larger groups, larger ranges, and greater flexibility in this habitat (Itani and Suzili 1967; Izawa 1970; Nishida 1968; Sugiyama 1968, 1969; Suzuki 1969).

The size of territories tends to be correlated with both trophic level and environmental productivity. The ranges or territories of fragivorous herbivores tend to be about four times as large as those of grazing herbivores of the same size, in accord with the different densities of their food resources (Rickleffs 1973:221). Moreover, the greater the productivity of the environment, the smaller the territory tends to be. Table 7.1 presents some figures for bird territories as they vary with habitat.

In part, the nature of defense show some correlation with the size of the territory: the smaller the area, the more active and constant the defense. In general, a carnivore often utilizes more area than it can quickly survey for intruders, and constant defense would be inefficient. In this case, a common solution is to defend aggressively only a small core area, to mark more peripheral zones, and to allow this core area to move in space rather than being fixed. The amount of defense observed also commonly increases with population density and competition for resources.

What does all this mean for human populations? The following might be suggested:

(1) Territories might be more clearly defined with denser and more stable resources (see the excellent discussion of this point by Dyson-Hudson and Smith 1978).
(2) Territories should vary in size with trophic level: larger for hunters than for gatherers or farmers, on a per capita basis.
(3) Territories should vary in size inversely with gross environmental productivity.
(4) The amount of overt defense might vary inversely with the size of territories.
(5) A pattern of core areas more rigorously defended than the margins may be more common than constant surveyance and aggressive defense of the total area.

(6) Markings, advertisements, and displays may be more common than aggression.
(7) Boundary maintenance, by aggression or markings, may increase with population density.

Turning to specific studies, according to Campbell, for the Nunamiut Eskimo:

> The tribal territorial border only approximately circumscribed Nunamiut range, and it is doubtful that for most of its length it was recognized by either the Nunamiut or their neighbors. It was essentially an economic boundary, which separated the resources most suited and necessary to the Nunamiut from either unoccupied lands or those resources that were less suited, and which were being exploited by Eskimos or Indians with different economic orientations and technologies [1968:3].

Among these people there was no overt defensive aggression between bands or, it appears, between the Nunamiut as a whole and their neighbors.

A contrast is provided by the Washo Indians centered around Lake Tahoe; the active defense, at least of a core area, was common. Not incidentally, the Washo derived only 30% of their diet from hunting, whereas the Nunamiut derived at least 70% of their diet from the more mobile animal resources.

> They viewed their territory as a series of layers. In the center was Lake Tahoe and the . . . valleys where they fished and hunted and regularly camped. This land was more or less vigorously defended. . . . Beyond this central zone was a much wider area in which the Washo wandered on hunting and gathering trips during part of the year. . . . It is certain that if one were interviewing Paiute, Maidu, or Miwok informants, the zones described as peripheral Washo would be described as peripheral Paiute, or Miwok, and so on [Downs 1966:5].

Other groups that are highly dependent on the nonmobile plant foods show some of the commonest examples of strongly defended territories (see King 1975).

An interesting point about the Washo is that the entire group territory enclosed all resources, whereas individual or family territories or ownership were defined primarily for plant foods and fish traps—the most stable and least mobile re-

TABLE 7.1

Bird Territories and Habitat Productivity[a]

Habitat (by increasing productivity)	Territory per breeding pair (acres)
Desert	4.5
Prairie	1.1
Chaparral	0.5
Pine forest	0.4
Hardwood forest	0.3
Floodplain forest	0.2

[a] After Ricklefs 1973: 222; reprinted with permission of Chiron Press, Inc.

sources. A similar pattern is seen among the Kaska and Dogrib of Canada: the large tribe or macroband maintained a territory by utilization, and within this area the extended families had territorial rights only to beaver lodges (Helm 1972; Honigmann 1964). Similarly, for the Northern Paiute, each village was a band whose unity and independence was expressed in the habitual cooperation in communal drives of game, in ownership of defined pinon and seed territories, in festivals, and in a common chief and name. Pinon areas were further subdivided into family plots (Suttles 1960).

It may be, consequently, that among many hunters and gatherers, rather stable resources are often owned by individuals or small groups, whereas access to more changing and uneven resources such as big game is usually open to all members of a larger group. There are some puzzling exceptions, however. Among the Kutchin, for example, fish traps are privately owned, whereas beaver lodges and bear dens are not (Osgood 1936). In this case, the fish traps represent not only fixed resources but also considerable concentrations of labor as fixed investments. Furthermore, it must be stressed that an environment may be so fluctuating and unpredictable that even groups dependent heavily on nonmobile plants may not be able to afford to maintain defined, exclusive territories. Defensible resources must be both relatively fixed and reliably productive. In arid regions such as the Kalahari or the Australian Desert, although territories may be defined around waterholes or totemic sites, it is noteworthy that a variety of cultural mechanisms exist to render these territories quite nonexclusive by facilitating the entrance of people into the territories of others. The patterns revealed by an examination of the human–spatial interactions are quite different from those presented by the cultural territorial divisions (Berndt 1972; Lee 1972).

Practices among the Indians of eastern subarctic Canada might also seem puzzling, in as much as family-owned hunting and trapping territories are common. Although some anthropologists have claimed that this practice is aboriginal (Speck 1915), others have argued more convincingly that definite, bounded hunting territories evolved with the introduction of the fur trade, with its competitive nature and its emphasis on smaller, less mobile game (Bishop 1970). In addition, Knight (1965) suggests that changes in the environment and its resources played a significant role in this development. Aboriginally, hunting areas were apparently regularly but not exclusively used.

A common feature of territories or home ranges of hunters and gatherers is that very often they seem to be centered on rivers, waterholes, or lakes, partly because these features form stable resource concentrations, and partly because they offer easy travel possibilities. In many areas, a watershed formed the approximate extent of the territory. Another common feature is that territories often crosscut many different habitats and thus contain a variety of different resources, thereby, providing greater subsistence security. The spatial arrangement of different habitats and resources therefore would be quite important in determining the size and shape of territories.

There also seems to be good correlation between the size of territories and environmental productivity, which is to be expected if territoriality ultimately involves security access to resources. Within the subarctic region of Canada, for example, the hunting territories of two groups have been compared (Hallowell 1949). The Berens River region in the west is quite a bit richer in animals than the Grand Lake Victoria region in the east; in conjunction with these differences, the average hunting territory in Berens River is 93 square miles, while in Grand Lake, the average is 316 square miles for groups of similar size.

Among the Tsembaga and most other agriculturalists, territoriality seems to be much more rigid, with greater fixity of boundaries and more overt defense. As Rappaport states

> The Tsembaga form a single territorial unit as far as defense is concerned and all Tsembaba may hunt, trap and gather in any part of the territory. These rights in nondomesticated resources are exclusive.... Although the entire territory is open to the hunting and gathering activities of all Tsembaga, it is divided into "subterritories," smaller areas claimed by less inclusive groups.... Subterritories are subdivided into smaller areas claimed by smaller patrilineal units.... In the arable zone, these areas are further subdivided into garden sites, generally less than an acre, claimed by individual men [1968:17–19].

The Tsembaga thus have a fixed and hierarchical system of territoriality primarily related to agricultural resources, whereas the wild resources are held in common with little subdivision. Again, the agricultural resources are stable and fixed and like fish traps or deer fences represent an investment of labor in a fixed location also. Because even agricultural plots are not totally secure, some flexibility in this system of territoriality exists: land can be transferred between individuals, subclans, or clans to equalize man–land relationships. Similarly, among the Pokot and many other East African groups, there exists a ranking of land according to the reliability of its agricultural productivity, and the intensity of territoriality correlates with the production reliability (Schneider 1979:74).

Regarding the boundaries of Tsembaga territory, Rappaport makes it clear that aggression (warfare) defined the borders, and that the Tsembaga as a unit were distinguished from other units by joint participation in the fighting that defined these borders. Such borders were not arbitrarily imposed upon the natural environment, however; the east and west boundaries followed watercourses, whereas the others coincided with the major river and the crest of the mountains.

The ultimate cause of such warfare is stressed by Rappaport to be competition over resources. Almost every Maring group shared at least one border with an enemy, and enemies most often occurred on the same side of the river. In other words, an enemy was often the holder of some of the nearest available agricultural land. Relationships across the mountains or the main river more often were friendly, perhaps because the separated groups would not be in direct competition for land. Increasing population density caused people to look to adjacent land first.

The Tsembaga territory, incidentally, was 3.2 square miles in area, with a population of about 200. Compared to the figures for the territories of Canadian Indians (whose group sizes ranged up to about 50), not only is Tsembaga population density much greater, but the territory is also significantly smaller in absolute terms. This Tsembaga territory, in fact, approximates a circle of 1-mile radius, a figure recurring among many other horticultural groups in New Guinea, even those with quite different population densities and sizes. The relative constancy of territorial size may be related to the costs of travel and the ease of communication and defense (Brown and Padolevsky 1976:234). Given a relatively sedentary focus on a fixed resource center, travel costs would limit the defendable area. Among many hunter-gatherers, by contrast, group size and density are much less variable—perhaps related to the greater inelasticity of production and the less developed means of integrating large groups—and so the territory size is more variable (Birdsell 1953).

The boundaries marked by stakes and actively defended by the Tsembaga are those with neighbors on the same side of the main river and mountains, and although they may coincide with streams or other natural features, they do not indicate any significant discontinuity in the distribution of resources. They apparently do not represent any discontinuity in human occupation either. Rappaport mentions that "some of the garden land of the neighboring group is likely to be as close to a man's residence as some of his own" (1968:101). This proximity of members of different groups is even more marked among other New Guinea groups (Healey 1978:204).

Spatial boundaries, consequently, are marked by a variety of means among different groups. Many horticulturalists show fixed, linear territorial borders. For the Nunamiut bands and the Washo, the boundaries took the form of bands of territory claimed by both and used by each: an overlap of home ranges not defended. In these cases, the uncontested zone of overlap appears to consist of heights of land of only marginal subsistence importance. Each group had an exclusive core area capable of providing the major resources.

A different kind of spatial boundary is seen between the Peel River Kutchin and the MacKenzie Eskimo, and between the Chippewa and Sioux in Minnesota, as described by Hickerson (1965). In the latter case, the boundary zone coincided with an ecotone—the transition between forest and prairie—and consisted of a buffer zone virtually empty of human settlement. Both the Chippewa and Sioux made hunting trips into this region after the Virginia deer, but the region was hotly contested, and aggressive warfare characterized any meetings between the two groups in this zone. Hickerson's major point is that this overt aggression was "functional" in an ecological sense. By preventing human settlement in the region, the aggression created a buffer zone that provided a refuge for the major resource, and deer could be maintained against overexploitation. The fact that this refuge was in fact an ecotone meant that it was an extremely productive habitat that was saved from overexploitation: it comprised a zone of concentrated conservation of resources.

The boundary between the Kutchin and the Eskimo also coincides with an ecotone: the border between forest and tundra, between river valley and delta flats (Osgood 1936). The lower 50 miles of the Peel River and the head of the MacKenzie Delta was a neutral no-man's land between the two groups, unoccupied except for occasional summer hunting trips. Meetings between the two groups were marked by fighting in most cases. It may be that this no-man's land had the same effect here as in Minnesota, providing a refuge for resources such as caribou that served to maintain their populations from overexploitation.

This unique kind of spatial boundary between groups, a contested buffer zone, might be expected to exist only in certain situations: where there is extreme variation in the distribution of habitats and where the principal resources underlying competition are highly mobile, such that they can flee to these refuges. Subsistence security is thus not guaranteed by maintaining just a core area, and different groups would be brought into direct competition at their borders. Since their low population density and organizational simplicity preclude permanent maintenance of extensive boundaries, a pattern of sporadic aggression developed.

For the Tsembaga, by contrast, the major contested resource is agricultural land, and leaving a band of unused land between populations does not help increase this resource, although it might conceivably have the effect of enforcing a fallow to restore soil fertility. Some farming groups do, in fact, maintain boundaries similar to those shown by the Chippewa and Sioux. Among the Kofyar of northern Nigeria, two neighboring groups of allied villages carried out intermittent warfare over a period of 23 years (Netting 1974). One of the first effects was the abandonment of villages on the border of the two groups and the subsequent destruction of the buildings and gardens to create an empty strip of wasteland between the two alliances. This no-man's land persisted for the entire period, but instead of having the effect of conserving resources, it led to their destruction, at least in the short run. In fact, the buffer zone did serve as a refuge of sorts: it proved to be an excellent breeding ground for mosquitoes that were major disease vectors.

In this case, as among the Tsembaga and the Chippewa and Sioux, competition for resources led to attempts to assert control, but these attempts assumed differing forms depending on the nature of the contested resources and the size and organization of the contending groups. Fixed linear boundaries imposed on the landscape are more likely with agriculturalists, for whom land is the primary resource, than for hunter–gatherers, whose resources are more mobile. Depending on the effectiveness of aggressive boundary-maintenance activities, however, agricultural territories may take several forms, including contiguous marked regions and areas separated by buffer zones in which opponents have displaced one another. The latter may not appear to be as "rational" a use for the land, but it can follow logically from the competitive processes and the attempts to insure control of adequate resources.

1.1.2. Conservation

Territoriality is essentially a long-term anticipatory strategy of defining and claiming resources. Closely associated with territoriality, and similarly long-term in their orientation, are strategies of resource conservation. Conservation consists of those activities aimed at preventing resource loss or wastage and insuring continued resource productivity in order to assure future human-resource balances. Included among these activities might be such hunter–gatherer practices as rotation of hunting areas, establishment of game refuges, and the regulation of exploitation rates by general norms against overkill or specific limitations on the harvest of particular resources. Horticulturalists may practice conservation through the fallowing of fields and the rotation of plots or crops. Conservation among pastoralists could take the form of the avoidance of killing livestock for meat, the rotation of grazing areas, and the attempt to maintain herd size far above the critical level of reproductive viability.

True, intentional conservation is a long-term, security-oriented strategy, and as such has a number of characteristics. Reinforcement for this type of behavior is necessarily delayed: success can only be assessed after a considerable length of time. For this reinforcement to occur, consequently, there must be a long-term reliable association between the resource and its conservator. Such an association is most reliable with a developed system of territoriality and exclusive ownership of land and herds. Environmental unpredictability, which discourages territoriality, would further discourage conservation by separating the reinforcement from the behavior: a single, unanticipated drought could disrupt any long-term plan of crop rotation. Competition, if it does not result in exclusive territories, may mitigate against conservation, since others might later benefit from one's current practices. In addition, conservation requires an ability to monitor the resources, to detect deterioration. Constant spatial association with the resources by means of sedentism (or traveling with herds) would allow more effective monitoring than periodic encounters typical of nomadic settlement patterns. The monitoring process requires some awareness of the resource's potential for exhaustion and renewal, and hence may be less applicable to certain resources, the productive state of which is hard to estimate. Wild resources, particularly those of oceans and rivers, for example, may be more difficult to assess in this manner than are cultivated plants and domestic animals. In brief, conservation should be more likely as environments become more predictable, as territories and property claims become more exclusive, and as sedentism and dependence upon domesticated resources increases.

A number of practices that have been suggested to function as conservation strategies do not occur in these contexts or seem motivated by concerns other than long-term conservation. Certainly, among the *effects* of various activities may be some conservation of resources, but to label such an effect a "function" suggests that the activity is thereby partially explained. If explanation of behavior implies the ability to predict other occurrences of that behavior, then such functional explanations must be put to this test. For example, divination using caribou shoulder-blades as a guide to the choice of hunting areas among the Naskapi of Labrador has been suggested to function in the conservation of game by randomizing hunting pressure (Moore 1957). Divination is an attempt to increase hunting success not to preserve resources. It may randomize hunting pressure, but only among those few areas already judged most likely to be productive. It is a technique used in conditions of uncertainty, when the available knowledge is insufficient to allow the designation of one area most likely to be productive. In this situation, the environment is sufficiently variable to give rise to such uncertainty, and the game resources are mobile, which precludes their long-term monitoring and exclusive claiming. This is precisely a context in which conservation is unlikely to be reinforced. Any positive effects of randomizing areal hunting pressure are too uncertain, and any benefits from such conservation may not be realized by the persons responsible. Divination would persist in this context, not because it serves an "adaptive (latent) function" of conservation, but rather because it directs hunting with sufficient frequency to productive areas. Such areas may be productive largely because they have been chosen (by divination) from a previously selected (by knowledge, experience, environmental cues) group of areas having high probabilities of success.

Just as it may not be useful to attempt to explain the practice of divination in terms of conservation of resources, so, too, explanations of many other practices by reference to their conservation effects are inappropriate. The fallowing of fields and rotation of plots by swidden farmers, for instance, does indeed have the effect of restoring soil fertility and vegetational growth amenable to easy clearance, and thus might be interpreted as a form of conservation of long-term land productivity. Yet field abandonment is characteristic of all swidden farmers, both those who practice a fairly stable, cyclical field rotation and pioneering groups who constantly clear new ground. The latter, pioneering groups, however, are in no position to benefit from any long-term conservation of the productivity of a particular plot. They are unlikely to return to it to reap the benefits. Consequently, it is more profitable to view such behavior in terms of short-term returns for effort. The cues for field abandonment include declining harvests, greater incidence of pests, and harder work required for weeding. Reinforcements for the abandonment of plots would consist of the higher yields and reduced work of new fields. Land scarcity, by precluding the possibility of new fields, would also preclude reinforcement of field abandonment, leading to permanent cultivation of plots regardless of the negative effects on land conservation.

1.1.3. Storage of Resources

If territoriality and conservation represent long-term maintenance strategies, resource storage is, by contrast, a relatively short-term anticipatory strategy. Through the preparation of meat by freezing, drying, or smoking, and by the stockpiling of grains, storage represents a security strategy aimed at providing sufficient resources for anticipated lean seasons. Storage may also represent a strategy of time efficiency, designed to take advantage of the short-term availability of particular resources. In either case, it implies significant environmental seasonality—strong seasonal contrasts in resource availability and sufficient seasonal regularity that lean seasons may be anticipated. As a result, northern- and temperate-latitude groups of farmers and hunter–gathers should be more likely to practice food storage than tropical groups would be. In the Tropics, moreover, food storage is more difficult because of the rapid rates of deterioration and decay. In low-latitude environments, horticulturalists can frequently spread out planting and harvesting throughout much of the year, whereas harvests are much more temporally restricted in more seasonal environments. Tropical wild resources similarly tend to be available most of the year, obviating the necessity of food storage.

Storage is more likely and necessary not only in predictably and strongly seasonal environments, but also among groups who are relatively sedentary or who show a significant predictability in their seasonal movements. Stored foods represent fixed concentrations of resources. Realization of the benefits of food stores requires that they be accessible during the lean season. Settlement within their vicinity or a certain return to their location insures this accessibility. It has been suggested, for example, that the Chipewyan of the Canadian Barren-Grounds, although coping with a strongly seasonal environment, did not practice much food storage because their highly variable settlement patterns (related to the unpredictability of caribou movements) made it difficult to return to food caches with any degree of certainty (Morris 1972). Sedentism at the site of food stores has the additional advantage of permitting their protection from predators and human competitors. Such sedentism may impose a degree of land efficiency on other productive decisions as a result of the limitations on land availability close to food stores. In a strongly seasonal environment, consequently (manifested by a short rainy season, for example), farmers may increase their security through grain storage, which may require time efficiency during the growing and harvest seasons, and which may impose land efficiency on other resource-use practices. The subsistence economy would represent the outcome of the combination and complex interaction of these environmental factors and such context-related goals.

1.1.4. Storage of Credit and Value

There are a number of contexts in which food storage is not possible, reliable, or sufficient as a means of anticipating resource shortages. Major resources, such as root crops, may be difficult to preserve at all. The abundance of pests and the rapidity of decay—especially in the humid Tropics—may preclude storage even if the resources themselves are amenable to preservation. The natural distribution of wild resources or the production techniques and labor supply of horticulturalists may render surplus production in anticipation of lean seasons difficult. Environmental variability may be such that seasonal shortages, although frequent, may not be predictable and therefore adequately anticipated. In such unpredictable environments, moreover, settlement may need to be so flexible that a certain return to food caches cannot be relied upon. Competition among groups may be sufficiently intense that fixed food stores frequently may be seized and thus cannot be dependable.

In all of these contexts, some alternative to food storage may be required to anticipate resource shortages. A common strategy in such situations is to develop systems of delayed exchange (e.g., Heider 1969). By exchanging a current excess for a future return, people store credit and can expand the time utility of their production into lean periods. Delayed exchange is essentially a strategy that expands the productive base of the practitioner. Intraband food sharing allows individuals to draw upon the production of their fellow band members. Intergroup feasting and counter feasting provides each group with access to the resources of the others.

In discussing delayed exchange as a strategy of anticipating resource shortages, it must be clearly realized that there exist many varieties of exchange transactions at many different levels of social and spatial organization. As an anticipatory strategy, delayed exchange represents a two-way transfer of goods, separated by some timelag, and so must be distinguished from immediate trade, which involves the simultaneous transfer of materials. As a means of dealing with resource scarcity, delayed exchange must represent transactions in goods that are utilized to compensate for their absence or scarcity, and so must be distinguished from ceremonial exchange, which may involve the continuous circulation, without consumption or utilization, of goods that are not necessarily scarce at any point along their flow path.

By focusing on delayed exchange as a strategy, it should be possible to examine its occurrence, organization, and implications in various contexts. As suggested earlier, it may represent an alternative to storage when the latter is not possible or adequate because of resource unsuitability or environmental unpredictability. Like storage, delayed exchange represents an insurance policy with certain costs. Some surplus must be available for exchange—through irregular, accidental abundances (a beached whale, for example), regular natural concentrations (fish runs, nut ripenings), or intensified production (crop harvests, game kills). Unlike storage, delayed exchange necessarily entails a dependence upon others. It represents a structured form of interaction between individuals or groups and must necessarily be conditioned by the characteristics of the parties involved.

For delayed exchange to be effective, for example, exchange partners cannot have the same schedule of shortages. If they practice the same subsistence activities, this means that they must have some differences in production timing, perhaps largely due to environmental variation. Farming groups in close proximity but at different elevations, for example, may have quite different harvest times (Schneider 1979:95). Groups of adjacent desert Aborigines may encounter quite different rainfall patterns. Neighboring Northwest Coastal Indians may have suffered periodic fish shortages at varying times (Piddocke 1965; Suttles 1962). Individual hunters within the same group may have significantly different schedules of success. In each case, one individual or group can share its excesses because its partners are likely to be suffering from relative shortages. Conversely, at a time of shortage, one's partners may be more likely to have an excess. Such differences in production timing may be accentuated when partners practice different activities because of differences in habitat or economy. Many instances of coastal/inland or highland/lowland exchange represent delayed transactions compensating for varying local shortages. The Pomo of California would periodically exchange their local food surpluses in anticipation of later returns from neighbors with different resources (Vayda 1967). Exchange between farmers and herders or farmers and hunter–gatherers similarly depends on the differences in resources and the timing of production between the groups. Some differential in the timing of risk or production is essential to the practice of delayed exchange as a strategy of anticipating resource shortages.

Similarly important is the scheduling of the transactions. Most important, the timing of receipt must coincide with a shortage. If this is not the case, then exchange cannot compensate for local scarcity (it may, of course, be accomplishing other things). In effect, the recipient, the individual or group suffering the shortage, must be able to initiate the incoming transaction, to call upon the stored credit. Among the Usino of Papua New Guinea, for example, a parish leader can initiate a ''wau'' exchange by contacting another parish leader and making his needs known. Specific groups traditionally served as providers of particular goods—that is, sago, sweet potato, meat, coconuts, or taro (Conton and Eisler 1976:141). In many situations, however, the reverse appears to be true: the donor initiates the transaction. If the recipients have no shortages at that time, and yet must accept the goods (as is true, for example, in some ceremonial exchange systems of Melanesia, where big-men are tricked into accepting gifts, Hogbin

1970), then it is doubtful that such a system could provide the necessary subsistence insurance to the groups involved. Frequently, on the other hand, there are sufficiently regular patterns of natural differences in resource productivity between areas that an abundance in one area usually does coincide with a shortage in another. If such is the case, then regardless of who initiates the transactions, a sharing of surpluses will almost automatically help overcome shortages elsewhere. A successful kill by an individual hunter may rarely coincide with that of another of the same group, so that a necessary sharing of the kill may virtually always compensate for shortages encountered by other hunters. Moreover, even in systems where the donor does initiate the transaction, the recipient may be able to refuse and so assume credit debts only when local shortages dictate.

Another implication of delayed exchange serving as a strategy of anticipating resource shortages is that the organization of exchange should reflect the scope of shortages. If shortages occur at different times for different individuals, then exchange by individuals should be more common. Often such individual variation depends on individual differences in skill or luck, as among different hunters. If, on the other hand, shortages are suffered by entire groups, such as droughts affecting whole villages of farmers or whole bands of desert foragers, then exchange at the group level with other groups may be more likely. The level of organization responsible for the transactions should show a direct relationship with the scope of risk and scarcity. Hunters, fishermen, and farmers tend to practice more frequent within-group delayed reciprocity on an individual basis than do gatherers and pastoralists, perhaps due to the greater individual risks associated with the former activities (Pryor 1977:204).

The organization of exchange should also reflect the severity of shortages. The more severe the shortage, the more important becomes the income from delayed exchange. As dependence upon the exchange increases, the more necessary it may be to insure the reliable and timely flow of goods. This insurance may take many forms: reinforcement of the proper reciprocal behavior with high moral status, prestige, and gifts; or institutionalization of the exchange process through the development of specialized coordinators; or threats of physical, social or supernatural sanctions. As shortages become more severe, the exchange should become more structured and more highly sanctioned. The observation that norms of food-sharing become more important toward northern latitudes is in accord with the similar directional increase in seasonality and the harshness of lean seasons (Eggan 1968; Leacock 1973). Similarly, among the Warao of the Orinoco Delta of Venezuela, those local groups who had the most spatially dispersed resources and the poorest and most variable supplies of palm starch had the most elaborate and ritualized systems of food storage and redistribution (Heinen and Ruddle 1974).

In addition, the severity of shortages should directly influence the volume of goods and the number of partners involved. Large shortages require large imports. In an area where intergroup habitat or economic differences are great, group investment in large-scale delayed exchange with one or a few other groups may be possible. In regions where neighboring groups show only slight and unpredictable differences in production, on the other hand, a group may need to maintain exchange relationships with a larger number of groups, to gain access to the productivity of a larger area. It may be that a group could most efficiently maintain such multiple contacts through a number of different individual exchanges rather than acting as a group in exchange. Thus, in some cases, even if shortages affect an entire group, the networks of exchange may be individually maintained. When such a group suffers a shortage its members would then activate their stored credit in other regions, and any incoming goods at the individual level could then be further distributed within the group through strong norms of sharing.

These responses to severe shortages and a heavy dependence upon delayed exchange as subsistence security could, when sufficiently important, provide a context favorable to the storage of value and credit in some type of currency. Sahlins (1972:228–229) notes that "primitive money" seems to be most important among those groups for whom delayed, balanced reciprocity with other groups is most significant. It can be suggested here that such groups can be found largely in certain contexts: where periodic shortages occur and storage is inadequate to deal with them, and social organization is such that any group cannot control regions with sufficient environmental heterogeneity to compensate for local shortages. In these contexts, if the shortages are severe enough, delayed exchange becomes more important and structured, higher volumes of goods may be exchanged, and wider areal networks linking different groups may be necessary. A currency or medium of exchange would be useful in these contexts because it would (1) facilitate the translation of exchange values among the numerous interacting groups; (2) help keep track of the large values exchanged; and (3) help insure the completion of transactions in which it is involved by its identity as an object constantly and everywhere of high value. Furthermore, a medium of exchange would be particularly useful in situations with long time lags between transactions: the longer the delay, the more difficult it may be to keep track of debts without such a device. Primitive money helps store value, translate values, and insure exchange, all of which may be necessary with crucial, widespread, high-volume, delayed exchanges.

This discussion of delayed exchange as a strategy of anticipating resource shortages has concentrated on relating this strategy to its context. As the context varies, so should the importance and organization of delayed exchange. Few specific cases of exchange have been examined in favor of an attempt to isolate characteristics of exchange that vary and that should be studied. All types of exchange do not compensate for resource shortages, nor are all shortages anticipated by systems of delayed exchange. An understanding of how exchange behavior related to human-resource balances requires investigation of the goods transferred, the frequency and timing of exchanges, the process of initiation of transactions, the volume of goods, the number and situation of partners, the scale and organization of exchange, and the degree of management and reinforcement.

1.1.5. Population Control

Other practices that, in part, may represent strategies of anticipating resource shortages are the various forms of population control. When confronted with the probability of imbalances between population and resources, groups or individuals may focus on the population side of the equation rather than on the resource side. This may be particularly likely when there are few options available for making more resources available. Depending on the situation, for example, there may be few alternative or additional resources to exploit, the intensification of production may be restricted by limited knowledge or means, storage may be impractical or insufficient, and neighbors may be unreliable providers during times of need. This latter situation may prevail in areas where adjacent groups have few differences in environment or economy, or when potential surpluses in good seasons are barely larger than a local group's needs, and hence any networks of delayed exchange would be unreliable or inadequate insurance. In such situations, the maintenance of population levels well below those supportable in the present—and geared to anticipated lean times—may represent one of the few strategies available.

A frequent observation about the population levels of hunter–gatherers (Ammerman 1975; Birdsell 1953; Casteel 1972; Hassan 1978) and horticulturalists (Carneiro 1960; Rappaport 1968) is that they often do tend to be much lower than the environment and economy would seem capable of supporting. A common ecological interpretation of this phenomenon invokes some form of Liebig's "Law of the Minimum": population levels of organisms are generally determined, not by the average or best food conditions, but rather by the worst conditions normally encountered within a period corresponding to the breeding cycle of the organism. That is, although once-a-century catastrophes may not be critical to most organisms, yearly or biannual lean periods may be crucial in determining population levels of many animals. If this Law of the Minimum applies to humans as well, then the worst conditions encountered within each generation—perhaps over a 20-year period—may be more important to population levels than are more usual conditions. A crucial difference between humans and other animals, of course, is that cultural transmission can augment individual experience, so that individuals may be aware of conditions in the past, enlarging their time frame of reference. For humans it may well be that the worst conditions over the past 100 years are remembered and are, indeed, of some significance to current population levels. A determination of the time scale relevant to human behavior remains an important research objective.

Demographic anthropology is clearly a large topic, complicated by controversies about carrying capacities (Brush 1975; Hayden 1975; Street 1969; Zubrow 1975), population equilibria (Ammerman 1975; Birdsell 1953), population growth (Cohen 1977; Cowgill 1975; Spooner 1972), and population control (Baumhoff 1963; Divale 1972; Douglas 1966; Dumond 1975; Hayden 1972; Nag 1962; Stott 1962). Whatever the time frame one utilizes, and however one measures resource abundance, there does, at least, seem to be some patterned relationship between resource availability and population size and density. Such a relationship is a necessary result if population control is used as a strategy to anticipate resource shortages. Another necessary implication of such a strategy is that there be a clear linkage between the initiation of population-control techniques and the perception of anticipated shortages. Such shortages may be anticipated in two general ways. First of all, a single gradual process of increasing relative scarcity may be perceived, so that a subsequent more severe shortage appears likely. Second, a repeated series of shortages may be experienced, so that future shortages come to be expected. In either situation, a relative shortage (chronic or acute) in the present serves as a cue for shortages in the future. Acute shortages, if they result in significant malnutrition, may have marked biological effects depressing fertility, whereas chronic scarcity may have few such biological effects (Bongaarts 1980). In both cases, cultural population control measures may be initiated once the shortage is perceived.

Scarcity may be perceived through hunger and declining resource variety, but in general, shortages—particularly chronic and gradually increasing scarcity—are rarely experienced through starvation (Hayden 1972). Consequently, famine is rarely the cue initiating population control. Rather, a variety of measures of procurement effort would show changes as the human–resource balance gradually worsened, and these changes in work load may be the most common means by which shortages are perceived and to which population-control measures are linked. Such measures of work might include work hours per day, distance traveled in procurement per day, and frequency of necessary shifts of camp or procurement areas (Hayden, 1972). Another measure of relative resource shortages might be provided by the intensity of competition and frequency of disputes over resources.

With the onset of relative scarcity, consequently, a number of processes may begin, each with potential effects on population. Acute malnutrition, if it occurs, may biologically depress fertility. Decreasing resource abundance and variety may encourage longer nursing of infants so that additional foods need not be provided to them. One of the major effect of such prolonged lactation seems to be a biological depression of fertility (Bongaarts 1980). Competition and disputes may increase, leading, perhaps, to aggressive conflict and some adult mortality, reducing population levels. None of these processes, however, is invitable, and none needs to be viewed as a strategy of population control. In each case, the effects on population levels appear to be secondary effects of the process. Prolonged lactation will be reinforced if it channels more food to older children and adults and simultaneously allows the survival of infants. Conflict will be reinforced if it results in higher food intakes or greater access to other resources for the initiating group. Any dampening of population represents a delayed, secondary effect that may happen to contribute to the conditions of reinforcement.

Each of these processes may be avoided in some situations of scarcity by behavioral responses that entail more work. Hunger and conflict may be avoided by increasing resource procurement through expanded effort. It is this higher work load, whether experienced through longer hours or greater travel, that may ultimately trigger specific strategies of population control.

These specific strategies are those practices that have as their primary observable effect the reduction of population, either by decreasing fertility or increasing mortality. The major forms of such specific controls are abstinence, contraception, abortion, and infanticide. If viewed as strategies of population control anticipating resource shortages, then these practices should vary in their importance and frequency with the context of scarcity. For example, they all represent essentially individual behavior and thus may be strategies most suitable in situations of varying individual shortages. If the resource imbalances are widespread and affect entire groups, then such practices may be embedded in more formally articulated population policies. Elaborate and strongly sanctioned rules of abstinence and sexual segregation, for example, may be more common in contexts of generalized occurrences of shortages. Moreover, these techniques of population control, especially abortion and infanticide, are largely female responsibilities, and so may be initiated more often when female work load increases. It might even be worth investigating to what extent the availability of wild or domesticated plants and thus the effort of gathering or weeding might be more significant to population levels than is the availability of wild game or domesticated livestock, given the usual sexual division of labor.

The four practices of abstinence, contraception, abortion, and infanticide interrupt the normal reproductive process at different times: at conception, during gestation, and at birth. The longer this process is allowed to continue, the greater the biological or energetic investment in the infant. Infanticide, especially, appears to be a costly and wasteful practice; its widespread occurrence must derive from particular benefits it offers. By viewing infanticide and the other techniques of population control as strategies, their differing contexts of suitability may be suggested. First of all, the strategies differ in the certainty of their effect. Infanticide can be always successful: killing an infant by smothering, impaling, or bashing its head can remove it from the population with certainty. Abortion is not so reliable. The various techniques of administering herbal inducers or inflicting abdominal trauma cannot be guaranteed to work. The same can be said for most methods of contraception. Abstinence must surely be the least effective, regardless of the rules and sanctions established. The differing efficacy of these techniques would render them suitable in different contexts. The more imperative the control of population, perhaps, the more reliable the technique chosen. On the other hand, if elaborate rules of abstinence tend to be a group strategy, then the net effect of even weak compliance may be some reliable reduction in birth rates for the group.

Another difference among the techniques concerns the risks they impose. Abortion is notoriously risky to mothers; the use of this technique would regularly remove both fetuses and some women from the population. Although one effect would be even more effective population reduction, this may be intolerable for a number of reasons. If women control the practice, they may be willing to take the risk only in certain circumstances, when the work of maintaining the infant, the emotional trauma of killing a live baby, or the wrath of husbands in cases of adultery outweigh the personal danger. Moreover, men may not want to risk losing a wife they know, finding it easier to wait and kill a live baby who is effectively a stranger. On a more materialistic level, women may be sufficiently scarce or sufficiently economically important that they cannot be risked by abortion. The presence of other children and the nature of female economic contributions may be factors relevant to the choices of abortion over other methods of population control.

In addition, these various techniques have different characteristics in terms of the degree of anticipation and the flexibility of response. The sooner the shortages can reliably be anticipated, the more efficient (in terms of biological costs) it is to interrupt the reproductive process early. Abstinence and contraception would be most suitable in situations where shortages can be predicted well in advance. Abortion requires less anticipation, whereas infanticide can be activated relatively much later. All these methods would have long-term effects, but they pose different requirements in terms of the lead-time in anticipating the needs. Infanticide may be more common in situations of acute, rapid-onset shortages. Furthermore, by delaying the interruption of reproduction, infanticide may provide much more flexibility of responses than does abortion or especially abstinence. By relying on abstinence, people commit themselves to a course of action 9 months earlier than they would if they relied on infanticide. If the environment or the economic situation changes in the meantime, the limiting of population may become unnecessary or even inappropriate. A reliance on infanticide allows people to change their minds, to respond to more recent and complete information. This flexibility offered by infanticide would be most valuable in variable environments where shortages are difficult to predict. The fact that in the cross-cultural distribution of different population-control techniques there are "regional differences, for which we still lack explanation" (Dickeman 1975:114), should prompt an investigation of the different regional contexts as they relate to the strategic characteristics. The high frequency of infanticide in

Australia and among the Eskimos may be related to the degree of variability and unpredictability in the desert and arctic environments. The fact that Eskimo children may be abandoned to die, only to be subsequently adopted by others, exemplifies additional flexibility in population-control methods. The relative rarity of both abortion and infanticide in much of agricultural Africa may suggest a less frequent occurrence of shortages, a greater importance of abstinence related to the occurrence of more predictable shortages, or the practice of strategies other than population control for coping with shortages.

Some of these other strategies have been discussed: territoriality, storage of resources, and storage of credit by delayed exchange. Each of these has a different set of requirements and implications, and hence, each may be more or less possible and reinforced in different contexts. Territoriality and food storage require certain characteristics of resources and their distribution and both have implications for settlement behavior. Delayed exchange requires some differentiation among interacting groups and has implications for regional social and economic behavior. Population control also has its specific characteristics. As a strategy it requires varying degrees of anticipation, but its effects are uniformly long term. It may be a slower acting response to anticipated shortages, requiring more lead time to initiate. It carries a risk of being too successful, of reducing population sufficiently that random, unanticipated population fluctuations can then lead to extinction of the family or group. Moreover, by reducing the number of mouths to feed, it also reduces the number of laborers available. In contexts of higher labor needs, this effect may be intolerable. Population control, therefore, may be a strategy most common when there exist few needs for large, concentrated labor forces, as is the case among the Aborigines and Eskimos. A frequent use for large labor forces is for defense, which may be most common in situations of competition and high population densities. Pardoxically, then, it may be that high population densities mitigate against population control, all other things being equal. In those situations where both defense and population control are found to be important, a common compromise strategy is to practice selective female infanticide, which reduces population but selectively provides the male work force necessary for defense (Chagnon 1968; Divale 1972).

1.2. Compensatory Strategies

Individuals and groups will frequently face resource shortages that are unexpected. If existing anticipatory strategies have not been or cannot be initiated, or are inadequate, then some immediate responses are necessary to correct the human–resource imbalances. Such responses may take one of two general forms: the redistribution of resources or the redistribution of people. Resources can be redistributed peacefully through trade or aggressively through confiscations and conquest. People may be redistributed through voluntary migration or forceful expulsion. Compensatory strategies, consequently, may involve forms of exchange, warfare, and migration. Each of these represents complex behavior of which only certain general aspects will be discussed here. Not all forms or instances of trade, fighting, and movement are strategies for correcting relative resource deficiencies, but some of the contexts in which this does occur may be suggested.

1.2.1. Redistribution of Resources

The redistribution of resources involves the transfer of goods from areas of abundance to areas of scarcity. As an alternative to the redistribution of people, it should occur in contexts in which the latter is less efficient, less reliable, or less feasible. If, for example, a shortage represents a scarcity of particular goods rather than a generalized resource failure, the movement of just these few goods may be the more efficient response. When the scarce goods are highly portable, their exchange may be relatively easy, whereas a shortage of land or water may require the redistribution of people. If a shortage is expected to be quite short-term, then the import of supplies may be much cheaper than a shift in residence. A relatively sedentary settlement pattern with large·investments of energy and capital in fixed locations may anchor people to these sites and render the redistribution of materials cheaper and more likely. Spatial diversity in the environment may cause each of several important resources to be discretely distributed with little overlap. When coupled with a lack of seasonal mobility (as may be true of settled farmers), utilization of all resources may make the exchange of goods necessary, especially if such spatially separated resources are available briefly and simultaneously, as may be true in highly seasonal environments.

On a general level, then, the movement of goods is increasingly likely when (1) the scarcity involves fewer goods, (2) the scarce goods are increasingly portable, (3) resources are increasingly nonoverlapping in spatial distribution, (4) resources are increasingly overlapping in temporal distribution, and (5) human residential mobility becomes increasingly difficult. Trade and raids, consequently, should involve only a few of the total spectrum of resources utilized, most particularly, lightweight materials, small processed or manufactured goods, or resources such as livestock, which are themselves mobile. Trade and raids should be more common in environments with pronounced spatial heterogeneity and temporal seasonality and among groups with substantial residential stability.

The movement of goods through either trade or raid has a number of requirements. Transportation routes and means must be adequate to the level of interaction required. If groups are separated by obstacles such as swamps or mountains and travel is by foot, then the high transportation costs may limit trade to infrequent exchange of goods of high value. In such situations of high costs, trade would become increasingly unlikely as the needs increase in volume or frequency; a group isolated by such transportation barriers and facing a shortage would more likely resort to out-migration or to local subsistence intensification and changes. If two groups differ significantly in their potential mobility as a result of access to differing modes of travel, then raiding becomes a more likely option for the more mobile group, since retaliation by the other would be difficult. The frequency of raids by mounted hunters or pastoralists on sedentary farmers is due largely to this mobility difference, as is clear in a study of the Hehe of East Africa, where "the greater the agricultural involvement the greater the risk of domination by more mobile neighbors" (Winans 1965:437). Raiding becomes increasingly feasible as the goods are more movable. Cattle and other livestock are the most frequent plunder obtained by raiding, and there exists a high correlation between pastoralism and raiding activities (Goldschmidt 1965; Pryor 1977; Schneider 1979).

Furthermore, the movement of goods requires neighbors, a context that is not necessary for the movement of people. The choice of trading or raiding then might depend, not only on transportation facilities, but also on the resources available to both groups. Trading requires that each group have a surplus to exchange at the same time. Differences in environment or subsistence economy between the groups may easily permit such simultaneous surpluses, in which case some degree of specialized economic intensification may be encouraged among both, with a consequent greater land efficiency of exploitation overall. If one group does not have a surplus of natural resources or subsistence products, then the production of specialized manufactures may be necessary in order to have goods to exchange for desired materials, thereby creating economic differences between the groups. Trade requires such differences and may serve as the context for increasing specialization and productive efficiency by both parties.

Raiding, on the other hand, requires no surpluses by either side. The raiders simply need sufficient mobility, organization, and manpower to carry out the attack. If their targets have surpluses of livestock or stored goods, this may make the raid more rewarding, but raided groups need not have such excesses: their everyday stocks of goods and animals may provide sufficient plunder. In a sense, raiding represents a specialized procurement technique that may be more efficient in some contexts than is producing a surplus for exchange. The productive efficiency and security of the raided groups, of course, are decreased in this situation. Trade represents a symbiotic relationship that is reinforcing to both sides; raids are a parasitic or predatory relationship of advantage only to the raiders. Raids represent aggressive competition for the same resources, whereas trade is mutualistic exploitation of multiple resources, avoiding competition.

Trade is often accompanied by or blends into two other similar forms of behavior: delayed exchange and ceremonial exchange. As strategies, these three types of activity can be differentiated. Trade is the immediate exchange of goods to be utilized or consumed. To the extent that it widens the food base or represents a compensation for shortages or deficits of vital subsistence goods, it enhances security. At the same time, however, it may be a strategy chosen not so much out of absolute necessity but because it enhanced efficiency. It may be a relatively cheap way of increasing resource variety or obtaining desired goods. It may stimulate efficiency of land or time use to produce a surplus for exchange. It may have the effect of enlarging the resource base of the participants, overcoming local shortages, and raising the regional carrying capacity accordingly. Delayed exchange, as previously discussed, also involves the transfer of goods for use, but with a time lag between the component transactions of the exchange. Like trade it can augment subsistence security and may encourage productive efficiency. The inclusion of a time lag, however, allows much more flexibility in matching supply with demand, and thus delayed exchange can more effectively anticipate and compensate for shortages, thereby contributing more to subsistence security. As subsistence risks become less predictable, therefore, delayed exchange should be favored over immediate trade.

Ceremonial exchange is quite different (Healey 1978; Sillitoe 1978). It largely entails the transfer of goods that are frequently exchanged further without being utilized or consumed, so that they simply pass through an individual or group, often in a cyclical fashion. The transfers occur in a context of prestations involving elaborate display and formalized behavior. Commonly the goods involved show little variation in local occurrence or abundance, so that their movement cannot compensate for local scarcity. Ceremonial exchange is less concerned with the goods themselves than with the social relations generated by the interaction. Among the Wola of Papua New Guinea, for example, ceremonial exchange never occurs between strangers, whereas 44% of the trade is, in fact, between individuals with no other or previous ties (Sillitoe 1978). In this form, ceremonial exchange is not a maintenance strategy to overcome human–resource imbalances, but rather a strategy of management, aimed at reinforcing other behaviors crucial to survival and at avoiding or resolving conflict. As such, it will be discussed in the next chapter.

Some attention, nevertheless, must be given here to ceremonial exchange, since it frequently occurs simultaneously with and supports trade or in some instances includes or supplants it. That is, ceremonial exchange can provide the vehicle and context for the movement of goods from areas of abundance to areas of scarcity and can involve goods that are utilized or consumed rather than passed on. In many parts of New Guinea, in fact, both trade and ceremonial exchange involve the same goods: pigs, pork, shells, plumes, axes, and salt (Healey 1978). The intertwining of social and material exchanges is a frequent observation in the literature (Alkire 1972; Harding 1978; McCarthy 1939; Sahlins 1965; Whitten and Whitten 1972). If these can be conceptually separated, however, then perhaps their differing strategic importance can be analyzed. When ceremonial exchange does account for the movement of goods to be utilized, it tends to show a number of differences as discussed here. Although trade tends to be immediate, ceremonial exchange is usually delayed. As suggested in the discussion of delayed exchange, when there exists a time lag, there is a risk of a failure to reciprocate. In this case, the ceremonial context may help to insure the return on an investment by channeling the transaction into a defined set of roles and activities, by placing it in a public arena, and by subjecting it to heavy social rewards and sanctions. Moreover, ceremonial exchange, unlike trade, often involves the concept of interest. Repayments are often expected to be somewhat larger than the original transaction (Healey 1978). The expectation of interest also acts as an incentive for repayment because the subsequent return will be even larger; it helps to perpetuate debt and thereby the ongoing series of exchanges.

In addition, trade tends to be a more individual activity, whereas ceremonial exchange is more often group organized. By its very nature, that is, by placing material transactions in public view and investing them with social significance, ceremonial exchange requires group participation and group agreement. There exist differences, however, in the level of group involvement. Strathern (1969) has discussed these differences in terms of a continuum between reliance upon "production" and use of "finance" to underwrite ceremonial exchanges in New Guinea. A big-man or aspirant who relies upon production derives the goods for prestations from his own household or settlement. One who depends on finance, on the other hand, draws upon the additional productivity of a number of others from different settlements who stand in partnership in relation to him. Production depends on the work and decisions of only a relatively few people, but its potential volume of goods is limited, and hence it is a technique not conducive to exchange systems involving interest accumulation that would consistantly increase the demands on productivity. Finance, by contrast, offers the potential for expanded productivity, and therefore, may be more suitable when exchanges involve the spiralling of interest accumulation. On the other hand, finance is riskier: it necessitates the dependence on the work and decisions of many people whose continued cooperation must be maintained. One further difference between the two techniques concerns the goods exchanged. Production often involves slaughtered pigs, whereas finance more frequently deals in live pigs and shells. These latter goods can circulate over much greater distances and longer periods than can pork without adequate preservation techniques and so are compatible with larger regional exchange networks.

In discussing these different forms of ceremonial exchange, Strathern arranges in order six New Guinea groups according to an increasing reliance on finance rather than production: Maring, Siane, Chimbu, Mendi, Hagen, and Enga. Interestingly, this arrangement of groups tends to order them according to increasing population density as well. Furthermore, Healey (1978) has compared the importance of trade and ceremonial exchange in general, and for three groups

(Maring, Melpa, and Enga) he has demonstrated a decreasing reliance upon trade and an increasing importance of ceremonial exchange as population density increases. We have, then, the suggestion of a pattern. Groups with relatively low population densities (such as the Maring) emphasize trade, and what ceremonial exchange does occur is based on local production, involves pig slaughters, and has a relatively small area of distribution. Groups with higher population densities, by contrast, increasingly emphasize ceremonial exchange at the expense of immediate trade, and this ceremonial exchange tends to be based increasingly on regional financing partnerships, involves greater use of live pigs and durable valuables, and has an increasingly larger spatial extent.

The determinants of this pattern must be exceedingly complex. Since ceremonial exchange is largely a management strategy for reinforcing a variety of types in interactions and avoiding conflict, then its importance depends largely on the necessity of such reinforcement and the risk of conflict. Since ceremonial exchange can also represent a maintenance strategy of highly formalized delayed exchange, then its importance also depends on the nature of anticipated shortages and the means available to deal with them. On a very general level, at least, the following may be suggested in contexts of high population density:

(1) Individuals and groups have many potential interpersonal contacts and a greater choice of interaction channels; the perpetuation of their participation in just a few of the possible networks—the limitation of their choices—requires that the desired behavior be strongly reinforced.

(2) The potential for competition and conflict is high, simply because of the large numbers of potentially competing and conflicting demands, aims, and strategies; the need to avoid and resolve conflict would be correspondingly high.

(3) Individuals cannot be dispersed to any significant degree; thus any shortages due to natural factors are likely to affect a number of people simultaneously, and hence, responses are likely to occur on a group level.

(4) The balance of resources to population may be relatively precarious because of either high relative demand or intensified production with a resulting lack of production flexibility and diversity, so that any stresses may cause relatively severe shortages; delayed systems of exchange, consequently, should be more crucial and therefore more formalized, highly sanctioned, and more likely to involve interest accumulation.

(5) The potential for relatively severe shortages may require that large volumes of goods be transferred; such high-volume exchange may be organized most profitably at the group level, and may need to extend over large areas.

Investigations of exchange must take into consideration the types, amounts, distribution, and uses of goods; the costs, timing, and organization of transactions; and the nature of similarities and differences among participants. Functions of exchange cannot be assumed without an examination of such factors.

1.2.2. Redistribution of People

An alternative compensatory response to resource shortage is to redistribute people rather than goods. This alternative would appear to be more suitable in a variety of situations. Generalized resource shortages or a scarcity of a few crucial subsistence goods may pose problems for which exchange is inadequate or too unreliable. Exchange may be incapable of compensating for shortages of relatively immobile goods, particularly land, and be unable to deal with long-term scarcity on a large scale. Movement of people may be relatively easier than trade mechanisms in contexts of normally high residential mobility and limited material culture.

An example of the differential emphasis on moving goods or moving people depending on the context is provided by Suttles' (1968) discussion of Northwest Coast cultures of North America. From south to north along this coast there exists a resource gradient of decreasing variety and increasing seasonal and local variation and spatial concentration at a few fixed locations. Corresponding to this resource gradient and in accord with general principles of territoriality, there is also a northward tendency toward more rigidly defined resource ownership, greater sedentism, and more clearly defined group membership. More northerly groups are marked by more frequent endogamy and greater institutionalization of leadership and ranking. More southerly groups, by contrast, are more fluid: they tend to stress local exogamy, have less rigid group membership, and give greater emphasis to affinal ties among individuals of different groups. The northern groups, therefore, are more fixed in spatial and social units. Their normally low mobility and ties to relatively few fixed resource locations impede the movement of people in times of stress. As a result, northern groups emphasize the redistribution of goods as a coping device: individual mobility is rare, but food and wealth generally move quite freely. Potlatches are brief but more frequent and more important in moving foods than are potlatches further south. The more southerly groups, on the other hand, stress the movement of people as a strategy of adjustment. They have more abundant and varied resources that are less spatially concentrated, and so territorial claims and property rights are less rigid and seasonal mobility is more pronounced. Flexible and indistinct rules of group membership and intergroup affinal ties help make the redistribution of people possible.

On a more general level, consideration must be given to the fact that some groups have access to adjacent lands that are unoccupied, and so a strategy of redistributing people may promote the colonization of these empty lands. As the colonization process is frequently portrayed, normal local population growth leads to a "budding-off" of a portion of the local group and a migration into unoccupied regions. An increasing local population density would raise the potential for disputes and competition, and the development of antagonistic factions is often the factor responsible for the budding-off process. Local population growth and high population density, however, are not necessary to colonization: sparse local populations, if subjected to a sudden resource shortage, may partially or totally abandon their areas in favor of new, unoccupied lands, especially if the presence of such empty regions precludes exchange with any nearby groups. Such a shortage would, of course, increase the *relative* population density, but this situation may develop at any level of absolute numbers of people per square kilometer. The original peopling of North and South America occurred in a context of quite low absolute population densities, whereas later European and Asian movements into these continents derived from societies with rather high absolute densities. In each case, movement was from an area of high to one of low absolute density, but even this may not always be the case, as the frequent cases of urban inmigration from rural hinterlands indicate. All of these cases may be better understood if they are viewed as a movement down a *relative* population gradient. Absolute population densities must be evaluated in relation to the resources or opportunities available. Resource shortages as well as population growth can raise the relative density and encourage migration at any level of absolute population size and density.

The individuals who actually move from a local area, whether into empty lands or not, are those who have evaluated their local situation in relation to the perceived opportunities in other areas and have found them lacking. Disputes may not even be necessary as a precipating factor of the move; simply a reexamination of opportunities may lead to emigration. In cases of severe and widespread shortages, these individuals may constitute all of the original local group, and total abandonment may ensue. More frequently, however, such individuals make up a minority who have less access to local resources, less likelihood of success in intragroup conflict, and fewer investments in local facilities to tie them down. It is frequently, therefore, the younger, the poorer, and the less influential who choose to move out. In cases of coercive expulsion rather than peaceful emigration, it is also usually these individuals who leave, not because they choose to, but because those with greater access to resources and authority force them out because of threats to the established economy and society. By stressing the relative poverty (in goods and influence) of the emigrants, it is not being proposed that only the lowest tier of society (however this is defined—by status, wealth, or simply hunting success) emigrates. Rather, because social groupings are usually along kinship lines, and since extended kin groups may often contain a cross section of levels of wealth and influence, the emigrants often will represent such a cross section as well. It is only that, as a group, the emigrants will have less access to local goods and authority, and thus will both have the most to gain by moving away and offer the least effective resistance to expulsion.

Usually the redistribution of people does not occur in a context where empty land is available. More commonly, there are neighbors all around and people must seek refuge in times of stress with one of these adjacent groups. Whenever this strategy is advantageous to each of the neighboring groups (for example, in regions of generalized unpredictability, but where specific shortages tend to affect only one or a few groups at any one time, i.e., *spatial* variation in the *timing* of risks), one would expect that the groups would be characterized by a variety of mechanisms that facilitate the redistribution of people. Briefly, such mechanisms should include spatially extensive (rather than intensive) social relationships and flexible criteria of group membership. These are precisely the type of features—exogamy, an emphasis on interareal affinal ties, and loosely defined group membership—that differentiate groups of the southern Northwest Coast from their northern neighbors.

Social flexibility must be accentuated so that social paths can direct and facilitate spatial movement. In the earlier discussion of the composition of residential groups, it was stressed that flexibility of group composition is maintained in a variety of situations marked by environmental variability and unpredictability—precisely those contexts where shortages are likely. Correlating with this flexibility are extensive areal networks maintained through marriage ties, partnerships, section systems, name relationships, or exchange. Here, then, is another context for exchange (most commonly, ceremonial exchange). Ceremonial exchange, often involving the continuous circulation of nonscarce items, can be seen as a device for maintaining social ties that can be activated to allow the reception of refugees into other areas and groups. For the movement of people to occur, not only must social channels exist, but they must also be reaffirmed and reinforced. This reinforcement is one of the aspects of ceremonial exchange as a management strategy.

In several situations, however, the practice of redistributing people may not be advantageous to all groups in a region, and so extensive ties may not be maintained. On the one hand, the environmental unpredictability may be localized and the threat of shortages limited largely to one group. There may exist *spatial* differences in the *amount* of risk. No matter how much a group may want to extend its relationships and emigrate in times of scarcity, its more secure neighbors would not have similar needs. In this case, two options may be available to the group experiencing scarcity: the use of force against neighbors, either to obtain plunder or to expel them and appropriate their land, and the emigration to a neighbor's lands on the neighbor's terms. These terms would likely be very different from those of a group that is equally insecure and would probably take the form of some type of subjugation: the bartering of labor for food or some type of client–patron relationship. The client or laborer loses freedom of choice in the process because the patron controls the means of reinforcement. The alternatives of raiding or conquest are risky, with the specific costs and dangers depending on the size and organization of the groups involved.

Another context in which a strategy of redistributing people through social networks would not be advantageous on a regional scale would be one of widespread unpredictability combined with widespread simultaneity of specific shortages: *spatial uniformity* in both the *amount and timing* of risk. An afflicted group in such a situation may find emigration to other regions unrewarding and actively discouraged by its neighbors. No matter how close the ties to people in another village, individuals may find themselves quite unwelcome if those people are facing scarcity. In the absence of a secure and productive refuge, the alternative may be force, that is, raiding, warfare, and conquest.

1.2.3. Warfare

The use of force has been mentioned in several contexts. It may represent a strategy of redistributing goods in the form of raids and confiscation. It may, on the other hand, be one strategy of redistributing people through expulsion and conquest. In both cases, it would help to compensate for imbalances of people and resources. Warfare, like exchange, however, is a complex and multipurpose phenomenon. It may also help to deal with shortages of labor or mates by providing slaves and wives. Warfare may, in addition, be one type of management strategy, effective in settling disputes, resolving competing aims and strategies, and enhancing an individuals's or group's ability to control reinforcement and thus behavior. The discussion here will be focused on war as a maintenance strategy dealing with resource shortages. Although analytically difficult to separate, the management role of warfare will be considered in Chapter 8.

Warfare as a strategy of redistributing people and resources is one alternative alongside trade and emigration. Since the ease and effectiveness of these latter strategies vary according to context, one approach to understanding when warfare and raiding occur would be through the identification of those contexts in which trade or emigration are inadequate or difficult. Trade is most effective in alleviating limited deficits of specified items; as shortages become larger in magnitude and encompass a greater variety of goods, some alternative or additional strategy may be necessary. The redistribution of goods by either trade or raids requires that the goods be portable; when scarce goods are fixed, the redistribution of people through emigration or warfare is necessary. Emigration to neighbors' territories is most effective when all groups concerned face similar degrees of risk, but at different times; as shortages become more spatially localized or more temporally synchronized, emigration becomes less possible and desirable. Figure 7.1 summarizes these generalizations.

As a strategy of redistributing people in relation to resources, consequently, warfare should be most likely when (1) shortages involve large amounts of various nonportable goods; and (2) either neighboring groups have different degrees of environmental unpredictability and risk or neighboring groups tend to suffer shortages at the same time.

Generalized stress on all resources as well as specific scarcity of land,

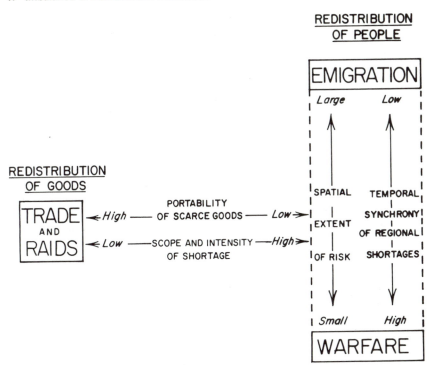

Fig. 7.1. Determinants of strategies for correcting human-resource imbalances.

waterholes, or productive fishing spots would represent likely contexts for aggressive warfare to compensate for these shortages. In such situations, if one group tends to face shortages much more frequently than its neighbors, it may be unable to build up peaceful relations with neighbors willing to accept its emigrants. This would occur because the neighbors would find little profit in such relationships unless they extracted labor in exchange. There may be gradients of increasing subsistence risk running from coasts toward the interior, from major river valleys inland, and from lowlands to highlands, and if so, then warfare may be relatively frequent among groups along these gradients. At the same time, groups along adjacent stretches of rivers or coasts, or within the same general lowland or highland region, may be more likely to experience simultaneous shortages, and thus more likely resort to warfare among themselves. In short, warfare is likely both *across* environmental boundaries because of differential risk and *within* environmental zones because of simultaneity of stress. One of the few possible categorical statements about the natural environmental context of warfare is that it is unlikely to be used to redistribute people in regions that are relatively homogeneous in terms of the degree of risk but heterogeneous in the timing of that risk. An environment that fits this description best is the desert. Warfare as a means of redistributing people may be unlikely within arid lands because rainfall tends to be scarce throughout large areas but varies in its spatial occurrence at any one time. All groups would face similar risks but at different times and so would all benefit from mutually supported strategies of intergroup ties and emigration. A "Golden Rule" of hospitality may be most advantageous to all concerned within desert environments.

Warfare is not, of course, impossible in deserts, but rather, it is unlikely to be practiced as a strategy for the redistribution of people because of the distribution of natural risks. Since warfare may do other things, it may well occur in such environments, but as a different strategy. In addition, subsistence risks depend on more than the natural environment; they depend as well on the subsistence economy and other factors. Where different economies are practiced with the same general arid habitat—for example, irrigation agriculture and pastoralism— differences are imposed on the habitat, and the nature and timing of risks among groups would vary considerably. Warfare to redistribute people within arid lands may be more likely as economic differences among groups increase.

A strict environmental approach to the occurrence of warfare, consequently, does not yield much insight. Logical arguments can be made to support the probability of warfare between habitats, within habitats that have simultaneous risks throughout, and within habitats that have locally varying timing of stresses if the groups involved show different subsistence economies. Among the Aborigines of Central and Western Australia is, perhaps, one of the few contexts in which warfare for redistributing people is unlikely.

A second approach to the delineation of contexts encouraging warfare would be to determine some of the requirements and implications of organized conflict as a means of redistributing people. As suggested earlier, this strategy should be confined largely to situations in which scarcity involves fixed resources such as land, for which readjustments require the movement of people. Since fixed resources are conducive to the development of territoriality, then warfare should be correlated with territoriality. Horticulturalists, consequently, should be more likely to practice this type of warfare than are pastoralists and hunter-gatherers. Among hunter-gatherers, moreover, those groups showing the greatest sedentism and most exclusive systems of territories, such as Northwest Coast Indians, should be most likely to practice warfare to redistribute people. In addition, it may be suggested that within the Northwest Coast, the more northerly groups who have a particularly limited number of fixed resource locations, the greatest sedentism, the most closed territories, the least individual mobility, and the greatest movement of goods, would be most likely to practice warfare to redistribute people when other mechanisms of adjustment fail. Ethnographic observations on the frequency of warfare and degree of territorial conquest tend to support these generalizations (Chagnon 1977; Driver 1969; Meggitt 1977; Vayda 1976).

Moreover, this type of strategic warfare implies expulsion of enemies and territorial conquest. It has been well demonstrated that many examples of warfare do not accomplish this (Hallpike 1973; Sillitoe 1977). If this result, however, is to be achieved, a number of additional implications are suggested. The conquered lands must be accessible and defendable, a situation most likely when these lands are adjacent to a group's own territory. Immediate neighbors should be the most likely targets of such aggression, which is true in many parts of New Guinea (Meggitt 1977; Rappaport 1968; Sillitoe 1977; Vayda 1976) and in Nigeria (Netting 1974). Among the Mae Enga, in fact, proximity is a good predictor of enmity regardless of the degree of kin relationship (Meggitt 1977:37). Furthermore, land shortages should increase with population density, suggesting a likely correlation between high density and warfare intensity. Such a correlation has been observed cross-culturally, both in terms of frequency of warfare, in general, (Netting 1974) and in terms of wars of territorial conquest (Healy 1978; Sillitoe 1977).

In contexts of relatively high density, therefore, warfare is a likely option and a significant environmental risk. Since both defense and aggression tend to be more effective as groups become larger and more organized, such contexts are likely to show a number of strategies for increasing the size of warring units. One of the most common of such strategies is the formation of alliances. Strong alliances both reduce the risk of attack and increase the probability of military success. Alliances are usually built through the extension of economic and social ties among the component groups, through trade, ceremonial exchange, and intermarriage, with the latter most effective (Chagnon 1977; Koch 1974). The risk of war, as a result, can act as a stimulus to trade even in the absence of significant environmental variation, by encouraging differentiation in craft manufacture to create objects of localized distribution. Because alliance formation would be most important with increasing population density and threat of war, the stronger social ties should be most developed in such contexts. Ceremonial exchange tends to replace or incorporate trade in New Guinea as population density increases (Healey 1978). Similarly, intermarriage among neighboring groups is stressed in regions with high population density. Among many highland groups there exist extensive kin networks, local exogamy, and a stress on interareal ties. On the other hand, one group, the Usino, which is exceptional in its low population density and abundant resources, prefers local endogamy and stresses intensive kin networks and local ties (Conton and Eisler 1976). Here, then, is another objective of extensive spatial relationships: to promote group cooperation in defense and aggression, most likely among sedentary, high-density groups. This is quite different from the extension of relationships in order to facilitate individual emigration. In fact, in New Guinea, individual mobility seems to be inversely related to population density (Sillitoe 1977). When land is scarce, acceptance by neighboring groups becomes less likely (Meggitt 1977).

A final approach to the delineation of contexts of warfare as a strategy for redistributing people is to view such warfare as the human equivalent of aggressive competition observed among other animals. Perhaps such an analogy would allow anthropology to draw upon generalizations derived from ecological studies. One major generalization in the ecological literature is that *intra*specific competition tends to be more severe than *inter*specific competition. Since a species is characterized by a certain niche in a given habitat, individuals of the same species will necessarily use the same resources, and in effect, be competing for them all. Individuals of different species will have only a limited number of resources in common, and their areas of competition will be similarly limited.

Applying this generalization to humans, it may be suggested that competition should vary with economic similarity. That is, the more similar the economies of two groups, the more similar their niches. Consequently, the closer they are to being similar "species," and the greater one would expect to be their competition. Among the Pokot of Africa, for example, relationships between farming korok are strained and disputes are common (Conant 1965). Warfare among the Tsembaga, Enga, and Yanomamo occurs between adjacent groups practicing the same economy (Chagnon 1977; Meggitt 1977; Rappaport 1968). The hostilities between Chippewa and Sioux involved the overlap in their economies on the major resource of Virginia deer (Hickerson 1965). In Swat, Pakistan, the Pathans fought the Kohistanis because they were in competition for agricultural land (Barth 1956). Vayda (1976) stresses warfare among slash-and-burn farmers of Oceania and South America as involving the scarce resource of secondary forest land desired by both sides.

By contrast, in many of these same areas, relations between groups with more differing economies—the "interspecific" relations—tend to be more peaceful. Farming and herding korok among the Pokot have generally close and easy interactions marked by much exchange and ceremonialism. The Tsembaga maintain relatively friendly ties to groups on the other side of the mountains who utilize and have access to slightly different resources. In Pakistan, the farming Pathans and herding Gujars have a stable and peaceful interdependence. Among humans, not only do interspecific relations often appear relatively peaceful, but they also assume the form of mutualism, the more so, the more diverse the niches or habitats. The Tsembaga and their neighbors over the mountains regularly exchange goods to the benefit of both, as do the farmers and herders among the Pokot and the Gujars and Pathans in Pakistan. Sometimes such mutualistic interactions can be quite complex and can be interpreted differently by different participants, as exemplified by Pygmy–Bantu relations (Turnbull 1963).

This view of warfare as the manifestation of competition over resources might be extended to include not only strictly economic resources such as land or game, but also women, which seem to be the object of many disputes. If so, however, it might be doubtful whether economic similarity between two groups would influence the frequency of disputes. In addition, competition could exist over land or water as economic resources even though two groups have quite differing economies; in this case, the resource in question has multiple uses, defined differently in each case. Economic similarity might be of some use in predicting probability of warfare, if only because significant economic differences make trade more likely. Economic similarity, however, is clearly not a necessary factor. All groups, regardless of their economies, have needs for land and water, and therefore, could come into competition and conflict over these resources. In fact, an opposing argument could be developed to suggest that economic differences among groups should increase the probability of wars of conquest. Differing economies show associated differences in size and organization of local groups. Successful warfare may be directly related to the superior size and organization of the victor, and thus warfare may be most likely to be reinforced in situations where the antagonists show major differences in social organization and settlement size—and by extension, differences in economy as well.

A summary of these various approaches to wars of conquest must present rather disappointing conclusions. An examination of the natural environment in terms of risk offers little help in predicting the probability of such warfare—virtually all environments are theoretically suitable contexts. An assessment of economic similarities or differences is equally unpromising, since antagonists may compete for identical resources for a variety of reasons. It can be suggested that such warfare is likely to be directed against nearby, fixed resources, and will increase in probability as relative population density increases. At the same time, a situation of greater probability of warfare and higher population density provides a context in which the elaboration of ties for alliance through ceremonial exchange and extensive marriage patterns is rewarded. Wars of conquest should be strongly associated with high population density, developed territoriality, elaborate ceremonial exchange, and extensive marriage networks, and this seems to be the case in much of New Guinea (Sillitoe 1977, 1978).

As will be mentioned in Chapter 8, however, other strategic forms of warfare should also increase in frequency with increasing population density, and so a context of relatively high population density cannot, by itself, demonstrate that observed cases of warfare are acting to redistribute people in relation to resources. The Kofyar of Nigeria, for example, present a situation in which population density is quite high, but no territorial conquest results from the warfare (Netting 1974). Warfare will persist if it is reinforced in a given context. One of the reinforcers may, indeed, be the acquisition of new land, but this should be observable as conquest. Every act of war, perhaps, need not end in conquest in order for this strategic function to be operating. Intermittent reinforcement in the form of occasional conquests may be sufficient to sustain the behavior, but it must be remembered that warfare is an expensive behavior that may be extinguished readily if reinforcement is too infrequent. In this regard, arguments suggesting that most warfare persists simply because it has the *potential* for conquest may need reexamination.

Furthermore, there exist many other possible reinforcers for the practice of warfare, which will be considered in discussions of the other strategic aspects of conflict. One of these other forms of reinforcement must be considered here, because it relates directly to the topic of coping with human–resource imbalances. Ecological interpretations of warfare, in fact, have generally emphasized one of two possible functions for this behavior. The first is the redistribution of population, which, as discussed above, certainly does not represent the only, and probably not even the most important, strategic aim of warfare. The second commonly suggested function of aggressive conflict is the reduction of population. In this view, warfare persists largely because it serves as a means of population control. The correlation of warfare frequency with population density can thus be interpreted in terms of a growing need for population control as density increases. Groups such as the Yanomamo have presented problems to this viewpoint because they have a high mortality rate without an obviously high population density (Chagnon 1977). This interpretative framework, however, has been maintained by attempts to identify specific resource shortages for this group, such as game as a protein source, for which the population density is relatively too high (Harris 1974). Counterarguments have largely concentrated on trying to falsify the proposition of protein scarcity (Chagnon and Hames 1979; Lizot 1977).

This viewpoint is clearly complex, but the framework presented in this book may suggest some directions for further research into the functions of warfare as a means of population regulation. The investigation into the importance of wild game as a limiting factor for the Yanomamo, for example, would be aided by a clearer distinction being made between protein as a biological need and game as a culturally valued good. If the scarcity of peccary meat (rather than protein) directly or indirectly serves as a cue for the initiation of population control, then all the grubs in the forest will not compensate for this scarcity.

On a more general level, however, proponents of warfare as a means of population control must demonstrate more clearly the behavioral links between reinforcement and function. That is, if population-control effects are to be used to explain the occurrence of warfare, then it must be demonstrated that there exist direct or indirect links between population decrease and the reinforcement of warfare. Although such links have not been investigated, a number of possibilities may be explored. Possible reinforcers for warfare may be identified through examining the stated motives of the participants, which include (1) insults, (2) adultery, (3) murder, (4) suspicion of sorcery, (5) trespass, (6) theft, (7) fights over property, (8) acquisition of booty, (9) acquisition of land, (10) acquisition of women, or (11) acquisition of slaves.

The first four constitute crimes against persons, the next three, crimes against property, and the last are desires for goods. Punishment for crimes and the acquisition of goods would represent the major types of reinforcers for warfare. It might be argued that high population density will increase the possible number and frequency of interpersonal crimes requiring punishment. Similarly, high population density relative to resources will increase the potential competition and thus the frequency of both crimes against property and forceful acquisition of goods. High density would provide a likely context for the development of the various motives for war. High mortality rates, by lowering the density, might then be seen as reinforcing through their alteration of this context. Both interpersonal crimes and competition for goods would be less likely as population density decreased.

There are certainly a number of examples of high mortality rates (through injury or crowding-induced disease) from warfare among certain groups, and many of these groups do, indeed, have quite high relative population densities (e.g., the Dani and Enga of New Guinea and the Kofyar of Nigeria—Heider 1970; Meggitt 1977; Netting 1974). The major problem with this generalized scheme, however, is simply that much of primitive warfare involves few fatalities. In the majority of situations, warfare necessarily must have a different strategic importance—that is, its reinforcement must derive from something other than the lowering of population density, however plausible this function appears. Among the Kofyar, in fact, warfare increases local densities and demands on resources because of the crowding of refugees and destruction of farms (Netting 1974). Since success in warfare may depend to a large extent on the size of the war party, such crowding (despite the strains on resources) may actually enhance the chances of successful warfare by making it easier to assemble large forces. *Increased* local density may contribute to the reinforcement of war. Part of the correlation between frequency of warfare and population density may derive from such factors rather than from a need to adjust population levels downward. As suggested earlier, many instances of warfare may actually represent strategies of management rather than maintenance, and as such will be considered in Chapter 8.

2. IMBALANCES OF LABOR, MATES, AND DEMAND

The emphasis in this chapter has been on responses to shortages of resources. It is clear, however, that much behavior serves to avoid or cope with scarcity of other factors, particularly labor and mates. Although these situations of scarcity will not be examined in detail, it should be possible to analyze such shortages in a manner similar to that used for investigating resource scarcity. That is, some of the contextual differences in spatial and temporal distributions of labor and mates can be suggested, along with some of the possible strategies for coping with local shortages. The value of this discussion should be the identification of some of the relationships between this coping behavior and its context.

Imbalances of labor supply and demand can develop in two general types of contexts: (1) patterns of demography and settlement may impose labor scarcity or (2) social and economic forces may intensify demand beyond the available labor supply. Underpopulation, which may be caused by disease (such as kuru among the Fore of New Guinea or smallpox among many native North American groups upon Western contact), by high mortality warfare, or by purposeful population control through infanticide, may pose a severe problem in relation to the traditional needs for labor. In addition to such absolute decreases in population, the distribution of population may also impose local labor shortages. Dispersed settlement as a strategy for most secure subsistence may preclude the collection of sufficient labor in one spot for most efficient exploitation of large or temporary aggregated resources. A lack of effective means for resolving conflict in large groups may impose mobility and dispersal despite the economic advantages of aggregation. Thus, a shortage of labor may develop in a number of contexts depending on the distribution of resources, the sociopolitical organization, and the intensity of warfare and infanticide.

Of equal importance to the labor balance is the structure of demands for labor. Intensified demands, overtaxing the supply, may characterize a number of situations. Contexts encouraging time efficiency—especially common in highly seasonal environments—may impose requirements for large seasonal work groups. Directly related to these contexts is the practice of food storage, for which large amounts of labor may be necessary. The high demands of salmon preparation on the Northwest Coast, for example, have been stressed by Schalk (1977). According to the context of resource security, production may be intensified in order to amass a surplus for trade or ceremonial exchange, representing another form of labor demands. Competition and warfare create a demand for both defensive and offensive labor. Highly variable and volatile resources, such as cattle, may create locally intense and varying needs for labor to exploit and manage them. All the strategies of procurement, settlement, and maintenance of resource balances contribute to the context of labor needs and supply, and shortages may arise in a variety of resulting contexts.

Wives, like workers, are also frequently scarce, and in fact, wives represent one of the most important sources of labor in many economies. Moreover, wives can provide not only their own labor, but also children, important for their labor contributions as well as for the perpetuation of the group. Many of the contexts promoting relative shortage of labor also may contribute to a relative shortage of suitable marriage partners. These would include depopulation, dispersal, and high demands on household production. In addition, situations encouraging small, dispersed populations frequently promote the development of spatially extensive marriage ties. Since such ties are often structured by elaborate rules of marriage pre- and proscriptions, the number of eligible partners may be further reduced.

Whenever labor and mates are relatively scarce, there should exist a number of strategies for anticipating and correcting these shortages. It is in this light that a variety of practices such as labor partnerships, the hiring of wage labor, competitive displays to attract followers, raids for slaves and women, and the various marriage rules and practices may be examined. Polygyny, for example, often represents a strategy of increasing domestic labor supplies, which may be necessary for financing ceremonial exchange (Strathern 1969), carrying out extensive swidden systems (Netting 1974), or managing large and growing cattle herds (Goldschmidt 1974). In addition, polygyny can compensate for an excess of women or may contribute to the scarcity of women already created by selective female infanticide, both of which, in turn, tend to be associated with high-mortality warfare and a demand for mates and high reproductive rates (Ember 1974; Harris 1974).

The scarcity of women may directly affect the level of bride prices (Goldschmidt 1974; Schneider 1979:82), which, in turn, will influence the level of demands on production. Labor forces will also be affected by policies of adoption, patron–client relationships, and bride service, and labor needs should exert strong influences on policies of family size and population control.

The procurement of labor and mates by exchange or force may be examined with attention given to the same factors considered in other transactions. The scale of exchanges, for example, should correspond to the degree of scarcity. Mating networks must have a certain minimum size in order to furnish mates reliably (Wobst 1974). Thus, the scale and degree of local endogamy should be directly related to the density and distribution of population: the lower the population density and the smaller the local groups, the larger the area that needs to be included in the marriage networks and the greater the need for local exogamy. Since exogamy may be used as a strategy for extending social alliances as well as for extending access to mates, however, this relationship between degree and scope of exogamy and population density often breaks down at relatively high densities when ceremonial exchange relations and warfare alliances are structured through exogamous ties.

Other factors important to general exchange behavior, besides its spatial extent, should also be significant in the procurement of labor and mates as well.

Research into marriage practices and labor transactions could profitably emphasize such factors as the scope of the shortage (e.g., whether on the individual or group level), the intensity and frequency of shortages, the dependence upon exchange relationships for the supply, the means of reinforcing and insuring supply lines, and the nature of competition for the supplies. Through such research, it should be possible to identify and explain the strategic aspects of many behaviors by reference to their natural and social environments.

DDT was developed to solve a problem (pests!), and the profitable production of this chemical was directly related to its success in solving the problem. However, in our society, the specific problem was separated from its total context, which included delayed adverse effects of DDT. These were eventually perceived, and ultimately there were few profits to be made within this country because of the legal banning of the pesticide. The production of DDT seems to have continued, however, with profits being made by dumping the pesticide on overseas markets. Even if this particular chemical ceases to be produced entirely, many others, of course, continue to be manufactured. No one, incidentally, has attempted to explain the persistent production of such chemicals by reference to their "latent functions" of poisoning the environment; latent functions are apparently only positive. In our market economy, the strength of cultural (monetary) reinforcement is greater than most consequences of activities themselves in perpetuating behavior. Anthropologists must examine behavior in other cultures in a similar manner, carefully distinguishing reinforcers from effects, before developing ecological assertions about the importance of unrecognized effects to the perpetuation of the behavior.

The focus of this discussion, consequently, is on the conscious perception and solution of problems. The basis of problem recognition is the gathering of information, which may be done in a number of ways. Direct, individual observation and experience form the core processes of information acquisition, but they may be quite limited in space and time. Different individuals within groups, however, will vary in their access to information due to their differing activities. Great individual mobility, for example, allows observation of the regional environment and is more characteristic of adult males in most groups. Such regional information would be particularly necessary when it concerns resources that are mobile or else localized and only briefly available. Many ethnographies document the importance of mobility among hunters and pastoralists to the collection of information about the state of resources. Future research could profitably examine two aspects of this process. First of all, it might be asked how the spatial movements of one season articulate with the information needs for later seasons. That is, are current movements dictated to any degree by the need for future information in addition to the need for current resources? Is scouting of regions of anticipated future use a regular component of nomadic movements? Among groups showing a regular transhumant pattern between highlands and lowlands, for instance, such scouting trips (perhaps up into the mountains early in spring) would have significant mobility costs that would be inexplicable if attention is confined only to current resource exploitation. A second research topic is the relationship between the gathering of information and decision making. Under what circumstances are those individuals with the greatest access to up-to-date regional resource information (the mobile young adult men) largely responsible for deciding future activities? The cross-cultural variability in the role of woman and older men in decision making should be examined in light of their roles in information gathering and the nature of particular decisions.

Such spatial information need not be gathered solely through individual observation: communication among groups is an important source of regional information. Ethnographic studies about intergroup communications are largely anecdotal and incomplete, but with the recent ecological emphasis on information exchange, there is a pressing need for systematic studies of information networks. Among the topics needing attention are the extent, composition, and distribution of such networks and the means and the regularity with which they are maintained. The more crucial and unpredictable the information (about caribou distribution or the onset of rains for summer pasture, for example), the more important the communication and the more formalized the networks should be. The shape of networks should depend on the direction of necessary information flow. For example, irrigation farmers would need to maintain upstream contacts, whereas salmon fisherman would have to emphasize communication with their downstream neighbors.

In addition to factors of spatial distribution, information about crucial temporal patterns must also be collected. Every individual has a fund of knowledge about linked natural phenomena based upon direct observation. Therefore, cues for later events can be recognized and utilized in decision making. The first green shoots of spring may have no economic significance of their own, but they may signal the onset of a host of other, more important seasonal changes. Older individuals will have had a longer personal experience of observing such cues, and so may contribute information unavailable to younger group members. The importance of older individuals in decision making should be examined in light of their access to information on such temporal patterns and past histories of successful decision. It may be possible to contrast situations in which information about temporal patterns is most important (and for which older individuals contribute most to decisions) with those in which information about current spatial patterns is more significant (and for which younger men contribute most in decision making). Certainly, contexts of rapid cultural change, such as contact situations, frequently render stores of past knowledge obsolete and lead to a "disenfranchisement" of older individuals.

Again, direct individual observation is not the only source of information about temporal phenomena. An important ecological consequence of the development of culture is the augmentation of the individual experience through the cultural transmission of information across generations. By means of stories and myths, such cultural transmission allows for an increase in an individual's knowledge of discriminatory stimuli and probabilities of reinforcement for various activities. History augments individual experience, and the degree to which such history is codified or sanctified depends in part upon the stability of problems through time. The environment and its problems need not remain static, however, for history to be valuable. By enlarging the time frame of information available, history permits the tracking of environmental variation and periodicity beyond the span of individual observations, increasing the predictability of events. Some attention must be directed to the nature of information contained within traditional lore and to its value in everyday decisions. Research could also be focused on the topic of the development of specialized practitioners of information collection and transmission, emphasizing the types of information involved and the role of such individuals in various decisions. It may be that as both the unpredictability and the importance of certain factors increase, the more likely they are to become the province of specialists. Greater uncertainty of problems would lead to a greater probability of differing perceptions of suitable solutions among individuals. The resulting disagreements could be avoided by delegating the tasks of defining the problem and choosing the solution to a single individual.

3. SOLVING THE PROBLEMS

The nature of the problems facing particular individuals and groups will strongly influence the decision-making procedures utilized. A goal of future ecological research should be the investigation of the relationship between attributes of problems and characteristics of the responsive decision-making organizations. Problems will, for example, vary in the number of people affected: if many individuals face identical problems, then group-level solutions (by consensus, cooperation, or coercion) become an option. Individually varying problems, by contrast, require responses at the individual level. At the group level, the composition of the deciding body has already been mentioned as a topic requiring research, focusing on such factors as the relative participation by age and sex, as well as the degree of specialization.

The types of decisions necessary are also important to determine. Many hunter–gatherers, for instance, must make frequent production decisions about both the timing and location of activities. The focus of such decisions among many sedentary farmers, on the other hand, is largely upon the timing of tasks, whereas among many pastoralists, choices of location are paramount. Surely, such differential emphases should have important implications for the relative extent of spatial information networks and the development of codified calendrical systems.

The frequency of decisions is another crucial topic for investigation. Certain groups have environments or economies requiring significant advanced planning of production. In contrast to many hunter–gatherers who practice year-round, foraging almost daily for example, some groups in highly seasonal environments, such as along the northern Northwest Coast of North America, must depend largely upon food storage and decisions made during limited seasons of production. Similarly, the subsistence of many farming groups depends largely on the decisions made at planting time. Since a few decisions can be so crucial to such groups, one would expect them to show an elaboration of techniques of information gathering and transmission, with an emphasis on the temporal patterns of climate and resources. Moreover, given the inherently greater uncertainty in long-term planning, one might expect that target production levels (of crops or wild harvests) would be established somewhat higher than anticipated needs. That is, in the context of necessary, long-term decision making, the planning of a surplus becomes a likely response to uncertainty. Such a surplus would provide a margin of safety, an extra amount that could be tolerably (and would be often) lost during years of bad weather.

The planning of a surplus would have significant implications. Not all years would be bad; in a few good years production would, in fact, exceed needs and a true surplus would exist. For this surplus not to be wasted (along with the time and labor devoted to its production), it may be converted into other goods or credit through various networks of exchange and distribution. Among highly seasonal economies of farming or foraging, consequently, one would expect an occasional surplus production due to the uncertainties of long-term planning, and therefore an opportunity for surplus conversion through trade, ceremonial exchange, or display.

A remarkable difference between most hunter–gatherers (who do not plan production amounts in advance) and many farming groups (who, along with some hunter–gatherers, are characterized by long-term production planning) is that prestige among the former is acquired and symbolized by *qualitative* factors, whereas among the latter, *quantitative* factors also assume importance. That is, among the most hunter–gatherers prestige is obtained, not by killing the most game, but by killing certain fearsome animals such as bear or elephant. The norms against material accumulations among such peoples are well known and further testify to their lack of quantitative measures of prestige symbols. Among many farming groups, by contrast, the amassing of material wealth and its distribution is a major source of prestige. The fervor of potential big-men in enlisting kin and allies in augmenting production is well documented in the literature. These different orientations toward prestige may depend ultimately on the difference between the two groups in the degree of planning inherent in their economic systems. If long-term planning tends to include a possible surplus, then in good years something must be done with this surplus. Prestige defined in terms of quantitative factors allows for the conversion of the surplus through various channels into wealth and influence. The possibility of such a conversion would also reinforce the planning of surpluses that may be necessary to long-term security in such economies.

In addition, a surplus becomes a source, not only of prestige, but also of power to the extent that it represents a concentration of goods that can be used as reinforcers to control others' behavior. In this light it must be recognized that long-term economic planning faces the problem of reinforcement for current activities since the natural reinforcers, such as a successful harvest, may be quite delayed. The manipulation of immediate, cultural reinforcers (money, beer, stored food) by the planners becomes a necessary part of planning and executing decisions. The development of a specialized class of decision makers should be examined in terms of both the complexity of decisions requiring specialization (see Fried 1967; Johnson 1979) and the importance of cultural reinforcers of behavior. The appearance of an elite with access to limited resources represents the development of a group able to control the reinforcers for others' behavior.

Two further implications of such long-term planning deserve mention. If such planning becomes the province of a specialized group who can manipulate cultural reinforcers, then such a group is in a position to impose its perceptions and goals upon others. The problems of the elite may become the focus of much of cultural behavior as social and political differentiation become more pronounced. Functionalist organic models of society and theories of group adaptation fail to recognize the importance of such special interests in guiding much of cultural behavior, and yet many events, including Aztec wars and Maya temple construction may only be explicable from such a perspective.

Second, the more behavior comes to be reinforced by cultural reinforcers, the more separated it becomes from its natural consequences. Just as with the production of DDT, many activities may persist because of immediate reinforcement despite negative long-term or secondary effects. Instances of permanent planting to the point of loss of soil fertility, of irrigating until salt buildup becomes problematic, of overgrazing to the point of desertification, of forest clearance to the point of severe erosion, and of pursuing wars to conclusions of land devastation and extreme mortality should be examined in terms of the source and nature of their reinforcement. The more divorced a behavior's reinforcements are from its effects, the more uncoupled it becomes from natural selection and the greater the potential for the persistence of "maladaptive" behavior.

There are clearly many other aspects of decision making that require investigation in an ecological framework. The process of selecting a course of action, for example, has been assumed to be a purposeful choice among options, and yet a variety of other techniques may be practiced. Divination and similar methods may be used to randomize the selection among various alternatives. Research needs to be directed to the frequency of such practices, to the types of decisions for which they are used, and to the extent to which they allow for manipulation and biased interpretation. It has already been mentioned in the case of shoulder-blade divination among northern hunters that a situation of uncertainty among a preselected set of best options forms a likely context for its use. Lawless (1975) has demonstrated how environmental changes have led to alterations in the divination systems among certain groups in the Philippines, suggesting a direct link between decision-making mechanism and their environmental context.

Rather than being actively chosen from among options, either by calculated selection or by some randomizing technique, courses of action may be prescribed by some ritualized procedure allowing few or no options. Rappaport (1971a; 1971b) has discussed such ritualized decisions and the sanctity that serves to reinforce compliance with their directives. As he suggests, such decision-making techniques help to reduce ambiguity and to simplify the decision-making process, but are relatively slow, imprecise, and inflexible. Given these characteristics, they would be suitable only to particular types of problems in certain contexts. Situations of rapid environmental change or great internal variability among individual circumstances, for example, would not be amenable to such techniques. Again, cross-cultural investigation of these ritualized decisions is required, with an emphasis on the types of decisions and the problem context in which they are practiced.

4. CONFLICT AVOIDANCE AND RESOLUTION

Disagreement and conflict are inevitable components of social life, and every society has mechanisms of avoiding and resolving such conflict. Humans have taken the almost universal biological responses of flight and fight and converted them into organized systems of dispersal and warfare. In addition, we have developed unique procedures of arbitration and adjudication that are insitutionalized in legal and religious systems. These aspects of cultural behavior have been extensively studied but rarely in an ecological framework. A few remarks may be offered here concerning the direction such studies might take.

Ecological anthropologists too frequently try to view most human conflict in terms of simple biological models of competition for resources. Using a framework of problem solving, however, in which various procedures of problem recognition, decision making, and decision enforcing must be carried out, it is possible to widen the view of the sources of conflict. Disagreements and conflict among individuals or groups may arise out of differences in (1) perception of problems or their magnitude; (2) aims or goals; (3) means available to solutions; (4) costs and benefits of various solutions; (5) access to reinforcers; and (6) perception of results and new problems. Variations among individuals and groups must be examined in terms of their implications for differences in the contexts of problem solving.

A number of generalizations about the context of such conflict may be suggested. The greater the environmental unpredictability, for example, the greater the chances of the development of different perceptions of problems and suitable solutions. Similarly, the greater the environmental or economic diversity among individuals or groups, the greater the likelihood of their having different perceptions of problems and different means available for solutions. Increasing population size and density leads to a greater potential for a diversity of perceptions. A scarcity of resources implies a scarcity of both means to solutions and reinforcers for behavior, as well as a concommitant potential for both competition and disagreement over their use. A scarcity of goods combined with their spatial concentration increases the possibility of their limited control and hence of the imposition of the goals of the controllers upon others. Because the types of cultural mechanisms for resolving conflict will be related to the intensity and nature of the conflict involved, they will also be related to the environmental characteristics mentioned before. Legal and religious systems could be studied profitably in light of such environmental features.

Various forms of cultural interaction could also be examined for their role in conflict avoidance and resolution. As suggested in Chapter 7, ceremonial exchange systems may be viewed, in part, as multipurpose management strategies. They may be instrumental in reinforcing the behavior of other groups to insure their participation in certain crucial networks of trade, alliance, or hospitality. Such a reaffirmation of selected social channels may be especially important in contexts of high population density in which a group would have many choices of partners. Furthermore, intensive interaction for trade or alliance leads to the development of role expectations and hence to the possibility of violations of these expectations by the partners. Such violations are an additional source of conflict that ceremonial exchanges may seek to avoid or resolve.

Warfare similarly may be a component of management strategies. Rather than a counterpart to the biological competition for subsistence resources, for example, wars may frequently represent a strategy of enhancing a group's (or an elite's) access to particular reinforcers useful for controlling the behavior of others. Wars may also, of course, represent a means of settling disputes and resolving competing aims and strategies. By viewing warfare in these terms, it should be possible to relate it to its context without reducing it to biological competition and without assuming that it must be functionally positive. Warfare, like ceremonial exchange and all the other aspects of behavior discussed here, is a strategy, that is, a course of action chosen to attain certain ends. If it is reinforced (by money, land, social promotion, or human heads or flesh), it will persist, regardless of its ultimate biological implications.

References

Acheson, J. M.
 1976 New directions in economic anthropology? *American Anthropologist* 78:331–335.
Alkire, W. H.
 1973 *An introduction to the peoples and cultures of Micronesia,* Module No. 18. Addison-Wesley, Reading, Massachusetts.
Ammerman, A. J.
 1975 Late Pleistocene population dynamics: An alternative view. *Human Ecology* 3:219–233.
Banfield, A. W. F.
 1954 Preliminary investigation of the Barren-Ground caribou. *Canadian Wildlife Service, Wildlife Management Bulletin.* Series 1:10A, 10B.
Barth, F.
 1956 Ecologic relationships of ethnic groups in Swat, North Pakistan. *American Anthropologist* 58:1079–1089.
Barlett, P. F.
 1976 Labor efficiency and the mechanism of agricultural evolution. *Journal of Anthropological Research* 32:124–140.
Basso, E. B.
 1973 *The Kalapalo Indians of Central Brazil.* Holt, Rinehart & Winston, New York.
Bates, D.
 1972 Differential access to pasture in a nomadic society: The Yoruk of southeastern Turkey. In *Perspectives on nomadism,* edited by W. Irons and N. Dyson-Hudson, pp. 48–60. Brill, Leiden.
Baumhoff, M. A.
 1963 Ecological determinants of aboriginal California population. *University of California Publications in American Archaeology and Ethnology* 49(2).
Bennett, C. F.
 1962 The Bayano Cuna Indians, Panama: an ecological study of livelihood and diet. *Annals of the Association of American Geographers* 52:32–50.
Berkes, F.
 1977 Fishery resource use in subartic indian community. *Human Ecology* 5:289–307.
Berndt, R. M.
 1972 The Walmadjeri and Gugadja. In *Hunters and gathers today,* edited by M. G. Bicchieri, pp. 177–216. Holt, Rinehart & Winston, New York.
Bicchieri, M. G.
 1969 The differential use of identical features of physical habitat in connection with exploitative, settlement, and community patterns. *National Museums of Canada, Bulletin* 230:65–72.

214

Binford, L. R.
 1968 Post pleistocene adaptations. In *New perspectives in archaeology*, edited by L. R. Binford and S. R. Binford, pp. 313-342. Aldine, Chicago.
 1978 *Nunamiut ethnoarchaeology*. Academic Press, New York.
 1980 Willow smoke and dogs' tails: hunter-gatherer settlement systems and archaeological site formation. *American Antiquity* 45:4-20.
Birdsell, J.
 1953 Some environmental and cultural factors influencing the structuring of Australian Aboriginal populations. *American Naturalist* 87:171-207.
Bishop, C. A.
 1970 The emergence of hunting territories among the northern Ojibwa. *Ethnology* 9:1-15.
Bongaarts, J.
 1980 Does malnutrition affect fecundity: a summary of evidence. *Science* 208:564-569.
Boserup, E.
 1965 *The conditions of agricultural growth*. Adline Press, Chicago.
Bronson, B.
 1972 Farm labor and the evolution of food production. In *Population growth: anthropological implications*, edited by B. Spooner, pp. 190-218. MIT Press, Cambridge.
Brookfield, H. C., and P. Brown
 1963 *Struggle for land: agriculture and group territories among the Chimbu of the New Guinea highlands*. Oxford University Press, Melbourne, Australia.
Brown, C. H.
 1977 Folk botanical life-forms: their universality and growth. *American Anthropologist* 79:317-342.
Brown, P., and A. Podolefsky
 1976 Population density, agricultural intensity, land tenure, and group size in the New Guinea highlands. *Ethnology* 15:211-238.
Brown, R.
 1963 *Explanation in social science*. Aldine Press, Chicago.
Browne, J.
 1940 Projectile points. *American Antiquity* 5:209-213.
Brush, S. B.
 1975 The concept of carrying capacity for systems of shifting cultivation. *American Anthropologist* 77:799-811.
Burch, E. S., Jr.
 1972 The caribou/wild reindeer as a human resource. *American Antiquity* 37:339-368.
Burton, B. T. (Ed.)
 1965· *The Heinz handbook of nutrition*. McGraw-Hill Book Co., New York.
Butt, A. J.
 1970 Land use and social organization of tropical forest peoples of the Guianas. In *Human ecology in the tropics*, edited by J. P. Garlick and R. W. J. Keay, pp. 33-50. Halsted Press, New York.
Butzer, K. W.
 1976 *Early hydraulic civilization in Egypt*. University of Chicago Press, Chicago.
Campbell, J. M.
 1968 Territoriality among ancient hunters: interpretations from ethnography and nature. In *Anthropological archaeology in the Americas*, edited by B. Meggers, pp. 1-21. Anthropological Society of Washington, Washington, D.C.
Carneiro, R.
 1960 Slash and burn agriculture: a closer look at its implications for settlement patterns. In *Men*

and cultures: selected papers of the Fifth International Congress of Anthropological and Ethnological Sciences, edited by A. F. C. Wallace, pp. 229–234. University of Pennsylvania Press, Philadelphia.

1961 Slash and burn cultivation among the Kuikuru and its implications for cultural development in the Amazon Basin. *Anthropologica,* Supplement No. 2:47–67.

1970 A theory on the origin of the state. *Science* 169:733–738.

Casteel, R. W.

1972 Two static maximum population-density models for hunter–gatherers: a first approximation. *World Archaeology* 4:19–40.

Chagnon, N.

1968 *Yanomamo: the fierce people.* Holt, Rinehart & Winston, New York.

1973 The culture-ecology of shifting (pioneering) cultivation among the Yanomamo Indians. In *People and cultures of native South America,* edited by D. R. Gross, pp. 126–145. Natural History Press, New York.

1977 *Yanomamo: the fierce people,* 2nd Ed. Holt, Rinehart & Winston, New York.

Chagnon, N., and R. Hames

1979 Protein deficiency and tribal warfare in Amazonia: new data. *Science* 203:910–913.

Childe, V. G.

1952 *New light on the most ancient Near East.* Grove Press, New York.

Chisholm, M.

1968 *Rural settlement and land use,* 2nd Ed. Hutchinson Press, London.

Clarke, W. C.

1966 From extensive to intensive shifting cultivation. *Ethnology* 5:347–359.

Cody, M. L.

1974 Optimization in ecology. *Science* 183:1156–1164.

Cohen, M. N.

1977 *The food crisis in prehistory.* Yale University Press, New Haven, Connecticut.

Colinvaux, P.

1973 *Introduction to ecology.* John Wiley and Sons, New York.

Conant, F. P.

1965 Korok: a variable unit of physical and social space among the Pokot of East Africa. *American Anthropologist* 67:429–434.

Conklin, H. C.

1961 Study of shifting cultivation. *Current Anthropology* 2:27–61.

Connell, J. H.

1978 Diversity in tropical rain forests and coral reefs. *Science* 199:1302–1310.

Conton, L., and D. Eisler

1976 The ecology of exchange in the Upper Ramu Valley. *Oceania* 47:135–143.

Coon, C. S.

1971 *The hunting peoples.* Little, Brown, Boston.

Cordell, J.

1974 The lunar-tide fishing cycle in northeastern Brazil. *Ethnology* 4:379–392.

Cowgill, G. L.

1975 On causes and consequences of ancient and modern population changes. *American Anthropologist* 77:505–525.

Dalton, G.

1977 Further remarks on exploitation. *American Anthropologist* 79:125–133.

Damas, D.

1972 The Copper Eskimo. In *Hunters and gatherers today,* edited by M. G. Bicchieri, pp. 3–50. Holt, Rinehart, & Winston, New York.

Denevan, W. M.
1971 Campa subsistence in the Gran Pajonal, Eastern Peru. *Geographic Review* 61:496–518.

Derman, W., and M. Levin
1977 Peasants, propaganda, economics and exploitation. *American Anthropologist* 79:119–125.

Diamond, J. M.
1973 Distributional ecology of New Guinea birds. *Science* 179:759–770.
1978 Niche shifts and the rediscovery of interspecific competition. *American Scientist* 66:322–331.

Dickeman, M.
1975 Demographic consequences of infanticide in man. *Annual Review of Ecology and Systematics* 6:107–137.

Dillon, J. L. and E. O. Heady
1960 *Theories of choice in relation to farmer decisions,* Research Bulletin 485. Iowa State University, Agricultural and Home Economics Experiment Station, Ames.

Divale, W. T.
1972 Systematic population control in the middle and upper paleolithic: inferences based on contemporary hunter–gatherers. *World Archaeology* 4:222–237.

Dobzhansky, T.
1974 Chance and creativity in evolution. In *Studies in the philosophy of biology,* edited by F. J. Ayala and T. Dobzhansky, pp. 309–339. University of California Press, Berkeley.

Douglas, M.
1966 Population control in primitive groups. *British Journal of Sociology* 17:263–273.

Downs, J. F.
1966 *The two worlds of the Washo.* Holt, Rinehart & Winston, New York.

Driver, H. E.
1969 *Indians of North America,* 2nd Ed. University of Chicago Press, Chicago.

Dumond, D. E.
1961 Swidden agriculture and the rise of Maya civilization. *Southwestern Journal of Anthropology* 17:301–316.
1975 The limitation of human population: a natural history. *Science* 187:713–721.

Durham, W. H.
1976 The adaptive significance of cultural behavior. *Human Ecology* 4:89–121.

Dwyer, P. D.
1974 The price of protein: five hundred hours of hunting in the New Guinea highlands. *Oceania* 44:278–293.

Dyson-Hudson, R.
1972 Pastoralism: self image and behavioral reality. In *Perspectives on nomadism,* edited by W. Irons and N. Dyson-Hudson, pp. 30–47. Brill, Leiden.

Dyson-Hudson, R., and N. Dyson-Hudson
1969 Subsistence herding in Uganda. *Scientific American* 220:76–89.

Dyson-Hudson, R., and E. A. Smith
1978 Human territoriality: an ecological reassessment. *American Anthropologist* 80:21–41.

Eder, J. F.
1978 The caloric returns to food collecting: disruption and change among the Batak of the Philippine tropical forest. *Human Ecology* 6:55–69.

Eggan, F.
1968 Discussions, part II. In *Man the hunter,* edited by R. B. Lee and I. Devore, pp. 83–85. Aldine Press, Chicago.

Ember, M.
1974 Warfare, sex ratio, and polygyny. *Ethnology* 13:197–206.

Erasmus, C. J.

1961 *Man takes control: cultural development and American aid.* University of Minnesota Press, Minneapolis.

Evans-Pritchard, E. E.

1940 *The Nuer.* Oxford University Press, London.

Feit, H.

1973 The ethnoecology of the Waswanipi Cree: or how hunters can manage their resources. In *Cultural ecology,* edited by B. Cox, pp. 115-125. Carleton Library 65, Toronto.

Firth, R. W.

1959 *Economics of the New Zealand Maori.* Government Printer, Wellington, New Zealand.

Flannery, K. V.

1972 The cultural evolution of civilizations. *Annual Review of Ecology and Systematics* 3:399-426.

Fried, M.

1967 *The evolution of political society.* Random House, New York.

Geertz, C.

1963 *Agricultural involution.* University of California Press, Berkeley.

Gilpin, M. E.

1975 *Group selection in predator-prey communities.* Princeton University Press, Princeton, New Jersey.

Goldschmidt, W.

1965 Theory and strategy in the study of cultural adaptability. *American Anthropologist* 67:402-407.

1974 The economics of brideprice among the Sebei in East Africa. *Ethnology* 13:311-331.

Gould, P. R.

1963 Man against his environment: a game theoretic framework. *Annals of the Association of American Geographers* 53:290-297.

Gould, R. A.

1969 Subsistence behaviour among the Western Desert Aborigines of Australia. *Oceania* 39:253-274.

1979 Exotic stones and battered bones: ethnoarchaeology in the Australian Desert. *Archaeology* 32:28-27.

Graburn, N. H. H., and B. S. Strong

1973 *Circumpolar peoples: an anthropological perspective.* Goodyear Publishing Company, Pacific Palisades, California.

Graham, A.

1969 Man-water relations in the East-Central Sudan. In *Environment and land use in Africa,* edited by M. F. Thomas and G. W. Whittington, pp. 409-446. Methuen, London.

Greenberg, J. H.

1969 Language universals: a research frontier. *Science* 166:473-478.

Gross, D. R.

1975 Protein capture and cultural development in the Amazon Basin. *American Anthropologist* 77:526-549.

Gross, D. R., G. Eiten, N. Flowers, F. Leoi, M. Ritter, and D. Werner

1979 Ecology and acculturation among native peoples of central Brazil. *Science* 206:1043-1050.

Gubser, N. J.

1965 *The Nunamiut Eskimos: hunters of caribou.* Yale University Press, New Haven, Connecticut.

Hallowell, A. I.

1949 The size of Algonkian hunting territories: a function of ecological adjustment. *American Anthropologist* 51:35-45.

Hallpike, C. R.
1973 Functionalist interpretations of primitive warfare. *Man* 8:451–470.

Hames, R. B.
1979 A comparison of the efficiency of the shotgun and the bow in neotropical forest hunting. *Human Ecology* 7:219–252.

Harako, R.
1976 The Mbuti as hunters. *Kyoto University African Studies* 10:37–99.

Hardesty, D. L.
1977 *Ecological anthropology*. John Wiley and Sons, New York.

Harding, T. G.
1978 Introduction: major themes of the conference. *Mankind* 11:161–164.

Harner, M. J.
1973 *Hallucinogens and shamanism*. London and Oxford Press, New York.
1977 The ecological basis for Aztec sacrifice. *American Ethnologist* 4:117–135.

Harris, D. R.
1971 The ecology of swidden cultivation in the Upper Orinoco rain forest, Venezuela. *Geographic Review* 61:475–495.
1972 Swidden systems and settlement. In *Man, settlement, and urbanism*, edited by P. J. Ucko, R. Tringham, and G. W. Dimbleby, pp. 245–262. Duckworth, London.

Harris, M.
1968 *The rise of anthropological theory*. Thomas Y. Crowell, New York.
1974 *Cows, pigs, wars, and witches: the riddles of culture*. Random House, New York.
1977 *Cannibals and kings*. Random House, New York.
1979 Our pound of flesh. *Natural History* 88:30–36.

Hart, J. A.
1978 From subsistence to market: a case study of the Mbuti net hunters. *Human Ecology* 6:325–353.

Hassan, F. A.
1978 Demographic archaeology. *Advances in Archaeological Method and Theory* 1:49–103.

Hatch, E.
1973 The growth of economic, subsistence, and ecological studies in American anthropology. *Journal of Anthropological Research* 29:221–243.

Hayden, B.
1972 Population control among hunter–gatherers. *World Archaeology* 4:205–221.
1975 The carrying capacity dilemma. In *Population studies in archaeology and biological anthropology*, edited by A. C. Swedlund. Memoir 30, pp. 11–21. Society for American Archaeology, Washington, D.C.

Healey, C. J.
1978 The adaptive significance of systems of ceremonial exchange and trade in the New Guinea highlands. *Mankind* 11:198–207.

Heider, K. G.
1969 Visiting trade institutions. *American Anthropologist* 71:462–471.
1970 *The Dugum Dani*, Viking Fund Publications in Anthropology No. 49. Viking Fund, New York.

Heinen, H. D., and K. Ruddle
1974 Ecology, ritual, and economic organization in the distribution of palm starch among the Warao of the Orinoco Delta. *Journal of Anthropological Research* 30:116–138.

Helm, J.
1972 The Dobrib Indians. In *Hunters and gatherers today*, edited by M. G. Bicchieri, pp. 51–89. Holt, Rinehart & Winston, New York.

Herskovits, M. J.
1952 *Economic anthropology.* Norton, New York.

Hiatt, L. R.
1968 Ownership and use of land among the Australian Aborigines. In *Man the hunter,* edited by R. B. Lee and I. DeVore, pp. 99–110. Aldine Press, Chicago.

Hickerson, J.
1965 Virginia deer and intertribal buffer zones in the Upper Mississippi Valley. In *Man, culture, and animals,* edited by A. Leeds and A. Vayda, pp. 43–65. American Association for the Advancement of Science, Washington, D.C.

Hirst, E.
1973 Living off the fuels of the land. *Natural History* 82:21–22.

Hogbin, I.
1964 *A Guadalcanal society.* Holt, Rinehart & Winston, New York.
1970 Food festivals and politics in Wogeo. *Oceania* 40:304–328.

Holmberg, A. R.
1950 *Nomads of the long bow.* Smithsonian Institute Press, Washington, D.C.

Honigmann, J. J.
1961 *Foodways in a Muskeg community.* Northern Coordinating and Research Centre, Department of Northern Affairs and Natural Resources, Ottawa, Canada.
1964 *The Kaska Indians: an ethnographic reconstruction,* Yale University Publications in Anthropology No. 51. Yale University Press, New Haven, Connecticut.

Horn, H. S.
1968 The adaptive significance of colonial behavior in the Brewer's blackbird. *Ecology* 49:682–694.

Hurst, M. E.
1972 *A geography of economic behavior.* Duxbury Press, North Scituate, Massachusetts.

Ichikawa, M.
1978 The residential groups of the Mbuti Pygmies. *Senri Ethnological Studies* 1:131–188.

Itani, J., and A. Suzuli
1967 The social unit of chimpanzees. *Primates* 8:355–382.

Izawa, K.
1970 Unit groups of chimpanzees and their nomadism in the Savanna-Woodland. *Primates* 11:1–46.

Jackson, H. H. T.
1961 *Mammals of Wisconsin.* University of Wisconsin Press, Madison.

Jacobsen, T., and R. M. Adams
1958 Salt and silt in ancient mesopotamian agriculture. *Science* 128:1251–1258.

Jarvenpa, R.
1977 Subarctic indian trappers and band society: the economics of male mobility. *Human Ecology* 5:223–260.

Jarvie, I. C.
1973 *Functionalism,* Basic Concepts in Anthropology Series. Burgess Publishing Company, Minneapolis, Minnesota.

Jochim, M. A.
1976 Hunter–gatherer subsistence and settlement: a predictive model. Academic Press, New York.

Johnson, A. W.
1971 Security and risk-taking among poor peasants: a Brazilian case. In *Studies in economic anthropology,* edited by G. Dalton. American Anthropological Association, Washington, D.C.
1972 Individuality and experimentation in traditional agriculture. *Human Ecology* 1:149–159.

Johnson, G. A.
1979 Information sources and the development of decision-making organizations. In *Social archaeology*, edited by C. Redman, pp. 87-112. Academic Press, New York.

Just, R. E., A. Schmitz, and D. Zilberman
1979 Technological change in agriculture. *Science* 206:1277-1280.

Keene, A. S.
1979 Economic optimization models and the study of hunter-gatherer subsistence and settlement systems. In *Transformation*, edited by C. Renfrew and K. L. Cooke, pp. 369-404. Academic Press, New York.

Kemp, W. B.
1971 The flow of energy in a hunting society. *Scientific American* 225:105-116.

King, G. E.
1975 Socioterritorial units among carnivores and early hominids. *Journal of Anthropological Research* 31:69-87.

Klima, G. J.
1970 *The Barabaig: East African cattle-herders*. Holt, Rinehart & Winston, New York.

Klopfer, P. H.
1969 *Habitats and territories*. Prentice-Hall, Englewood Cliffs, New Jersey.

Knight, R.
1965 A reexamination of hunting, trapping, and territoriality among the Northeastern Algonkian Indians. In *Man, culture and animals*, edited by A. Leeds and A. Vayda, pp. 27-42. American Association for the Advancement of Science, Washington, D.C.

Koch, K.
1974 *The anthropology of warfare*, Module in Anthropology No. 52. Addison-Wesley, Reading, Massachusetts.

Kormondy, E. J.
1969 *Concepts in ecology*. Prentice-Hall, Englewood Cliffs, New Jersey.

Kroeber, A. L.
1939 *Cultural and natural areas of native North America*. University of California Press, Berkeley.

Kroeber, A. L., and S. A. Barrett
1960 *Fishing among the Indians of Northwestern California*, Anthropological Records 21, No. 1. University of California Publications, Berkeley.

Kummer, H.
1971 Spacing mechanisms in social behavior. In *Man and beast*, edited by J. F. Eisenberg and W. S. Dillon. Smithsonian Institution Press, Washington, D.C.

Kunkel, J. H.
1976 Opportunity, economics and behavior: a comment on Acheson and Foster. *American Anthropologist* 78:327-331.

Langdon, S.
1979 Comparative Tlingit and Haida adaptation to the West Coast of the Prince of Wales Archipelago. *Ethnology* 18:101-119.

Lawless, R.
1975 Effects of population growth and environment changes on divination practices in northern Luzon. *Journal of Anthropological Research* 31:18-33.

Leach, E. R.
1964 *Political systems of highland Burma*. Beacon Press, Boston.

Leacock, E.
1973 The Montagnais-Naskapi band. In *Cultural ecology*, edited by B. Cox, pp. 81-100. Carleton Library 65, Toronto, Canada.

Lee, R. B.

1968   What hunters do for a living, or, how to make out on scarce resources. In *Man the hunter*, edited by R. Lee and I. DeVore, pp. 30–48. Aldine Press, Chicago.

1969   !Kung bushman subsistence: an input–output analysis. In *Environment and cultural behavior*, edited by A. P. Vayda, pp. 47–49. Natural History Press, Garden City, New York.

1972   !Kung spatial organizations: an ecological and historical perspective. *Human Ecology* 1:125–147.

1979   *The !Kung San*. Cambridge University Press, Cambridge, England.

Leibenstein, H.

1976   *Beyond economic man*. Harvard University Press, Cambridge, Massachusetts.

Lizot, J.

1977   Population, resources, and warfare among the Yanomami. *Man* 12:497–517.

Love, T. F.

1977   Ecological niche theory in sociocultural anthropology: a conceptual framework and an application. *American Ethnologist* 4:27–41.

MacArthur, R. H.

1972   *Geographical ecology*. Harper and Row, New York.

MacArthur, R. H., and E. O. Wilson

1967   *The theory of island biogeography*. Princeton University Press, Princeton, New Jersey.

Margalef, D. R.

1968   *Perspectives in ecological theory*. University of Chicago Press, Chicago.

Margolis, M.

1977   Historical perspectives on frontier agriculture as an adaptive strategy. *American Ethnologist* 4:42–64.

Marks, S. A.

1976   Large mammals and a brave people. University of Washington Press, Seattle.

1977   Hunting behavior and strategies of the Valley Bisa in Zambia. *Human Ecology* 5:1–36.

May, R. M.

1973   Stability and complexity in model ecosystems. Princeton University Press, Princeton, New Jersey.

McArthur, M.

1974   Pigs for the ancestors: a review article. *Oceania* 45:87–123.

McCarthy, F. D.

1939   "Trade" in Aboriginal Australia, and "Trade" relationships with Torres Strait, New Guinea and Malay. *Oceania* 9:405–438; 10:80–104; 171–195.

McCay, B. J.

1978   Systems ecology, people ecology, and the anthropology of fishing communities. *Human Ecology* 6:397–422.

McNaughton, S. J., and L. L. Wolf

1970   Dominance and niche in ecological systems. *Science* 167:131–139.

Meggitt, M.

1977   *Blood is their argument*. Mayfield Publishing Company, Palo Alto, California.

Middleton, J.

1965   *The Lugbara of Uganda*. Holt, Rinehart & Winston, New York.

Millenson, J. R.

1967   *Principles of behavioral analysis*. MacMillan Company, New York.

Moerman, M.

1968   *Agricultural change and peasant choice in a Thai village*. University of California Press, Berkeley.

Moore, O. K.

1957   Divination—a new perspective. *American Anthropologist* 59:69–74.

Moran, E. F.
1979 *Human adaptability*. Duxbury Press, North Scituate, Massachusetts.

Morgan, W. B.
1969 Peasant agriculture in tropical Africa. In *Environment and land use in Africa*, edited by M. F. Thomas and G. W. Whittington, pp. 241-272. Methuen, London.
1973 Farming practice, settlement pattern, and population density in Southeastern Nigeria. In *Peoples and cultures of Africa*, edited by E. P. Skinner, pp. 188-204. Natural History Press, Garden City, New York.

Morrill, R. L., and J. M. Dormitzer
1979 *The spatial order*. Duxbury Press, North Scituate, Massachusetts.

Morris, M. W.
1972 Great Bear Lake Indians: a historical demography and human ecology. *The Muskox* 11:3-27.

Moss, R. P., and W. B. Morgan
1970 Soils, plants and farmers in West Africa. In *Human ecology in the tropics*, edited by J. P. Garlick and R. W. J. Keay, pp. 1-32. Halsted Press, New York.

Murdock, G. P.
1969 Correlations of exploitive and settlement patterns. *National Museums of Canada Bulletin* 230:105-110.

Murphy, R. F., and J. H. Steward
1956 Tappers and trappers: parallel process in acculturation. *Economic Development and Change* 4:335-355.

Nag, M.
1962 *Factors affecting human fertility in nonindustrial societies: a cross-cultural study*, Yale University Publications in Anthropology No. 66. Yale University Press, New Haven, Connecticut.

Nelson, R. K.
1973 *Hunters of the Northern Forest*. University of Chicago Press, Chicago.

Netboy, A.
1968 *The Atlantic salmon: a vanishing species?* Houghton Mifflin, Boston.

Netting, R. M.
1965 Household organization and intensive agriculture: the Kofyar case. *Africa* 35:422-428.
1969 Ecosystems in process: a comparative study of change in two West African societies. *National Museums of Canada Bulletin* 230:102-112.
1974 Agrarian ecology. *Annual Review of Anthropology* 3:21-56.
1977 *Cultural Ecology*. Cummings, Menlo Park, California.

Newman, P. L.
1965 *Knowing the Gururumba*. Holt, Rinehart & Winston, New York.

Nietschmann, B.
1972 Hunting and fishing focus among the Miskito Indians, Eastern Nicaragua. *Human Ecology* 1:41-67.
1973 *Between land and water: the subsistence ecology of the Miskito Indians, Eastern Nicaragua*. Seminar Press, New York.
1978 Comment on Ross. *Current Anthropology* 19:23-24.

Nishida, T.
1968 The social group of wild chimpanzees in the Mahali mountains. *Primates* 9:167-224.

Oberg, K.
1973 *The social economy of the Tlingit Indians*. University of Washington Press, Seattle.

Odend'hal, S.
1972 The Energetics of indian cattle in their environment. *Human Ecology* 1:1-21.

Odum, E. P.

1971 *Fundamentals of ecology,* 3rd Ed. W. B. Saunders, Philadelphia.

1977 The emergence of ecology as a new integrative discipline. *Science* 195:1289–1293.

Orans, M.

1975 Domesticating the functionalist dragon: an analysis of Piddocke's potlatch. *American Anthropologist* 77:312–328.

Osgood, C. B.

1936 *Contributions to the ethnography of the Kutchin,* Yale University Publications in Anthropology No. 14. Yale University Press, New Haven, Connecticut.

Palmer, G. B.

1975 Cultural ecology in the Canadian Plateau: pre-contact to the early contact period in the territory of the Southern Shuswap Indians of British Columbia. *Northwestern Anthropological Notes* 9:199–245.

Parrack, D. W.

1969 An approach to the bioenergetics of rural West Bengal. In *Environment and cultural behavior,* edited by A. P. Vayda, pp. 29–46. Natural History Press, Garden City, New York.

Parsons, J. R., and N. P. Psuty

1975 Sunken fields and prehispanic subsistence on the Peruvian Coast. *American Antiquity* 40:259–282.

Pasternak, B., C. R. Ember, and M. Ember

1976 On the conditions favoring extended family households. *Journal of Anthropological Research* 32:109–123.

Pearson, O. P.

1964 Metabolism and bioenergetics. In *Readings in population and community ecology,* edited by W. Hazen, pp. 40–63. W.B. Saunders, Philadelphia.

Pianka, E. R.

1975 Do ecosystems converge? *Science* 188:847–848.

Piddocke, S.

1965 The potlatch system of the Southern Kwakiutl: a new perspective. *Southwestern Journal of Anthropology* 21:244–264.

Pielou, E. C.

1975 *Ecological diversity.* John Wiley & Sons, New York.

Popper, K.

1974 Scientific reduction and the essential incompleteness of all science. In *Studies in the philosophy of biology,* edited by F. J. Ayala and T. Dobzhansky, pp. 262–281. University of California Press, Berkeley.

Porter, P. W.

1965 Environmental potentials and economic opportunities. *American Anthropologist* 67:409–420.

Pospisil, L.

1963 *Kapauku Papuan economy,* Yale University Publications in Anthropology No. 67. Yale University Press, New Haven, Connecticut.

Post, R. H.

1938 The subsistence quest. In *The Sinkaietk or Southern Okanagon of Washington,* edited by L. Spier, pp. 11–33. George Banta Publ. Co., Menasha, Wisconsin.

Pryor, F. L.

1977 *The origins of the economy.* Academic Press, New York.

Radcliffe-Brown, A. R.

1931 Social organization of Australian tribes. *Oceania Monographs* 1.

Rapoport, A.
  1960 *Fights, games and debates.* University of Michigan Press, Ann Arbor.
Rappaport, R. A.
  1968 *Pigs for the ancestors.* Yale University Press, New Haven, Connecticut.
  1971a The flow of energy in an agricultural society. *Scientific American* 225:117-132.
  1971b Ritual, sanctity, and cybernetics. *American Anthropologist* 73:59-76.
  1971c The sacred in human evolution. *Annual of Ecology and Systematics* 2:25-44.
Rapport, D. J., and J. E. Turner
  1977 Economic models in ecology. *Science* 195:367-374.
Reese, E. P.
  1966 *The analysis of human operant conditioning.* William C. Brown Co., Dubuque, Iowa.
Reidhead, V. A.
  1977 Labor and nutrition in food procurement: did prehistoric people optimize?, paper presented
        at the 42nd Annual Meeting, Society for American Archaeology, New Orleans.
Renfrew, J. M.
  1973 *Palaeoethnobotany.* Columbia University Press, New York.
Reyna, S. P.
  1976 The extending strategy: regulation of the household dependency ratio. *Journal of An-
        thropological Research* 32:182-197.
Richards, A. I.
  1939 *Land, labour and diet in northern Rhodesia.* Oxford University Press, London.
Richerson, P. J.
  1977 Ecology and human ecology: a comparison of theories in the biological and social sciences.
        American Enologist 4:1-26.
Ricklefs, R. E.
  1973 *Ecology.* Chiron Press, Newton, Massachusetts.
Rogers, E. S.
  1962 *The Round Lake Ojibwa,* Occasional Papers 5. Royal Ontario Museum, Division of Art
        and Archaeology, Ontario.
  1963 The hunting group-hunting territory complex among the Mistassini Indians. *National
        Museums of Canada Bulletin* 195.
  1969 Band organization among the indians of eastern subartic Canada. *National Museums of
        Canada Bulletin* 228:21-50.
  1972 The Mistassini Cree. In *Hunters and gatherers today,* edited by M. G. Bicchieri, pp.
        90-137. Holt, Rinehart & Winston, New York.
Rogers, E. S., and M. B. Black
  1976 Subsistence strategy in the fish and hare period, northern Ontario: the Weagamow Ojibwa,
        1880-1920. *Journal of Anthropological Research* 32:1-43.
Ross, E. B.
  1978 Food taboos, diet and hunting strategy: the adaptation to animals in Amazon cultural
        ecology. *Current Anthropology* 19:1-36.
  1979 Reply to comments. *Current Anthropology* 20:151-155.
Ross, M.
  1977 Everyday information processing. *Science* 196:1309-1310.
Rostlund, E.
  1952 Freshwater fish and fishing in native North America. *University of California Publications
        in Geography* IX.
Rutz, H. J.
  1977 Individual decisions and functional systems: economic rationality and environmental adap-
        tation. *American Ethnologist* 4:156-174.

Sahlins, M. D.

1957 Land use and the extended family in Moala, Fiji. *American Anthropologist* 59:449–462.

1965 On the sociology of primitive exchange. In *The relevance of models for social anthropology,* edited by M. Banton, pp. 139–236. Tavistock, London.

1972 *Stone age economics.* Aldine Press, Chicago.

1976 *Culture and practical reason.* University of Chicago Press, Chicago.

Salisbury, R. F.

1975 Comment on Gregory. *Current Anthropology* 16:89.

Sauer, J. D.

1977 Biogeographical theory and cultural analogies. *World Archaeology* 8:320–331.

Savishinsky, J. S.

1978 Trapping, survival strategies, and environmental involvement: a case study from the Canadian subarctic. *Human Ecology* 6:1–25.

Schalk, R.

1977 The structure of an anadromous fish resource. In *For theory building in archaeology,* edited by L. R. Binford, pp. 207–250. Academic Press, New York.

Schall, J. J., and E. R. Pianka

1978 Geographic trends in numbers of species. *Science* 201:679–685.

Schneider, H. K.

1974 *Economic man.* Free Press, New York.

1979 *Livestock and equality in East Africa.* Indiana University Press, Bloomington, Indiana.

Schoener, T. W.

1971 Theory of feeding strategies. *Annual Review of Ecology and Systematics* 2:369–404.

1974a Resource partitioning in ecological communities. *Science* 185:27–39.

1974b Some methods for calculating competition coefficients from resource-utilization spectra. *American Naturalist* 108:332–340.

Sharp, H. S.

1977 The caribou-eater Chipewyan: bilaterality, strategies of caribou hunting, and the fur trade. *Arctic Anthropology* 14:35–40.

Sharp, L.

1968 Hunter social organization: some problems of method. In *Man the hunter,* edited by R. B. Lee and I. DeVore, pp. 158–161. Aldine Press, Chicago.

Silberbauer, G. B.

1972 The G/Wi bushmen. In *Hunters and gatherers today,* edited by M. G. Bicchieri, pp. 271–325. Holt, Rinehart & Winston, New York.

Simenstad, C. A., J. A. Estes, and K. W. Kenyon

1978 Aleuts, sea otters, and alternate stable-state communities. *Science* 200:403–411.

Sillitoe, P.

1977 Land shortage and war in New Guinea. *Ethnology* 16:71–81.

1978 Ceremonial exchange and trade: two contexts in which objects change hands in the highlands of Papua New Guinea. *Mankind* 11:265–275.

Slobodkin, L. B.

1977 Evolution is no help. *World Archaeology* 8:332–343.

Smil, V.

1979 Energy flows in the developing world. *American Scientist* 67:522–531.

Smith, E. A.

1979 Human adaptation and energetic efficiency. *Human Ecology* 7:53–74.

Smith, J. G. E.

1978 Economic uncertainty in an "original affluent society": caribou and caribou eater Chipewyan adaptive strategies. *Arctic Anthropology* 15:68–88.

Smith, J. M.
1976   Evolution and the theory of games. *American Scientist* 64:41–45.

Smith, P. E. L.
1972   Land-use, settlement patterns, and subsistence agriculture: a demographic perspective. In *Man, settlement and urbanism*, edited by P. Ucko, R. Tringham, and G. W. Dimbleby, pp. 221–244. Duckworth Press, London.

Speck, F. G.
1915   The family hunting band as the basis of Algonkian social organization. *American Anthropologist* 17:289–305.

Spector, W. S. (Ed.)
1956   *Handbook of biological data*. W. B. Saunders Company, Philadelphia.

Spooner, B.
1972   The Iranian deserts. In *Population growth: anthropological implications*, edited by B. Spooner, pp. 245–268. MIT Press, Cambridge, Massachusetts.

Stebbins, G. L.
1974   Adaptive shifts and evolutionary novelty: a compositionist approach. In *Studies in the philosophy of biology*, edited by F. J. Ayala and T. Dobzhansky, pp. 281–308. University of California Press, Berkeley.

Steensberg, A.
1943   *Ancient harvesting implements*. National Museum, Copenhagen, Denmark.

Steward, J.
1955   *Theory of culture change*. University of Illinois Press, Urbana, Illinois.

Stott, D. H.
1962   Cultural and natural checks on population growth. In *Culture and the evolution of man*, edited by M. F. Ashley-Montagu, pp. 355–376. Oxford University Press, New York.

Strathern, A.
1969   Finance and production: two strategies in New Guinea highlands exchange systems. *Oceania* 40:42–67.

Street, J.
1969   An evaluation of the concept of carrying capacity. *Professional Geographer* 21:104–107.

Strehlow, T. G. H.
1965   Culture, social structure, and environment in Aboriginal Central Australia. In *Aboriginal man in Australia*, edited by R. M. Berndt and C. M. Berndt, pp. 121–145. Angus and Robbertson, Sydney, Australia.

Sugiyama, Y.
1968   Social organization of chimpanzees in the Budongo forest, Uganda. *Primates* 9:225–258.
1969   Social behavior of chimpanzees in the Budongo forest, Uganda. *Primates* 10:197–226.

Suttles, W.
1960   Affinal ties, subsistence and prestige among the Coast Salish. *American Anthropologist* 62:296–305.
1962   *Variation in habitat and culture on the Northwest Coast*, Proceedings of the 34th International Congress of Americanists, pp. 128–141. Verlag F. Berger, Horn-Vienna.
1968   Coping with abundance: subsistence on the Northwest Coast. In *Man the hunter*, edited by R. B. Lee and I. DeVore, pp. 56–68. Aldine Press, Chicago.

Suzuki, A.
1969   An ecological study of chimpanzees in Savanna-Woodland. *Primates* 10:103–148.

Sweet, L. E.
1965   Camel pastoralism in north Arabia and the minimal camping unit. In *Man, culture, and animals*, edited by A. Leeds and A. P. Vayda, pp. 129–152. American Association of the Advancement of Science, Washington, D.C.

Tanaka, J.

1969   The ecology and social structure of Central Kalahari bushmen. *Kyoto African Studies* 3:1–20.

1976   Subsistence ecology of Central Kalahari San. In *Kalahari hunter-gatherers,* edited by R. B. Lee and I. DeVore, pp. 98–119. Harvard University Press, Cambridge, Massachusetts.

Tanno, T.

1976   The Mbuti nethunters in the Ituri forest, Eastern Zaire: their hunting activities and band composition. *Kyoto African Studies* 10:101–135.

Terrell, J.

1977   Biology, biogeography and man. *World Archaeology* 8:237–246.

Thomas, D. H.

1972   A computer simulation model of Great Basin Shoshonean subsistence and settlement patterns. In *Models in archaeology,* edited by D. L. Clarke, pp. 671–704. Methuen, London.

Thompson, S. I.

1973   *Pioneer colonization: a cross-cultural view,* Module in Anthropology No. 33. Addison-Wesley, Reading, Massachusetts.

Tindale, N. B.

1972   The Pitjandjara. In *Hunters and gatherers today,* edited by M. G. Bicchieri, pp. 217–268. Holt, Rinehart & Winston, New York.

Turnbull, C. M.

1963   The lesson of the Pygmies. *Scientific American* 208:302–311.

1965   *The Mbuti Pygmies: an ethnographic survey,* Anthropological Papers, No. 50. American Museum of Natural History, New York.

1968   The importance of flux in two hunting societies. In *Man the hunter,* edited by R. B. Lee and I. DeVore, pp. 132–137. Aldine Press, Chicago.

Turton, D.

1970   Response to drought: the Mursi of Southwestern Ethiopia. In *Human ecology in the tropics,* edited by J. P. Garlick and R. W. J. Keay, pp. 172–191. Halsted Press, New York.

Vayda, A. P.

1967   Pomo trade feasts. In *Tribal and peasant economies,* edited by G. Dalton, pp. 494–500. Natural History Press, Garden City, New York.

1976   *War in ecological perspective.* Plenum Press, New York.

Vayda, A. P., and B. McCay

1975   New directions in ecology and ecological anthropology. *Annual Review of Anthropology* 4:293–306.

Vayda, A. P., and R. Rappaport

1968   Ecology, cultural and noncultural. In *Introduction to cultural anthropology,* edited by J. Clifton, pp. 477–497. Houghton Mifflin, Boston.

Waddell, E.

1972   *The mound builders.* University of Washington Press, Seattle.

Wade, N.

1974   Green revolution (II): problems of adapting a western technology. *Science* 186:1186–1192.

Wandeler, A., and W. Huber

1969   Gewichtswachstum und Jahreszeitliche Gewichtsschwankungen bei Reh und Gemse. *Revue Suisse de Zoologie* 76:3–21.

Watanabe, H.

1968   Subsistence and ecology of northern food gatherers with special reference to the Ainu. In *Man the hunter,* edited by R. B. Lee, and I. DeVore, pp. 69–77. Aldine Press, Chicago.

1972   The Ainu. In *Hunters and gatherers today,* edited by M. G. Bicchieri, pp. 451–484. Holt, Rinehart & Winston, New York.

Watt, B., and A. Merrill
1975 Composition of foods. U.S. Department of Agriculture, Washington, D.C.

Watt, K. E. F.
1974 The end of an energy orgy. *Natural History* 83:16-22.

Werner, D.
1978 Trekking in the amazon forest. *Natural History* 87:42-55.

Westlake, D. F.
1963 Comparison of plant productivity. *Biological Reviews* 38:385-425.

Whallon, R.
1972 A new approach to pottery typology. *American Antiquity* 37:13-33.

Wharton, C. R. (Ed.)
1969 *Subsistence agriculture and economic development.* Aldine Press, Chicago.

White, L.
1949 *The science of culture.* Farrar, Strauss and Cudahy, New York.

White, T. E.
1953 A method of calculating the dietary percentage of various food animals utilized by aboriginal peoples. *American Antiquity* 18:396-398.

Whitten, N. E., and D. S. Whitten
1972 Social strategies and social relationships. *Annual Review of Anthropology* 1:247-270.

Wiegert, R. G.
1974 Competition: a theory based on realistic general equations of population growth. *Science* 185:539-542.

Wiens, J. A.
1977 On competition and variable environments. *American Scientist* 65:590-597.

Williams, B. J.
1974 A model of band society. *Memoirs of the Society for American Archaeology,* No. 29.

Williams, G.
1977 Differential risk strategies as cultural style among farmers in the Lower Chobut Valley, Patagonia. *American Ethnologist* 4:65-83.

Williams, T. R.
1965 *The Dusun: a North Borneo society.* Holt, Rinehart & Winston, New York.

Wilson, E. O.
1975 *Sociobiology: the new synthesis.* Harvard University Press, Cambridge, Massachusetts.

Winans, E. V.
1965 The political context of economic adaptation in the southern highlands of Tanganyika. *American Anthropologist* 67:435-441.

Winkler, R. L., and A. H. Murphy
1973 Information aggregation in probabilistic prediction. *IEEE Transactions on Systems, Man, and Cybernetics,* SMC-3 (2):154-160.

Wobst, H. M.
1974 Boundary conditions for paleolithic social systems: a simulation approach. *American Antiquity* 39:147-178.
1976 Locational relationships in paleolithic society. *Journal of Human Evolution* 5:49-58.

Woodburn, J.
1968a Ecology, nomadic movement and the composition of the local group among hunters and gatherers: an East African example and its implications. In *Man, settlement and urbanism,* edited by P. J. Ucko, R. Tringham and G. W. Dimbleby, pp. 193-206. Duckworth, London.
1968b Stability and flexibility in Hadza residential groupings. In *Man the hunter,* edited by R. B. Lee and I. DeVore, pp. 103-110. Aldine Press, Chicago.

Worsley, P.
   1961   The utilization of natural food resources by an Australian aboriginal tribe. *Acta Ethnographica* X:155–180.
Wynne-Edwards, V. C.
   1965   Self-regulating systems in populations of animals. *Science* 147:1543–1548.
Yellen, J. E.
   1977   Long-term hunter–gatherer adaptation to desert environments: a biogeographical perspective. *World Archaeology* 8:262–274.
Yellen, J. E., and H. Harpending
   1972   Hunter–gatherer populations and archaeological inference. *World Archaeology* 4:244–253.
Yellen, J. E., and R. B. Lee
   1976   The Dobe-/Du/da environment. In *Kalahari hunter–gatherers,* edited by R. B. Lee and I. DeVore, pp. 27–46. Harvard University Press, Cambridge, Massachusetts.
Yengoyan, A.
   1968   Demographic and ecological influences on aboriginal Australian marriage sections. In *Man the hunter,* edited by R. B. Lee and I. DeVore, pp. 185–199. Aldine Press, Chicago.
Young, G. L.
   1974   Human ecology as an interdisciplinary concept: a critical inquiry. *Advances in Ecological Research* 8:1–105.
Zubrow, E.
   1975   *Prehistoric carrying capacity: a model.* Benjamin-Cummings, Menlo Park, California.

Index